Regulating U.S. Intelligence Operations

Regulating U.S. Intelligence Operations

A Study in Definition of the National Interest

JOHN M. OSETH

With a Foreword by Roger Hilsman

THE UNIVERSITY PRESS OF KENTUCKY

Copyright © 1985 by The University Press of Kentucky

Scholarly publisher for the Commonwealth,
serving Bellarmine College, Berea College, Centre
College of Kentucky, Eastern Kentucky University,
The Filson Club, Georgetown College, Kentucky
Historical Society, Kentucky State University,
Morehead State University, Murray State University,
Northern Kentucky University, Transylvania University,
University of Kentucky, University of Louisville,
and Western Kentucky University.

Editorial and Sales Offices: Lexington, Kentucky 40506-0024

Library of Congress Cataloging in Publication Data

Oseth, John M., 1944–
    Regulating U.S. Intelligence operations.

    Bibliography: p.
    Includes index.
    1. Intelligence service—United States. I. Title.
II. Title: Regulating US intelligence operations.
JK468.I6084   1985   327.1'2'0973   84-22105
ISBN 0-8131-1534-5

237049

For MARILYN
and for CATHY and DEBBIE
who have lived with the silences

Contents

Foreword

This book is a study of how a free society may control the intelligence activities that are, however regrettably, vital to a society living not under a world government but in a world of sovereign nation-states.

Throughout most of its history, the United States dealt with the need for intelligence the way it dealt with the need for armed forces to defend itself – episodically, after war was upon it and the need became immediate and overwhelming. Thus in the Civil War, the United States government turned to the Pinkerton detective agency to build an intelligence service for the nation. In the Spanish-American War the government got what intelligence it could from friendly governments, its diplomats, its newsmen, and other Americans who lived and worked abroad. In World War I, the United States was almost totally dependent on the British secret intelligence service and the French *deuxième bureau*. In World War II, for the first time, the United States tried to establish an intelligence service before it actually became a combatant, when President Franklin D. Roosevelt commissioned General William J. ("Wild Bill") Donovan to set up an intelligence service in 1940 and 1941. Following the war the decision was finally made, as incorporated in the National Security Act of 1947, to turn Donovan's Office of Strategic Services into a permanent peacetime intelligence service, the Central Intelligence Agency, and at the same time to create intelligence research and analysis organizations in each of the three services and in the Department of State, and a special organization for electronic intelligence activities, the National Security Agency.

In the years that followed, the CIA, the research and analysis organizations of the Army, Navy, Air Force, and State Department, and the NSA did much of which they may rightly be very proud. The CIA in time successfully asserted its legal monopoly of espionage and other covert activities, which eliminated the spectacle of rival United States secret services stumbling over each other abroad. The NSA accomplished a number of wonders in the field of electronic intelligence. The CIA established highly efficient and effective organizations for collecting overt materials – newspapers, articles, books, and foreign broadcasts. The agency also brought about the development of the U-2, a high-altitude reconnaissance aircraft, and the related camera and film innovations that permitted pictures to be taken with such high resolution that the stripes on a supermarket parking lot could be distinguished at an altitude of fifteen miles. It was this remarkable intelligence system that permitted the United States to discover that there was in fact no "missile gap," as the intelligence community had believed in the latter years of the administration of Dwight D. Eisenhower (and which became an issue in the election of 1960), and so saved the American taxpayer untold billions of dollars and massively slowed down the arms race. It also permitted the discovery that the Soviets were deploying nuclear misiles to Cuba in time for the United States to deal with the threat effectively without the use of force.

But just as important were the accomplishments in the field of research and analysis. The CIA and the intelligence community have brought the best of the social sciences to bear on the problem of understanding the world today, from the Soviet Union and China to the Third World. In general the results have been good, although there have naturally been some failures and some notable omissions. But we can be certain that the United States has had an infinitely better understanding of the world than if there had been no CIA nor other intelligence organizations. There is simply no question but that the United States is the best informed government in the world.

Finally, the CIA can be proud of what it has accomplished in bringing abut a consensus – much of the time – in the intelligence community through the National Intelligence Estimates. By a patient and sometimes painful process of mutual education, the CIA and the departmental research and analysis organizations jointly address such problems as Soviet missile strength, the Sino-Soviet dispute, and the intentions and likely courses of action of all the powers in the world. Though not always as prescient and wise as one might hope, the results have achieved a level of sophistication and objectivity that has been admirable. And the intelligence community has, through this process of mutual education, prevented each of the services from developing independent intelligence estimates that would inevitably be biased toward parochial service interests and would exacerbate interservice rivalries even further. The alternative to this unifying procedure, especially on the major questions of Soviet missile and nuclear strength and Communist intentions throughout the world, would have been a contest between competing service estimates that would have torn policy asunder. General Curtis LeMay of the Air Force, for example, was a brave soldier and a great combat commander, but his understanding of the subtleties of international politics is suggested by his complaint that the United States was "swatting flies in South Vietnam when it ought to be going for the manure pile" in North Vietnam. What he wanted was to "bomb it back to the stone age." One can only imagine the consequences if the United States government had to contend with competing intelligence estimates of this kind.

But even though the successes of the CIA and the intelligence community have been great, so have the problems. The National Security Act of 1947 was passed and signed into law during the administration of Harry S Truman and with Truman's approval. Yet Truman himself came to be disturbed about what the CIA had become. "For some time I have been disturbed," he wrote, "by the way CIA has been diverted from its original assignment. It has become an operational and at times a policy-making arm of the government." Truman went on to say that he had never had any thought, when he approved of setting up the CIA, that it would be injected into peacetime cloak-and-dagger operations, but that he intended for it to be confined to intelligence work. "Some of the complications and embarrassment that I think we have experienced are in part attributable to the fact that this quiet intelligence arm of the President has been so removed from its intended role that it is being interpreted as a symbol of sinister and mysterious foreign intrigue – and a subject for Cold War enemy propaganda." President Truman's conclusion was that he would like to see the CIA restored to its original assignment as the intelligence arm of the president. "We have grown up as a nation," he wrote, "respected for our free institutions and for our ability to maintain a free and open society. There is something about the way the CIA has been functioning that is casting a shadow over our historic position and I feel that we need to correct it."[1]

President Truman's role in creating the CIA makes his criticism all the more sobering. But, stiff though his criticism was, others were even harsher. Article after article in magazines and newspapers catalogued a long list of charges: the CIA was a mass of bumbling inefficiency; it was a citadel of extreme conservatism; it had vast sums of money at its disposal for which it made no accounting; it had such an extensive empire and so many employees that in some of our embassies overseas the CIA agents outnumbered regular foreign service officers; the pervasive secrecy of intelligence activities permitted CIA to pursue its own policies without regard for the rest of the government or the American people. Some of these charges were undoubtedly motivated by nothing more than journalistic sensationalism. But some of the concern was very real. Two responsible journalists wrote a book charging that there were "two governments in the United States today," one visible and the other invisible. The two journalists were convinced that "the Invisible Government has achieved a quasi-independent status and a power of its own," with the result that one cannot help suspecting "that the foreign policy of the United States often works publicly

1. Harry S Truman in an article syndicated by the North American Newspaper Alliance, as it appears in the *Washington Post*, Dec. 22, 1963.

in one direction and secretly through the Invisible Government in just the opposite direction" — sometimes, they seem to suggest, against the wishes of the president himself.[2]

Even more disturbing to many people both inside and outside the government was "covert political action," CIA activities ranging from influencing elections by secret means and engineering *coups d'état* to secretly supporting invasions, such as the Bay of Pigs in the Kennedy Administration and the attacks launched by the *Contras* in Nicaragua in the Reagan Administration.

Allen Dulles, one-time director of the CIA, justified secret intelligence-gathering activities (espionage and the use of the U-2) on the grounds of national survival. The Communists say they are out to "bury us," Dulles pointed out, and they make extensive military preparations in the utmost secrecy. These facts alone, Dulles argued, justify our taking the measures necessary to uncover those preparations. Dulles justified covert activities on similar grounds. As long as the Communist countries continue to use subversive means to bring down non-Communist regimes, those who oppose the Communists must be prepared to meet the threat. But meeting it successfully, Dulles argued, means that our intelligence services must play their role early in the struggle, while the subversion is still in the plotting stage. "To act," Dulles wrote, "one must have the intelligence about the plot and the plotters and have ready the technical means, overt and covert, to meet it."[3] Citing the Truman and Eisenhower doctrines, which laid down policies that the United States would come to the aid of countries threatened by communism *whose governments requested help,* Dulles went on to enunciate a doctrine of his own. He argued that covert political action should be used to foil Communist attempts to take over a country, with or without a request for help. "In Iran a Mossadegh and in Guatemala an Arbenz came to power through the usual process of government," he wrote, "and not by any communist *coup* as in Czechoslovakia. Neither man at the time disclosed the intention of creating a communist state. When this purpose became clear, support from outside was given to loyal anti-communist elements in the respective countries. . . . In each case the danger was successfully met. There again no invitation was extended by the *government* in power for outside help."[4]

In abstract and theoretical terms, Dulles's position is not unreasonable. If a great power — Communist, Nazi, militarist, imperialist, or whatever — is openly antagonistic to the rest of the world and uses techniques of

2. David Wise and Thomas B. Ross, *The Invisible Government* (New York: Random House, 1964).

3. Allen W. Dulles, *The Craft of Intelligence* (New York: Harper and Row, 1963) pp. 48-51.

4. Ibid., p. 224.

subversion to bring down foreign governements, then the countries that are the targets of this hostility have both a right and a duty to protect and defend themselves by methods which are effective and appropriate and for which there is no effective and appropriate alternative.

The trouble has been, of course, that these qualifications have not always been observed. In the past the United States has too often used secret intelligence methods when they were *not* effective and appropriate or when there did exist effective and appropriate alternatives. Covert political action in particular became a fad, the answer to every kind of problem, and American agents became as ubiquitously busy as were the Communists.

The trouble finally was that it was not just the CIA and the intelligence community who were enthusiastically pushing for covert political action but also the policymakers. Indeed, in some cases, such as the CIA covert support of anti-Allende forces in Chile, the evidence indicates that it was not the CIA that was the most passionate and persistent advocate of covert action, but the policymakers – President Richard M. Nixon, in this particular case, and Secretary of State Henry A. Kissinger.

All this uneasiness about intelligence activities finally led to a search for ways of controlling them. After the Bay of Pigs fiasco – the failed invasion of Cuba by a brigade of Cuban emigrés trained by the CIA – President John F. Kennedy said, "It's a hell of a way to learn things, but I have learned one thing from this business – that is, that we will have to deal with the CIA." During the rest of the Kennedy Administration steps were taken to cut the CIA down to size. But the effort was internal to the administration and did not involve either Congress or the public. It was only during the administration of President Gerald R. Ford that public and congressional pressures began to mount, and they continued throughout the administration of President Jimmy Carter and into the administration of President Ronald Reagan. The Ford Administration responded by appointing a blue-ribbon panel headed by Vice-President Nelson D. Rockefeller, which culminated in an executive order laying down new rules for controlling the intelligence community. Congress, for its part, appointed select committees in both the Senate and the House, chaired by Senator Frank Church in the one and by Representative Otis Pike in the other.

John M. Oseth's study of how a free society may control the intelligence activities that are essential for survival and may prevent them from undermining the society they are intended to protect examines this debate in detail. His own feeling is that the "long and painful inquiry into intelligence control issues now appears as nothing less than a public probing of the nation's soul – a probing which uncovered sometimes disquieting perceptions of men, of the nation's needs, and of the nature of the world at large." The same can be said of Oseth's study.

ROGER HILSMAN

Preface

In recent years two sets of intelligence issues have bedeviled scholars, policymakers, and practitioners alike. One deals with regulatory matters – controls, constraints, and accountability procedures for intelligence operations. Decisions or judgments about those issues establish, essentially, the boundaries of operational permissibility for our intelligence agencies, and the mechanisms by which their activities are controlled. The other set of issues deals with effectiveness problems – how to improve the performance of the intelligence agencies and how to enhance their contributions to national security interests within the established boundaries. This book examines the first set of issues, not (at least not directly) the second.

I have chosen that focus because this inquiry into regulatory issues illuminates central policymaking dilemmas, indeed, central questions about our nation and its purposes that all of us – practitioners, scholars, students, or ordinary citizens – must answer in our own minds before we can deal sensibly with problems of effectiveness or quality. This, then, is a book about threshold subjects. With a study of rules issued by several administrations over a number of years, I hope to lead the reader into reflection about underlying societal values and national purposes, and also about how to deal with, and live with, the tensions among them.

As a practitioner, a professional intelligence officer for fifteen years, I know only too well that some of my colleagues and others are, and will forever be, impatient with this approach. Those who lived through the extended, often spectacular, public inquiry into intelligence "abuses" in the 1970s will not be eager to go back over that unpleasant terrain. Moreover, the policy and intelligence communities in Washington are vitally – and rightly – interested in the quality-of-performance issues which are beyond the bounds of this study. They need *good* and active intelligence agencies, and they know it.

But as one who has also been a college teacher of international relations and national security affairs, I feel strongly that the highest responsibility we have to our successor generation is to develop in them a sensitivity to the value-based tensions Washington policymakers must resolve as they make choices about what to do. Additionally, as one who has lived through the breakdown of the vaunted postwar consensus on America's role in the world and who has witnessed nostalgic calls for its revival, I also know that no semblance of that consensus can be revived unless we can attend to elusive – and frustrating – questions about national purposes, about what we are and what we want to be as a society and as a nation among nations. We cannot (and should not try to) eliminate all disagreement about how to answer those questions. But perhaps with greater understanding of the underlying sources of divergence and of the full range of societal values at stake, there can be a more enlightened search for reconciliation. In an important sense, ultimately, this book is not only about intelligence; it is about America and about the societal self-images that emerge in our national security politics and are expressed in our policies.

There is one more level at which I hope this book will operate productively. As a practitioner I hope that my explication of the rationales for intelligence capabilities will lead the public discussion of effectiveness/performance issues in directions more likely to serve the national interest. For many years intelligence professionals took public acceptance of those rationales for granted, and then receded from the public debate about them, to their great cost. It is now long past time to abandon reticence about rationales and to set aside defensiveness about criticism of them. The official, "insider" exposition of underlying principles can stand on its merits alongside other perspectives, and it should be made to do just that.

Though the origins of this project lie elsewhere, it first took shape on paper in 1982 and 1983 as my doctoral dissertation in the Political Science Department at Columbia University. To Professor Roger Hilsman of Columbia, my dissertation advisor, whose work I had already admired from a distance for many years, I owe a special debt of gratitude. Lively criticism by Professors Howard Wriggins, Robert Jervis, Sigmund Diamond, and Henry Graff also helped to sharpen my thinking, research, and writing.

One other influence needs to be acknowledged; it is the most prominent memory of my time as a law student at Columbia in the late 1960s. The scene is a classroom with about forty students gathered around the legendary Professor Willis L.M. Reese in a course about Conflict of Laws. Students are reciting, one after the other, responding to probes from the podium. They are trying to decide what rules ought to be applied to some problem for which there are competing sets of rules. Each student has an idea about a preferred outcome, but each has difficulty explaining and defending that preference in terms the professor is seeking. "What are the underlying public policies?" he asks repeatedly, impatient with the fledgling lawyers' tendency to justify outcomes only by reference to this or that prior decision or rule. "Which of those policies – or purposes – will your decision promote, and why does it make sense to do that?" How can you decide what rules to make or to apply, he was asking, unless you first comprehend what is really at stake and what you want to do? Down through the years those questions have echoed in my head, and they have in large measure shaped the study I have undertaken here.

1

Dimensions of the Intelligence Debate

In the 1970s Americans witnessed a sustained, spectacular debate about a subject never before submitted to public scrutiny, even in this most open of societies: the domestic and international operations of U.S. intelligence agencies. An intensive, widely publicized, and highly politicized inquiry, it examined in detail all three kinds of intelligence operations conducted by American agencies: the collecting of information needed to support national security decisions, activities undertaken covertly to influence persons and events abroad, and activities intended to protect against foreign intelligence services, saboteurs, and international terrorists.

For many years these tools of government had operated silently and unobtrusively at home and abroad, serving national interests as leaders in Washington saw them. Spies and counterspies went about their business in secret, without controversy or public credit. Their work helped decision-makers learn about – and occasionally try to shape – the world and the threats it seemed to present.

The debate of the 1970s brought the era of secrecy to an abrupt end. It opened a period in which three successive presidents, Ford, Carter, and Reagan, and political forces in Congress and elsewhere, sought to devise new institutions, rules, and procedures to control those operations and to supervise them sensibly in the national interest. From the very beginning there was sharp contention between critics of the agencies, who sought to restrain them or to monitor them closely, and others who sought to defend them from reforms that might impair their effectiveness. This book is a study of the choices made by the nation's leaders among the perspectives that emerged in that debate.

In a sense this concern for rationalized governance of intelligence was understandable, indeed inevitable, in the 1970s. For many Americans that decade was generally a time of individual and collective examination of conscience about their government's actions at home and abroad. In foreign affairs the national introspection resulting from the war in Vietnam gave rise to new sensitivities about limits and standards for using national power. At home, meanwhile, the prolonged agonies of Watergate had exposed abuses of power at the highest levels of authority within the nation's own borders. The domestic and international activities of the intelligence agencies touched growing concerns about the character and purposes of U.S. activities in both arenas.

Even aside from the convergence of these themes in public consciousness, the way the intelligence debate began virtually assured it a place high on the national policy agenda. The early years of the decade saw a veritable explosion of exposés which riveted public attention on exotic, and arguably unconscionable, operations. Americans learned, for instance, that covert action by the Central Intelligence Agency may have helped intensify the social and political turmoil in Chile which led to the death of President Salvatore Allende. They read, too, about reports of American spying which could hardly be justified as protection of the country from foreign enemies (e.g., clandestine spying on negotiations with Micronesia). And they were told, as well, that such operations may have frequently violated the law at home, intruded on civil liberties, and invaded America's most important civil institutions, such as the press and academia. If such activities as then described seemed challengeable, so too did the mechanisms and institutions that were supposed to control them. Proposals for reform were promptly set before Congress, the courts, and the leadership of the executive branch.

Each divergent regulatory perspective that emerged in these forums claimed to serve fundamental purposes and values – the national interest – better than the others. Some argued that active and aggressive intelligence agencies were needed to cope with serious international challenges. Others insisted on rules that would protect civil liberties at home and mandate decent behavior abroad. Still others hoped to devise constraints that would rein in an "imperial presidency," to make it accountable, and to assert rightful congressional roles in national security and foreign affairs.

This study examines the national decisionmaking process that tried to reconcile these perspectives. It has a twofold purpose: to explore the key ideas that shaped the intelligence debate and to survey the main regulatory themes emerging from the extended public scrutiny of these tools of American foreign policy and power. The intent is to identify the "value" ingredients of decisions about intelligence controls and to show how those ingredients were combined by successive administrations. To the extent that the intelligence debate involved issues of organizing and controlling governmental power at home, it implicated political values of the highest order in the American scheme. To the extent that the debate involved instruments of national power in the world at large, it touched also upon security imperatives and deeply-felt standards of decency. In exploring the contention among these values in the major forums where intelligence operations were debated, I have sought in the end to understand the directions in which policy choices moved the nation.

Three questions will be central to this inquiry: (1) What did the process of decision about intelligence controls look like: who were the major actors, and what did they do? (2) What were the main concerns of those who participated? (3) What were the choices made and what do they say about our nation and its larger purposes? Despite the great profusion of analyses of various intelligence issues in recent years, there has as yet been little effort to answer these questions. In part this failure is attributable to the curtain of secrecy which, though not totally impenetrable in an open society such as ours, has nevertheless shrouded much information from public view. Though some observers knew decades ago that this subject was far too important for serious students of public affairs to ignore, and though they did their best to understand it and enlighten others about it,[1] detailed analysis of the various intelligence agencies' operations was largely foreclosed because of government secrecy needs. Only former intelligence officials, or others who knew about the work of the intelligence agencies as a result of related government service, had access to extensive information about activities and capabilities.

Today, however, there is a wealth of important material available on the public record, including the memoirs and other publications of former intelligence officials, documents and reports produced by congressional investigations and oversight activities, and materials released through litigation and under disclosure requirements of the Freedom of Information Act. Regulatory decisions and judgments made by presidents, the courts, and Congress are widely available. But even with the veil of secrecy now in important respects drawn back, there has been concern, particularly among academics, that intelligence issues have not been given the attention they need and deserve.[2]

To be sure, a growing body of work has emerged on such important issues as the quality of analysis applied to information gathered by the agencies[3] and the relationship of intelligence to policy decisions.[4] But treatment of operations and the last decade's attempt to regulate them have not attracted comparable interest. Where intelligence operations have been addressed, moreover, analysis has often been subverted by preexisting normative predilections. Some studies of CIA manipulative operations abroad, for instance, have been infected throughout by undisguised revulsion of the agency as an institution and of such operations as evil, malevolent, and unworthy of the ideals central to American society.[5] The same has been true of many analyses of domestic intelligence activities, whose premises tend to align with the assertion in one study that "the history of intelligence in this country is dominated by a systematic invention, usurpation, and abuse of the power to engage in it."[6] Deeply felt attitudes have worked in the opposite direction, too, as supporters of the intelligence agencies have tried unceasingly to protect them from reform programs and, when that failed, to limit the damage they thought reform would do.[7]

Furthermore, a more subtle but equally disabling failing has emerged: a tendency to describe and evaluate intelligence operations and their rationales only in terms of one or the other (but not both) of the arenas in which intelligence agencies must operate, the domestic and international environments. In narrowing their focus to either domestic or international activities, some students of the intelligence agencies have tended artificially to circumscribe description of the operational challenges addressed and the national values at stake. They fail to perceive that the rationales for intelligence capabilities exercised in one arena are intertwined with perceived imperatives and constraints emerging from the other. Domestic activities are then too easily characterized and evaluated as purely domestic in purpose and effect ("spying on Americans"), and activities abroad can be too easily seen and evaluated in terms of presumed external threats without reference to equally vital internal interests in limiting and regulating governmental behavior.

Wherever it appears, this error fails to comprehend the overall operational context and dimensions of intelligence activity. On the one hand, it may fail to understand the place of the intelligence community as a tool of the American nation-state in a world of other nation-states.[8] It may then argue for policies which others believe would unnecessarily and unwisely disable the nation or appreciably reduce its capability to navigate in a confused and competitive world. A classic example here has been the tendency to use constitutional principles mainly to support arguments that the instruments of government must be constrained, rather than to find in them also support for the view that America must have a national government capable of coping with its external environment.[9]

On the other hand, some have sought to take bearings only from perceived or presumed imperatives of international politics, with too little regard for rules and behavioral imperatives derived from domestic political and social values. Resulting policy prescriptions may then call for excessive strengthening and concentration of powers capable of infringing civil liberties at home and abusing human rights abroad.

A few studies of intelligence activities have managed to avoid these errors of prejudice or limited scope.[10] But to this point no one has attempted a comprehensive, longitudinal analysis of the regulatory responses to the control and oversight issues raised in the last decade, nor has anyone tried to explain those responses in terms of choices about societal purposes and interests. As a result, we lack an understanding – beyond scattered impressions that may be gathered from recurrent criticism and defenses of intelligence rules — of what the intelligence debate has produced and of what it has revealed about the forces that shape American decisions about instruments of national power. This study attempts to remedy that deficiency, reaching all of the operational capabilities of the intelligence agencies, identifying the regulatory tensions they produce, and describing how a succession of policymakers have dealt with those tensions over a period of years.

This study takes its most basic investigative and analytical bearings from the proposition that the national security decisionmaking process is a classically political one in which the preferences of multiple governmental and nongovernmental actors contend for influence on the outcome.[11] Decisionmakers need ultimately to accommodate these more or less influential advocates of competing ends and means, and to choose among their views about how the United States should act.[12] As Roger Hilsman observed: "The business of Washington is making decisions that move a nation, decisions about the directions American society should go and about how and where and for what purposes the awesome power — economic, political, and military — of this, the world's most powerful nation, shall be used."[13]

For such business the process of decision unfolds not as a rationalized, dignified, elegantly logical matching of available means with agreed and obvious ends, but as a series of contests in which alternative preferences clash and contend for various reasons and in various forums.[14] Within this process there is a high degree of turbulence at two levels: procedural turmoil in the multiplicity of official and nonofficial actors and interests seeking to make their views heard, and substantive turmoil in the clash of arguments about the directions decisions should take. Though hardly systematic, the process is given a certain shape, and many patterns of activity are regularized, by the formal structures, institutions, and decisionmaking practices of government. But even more than this, there are factors at work which press together the competitors for power. Counterpoised against the centrifugal forces of conflict are the centripetal forces of a striving toward consensus. Those involved in the competition "are oriented to the prospect of agreement, and conflict is marked by a high propensity to search for a way of resolving it." The product of that process — policy itself — inevitably reflects the clash of these contending forces and the accommodations reached between them.[15]

On the surface the last decade's discourse on intelligence operations appeared, for even the most attentive and knowledgeable observers, to resemble nothing so much as a verbal battleground of nearly hopeless disorder. But with the orientation taken here, we can look out on that apparent disorder and search for its underlying coherence. We are also alerted to the truly fundamental level at which we must search for contention: the level of national goals, where we must expect to find multiple interested actors, each striving to pull the policy product closer to his own concept of overarching societal purposes. And it is those purposes themselves which provide the meeting-ground on which ultimate reconciliation must be sought.

In this inquiry I am concerned with more than tracing the process of decision about intelligence rules, and with more than showing that the process of decision may have involved important contention at the level of national purposes. I am interested, more particularly, in the specific kinds of purposes which entered into the policy calculus, and which ultimately shaped the regulatory postures taken. Whatever the process of decision may have looked like, and whoever the actors were who became involved, what were the substantive points of contention about national directions? Which path did policymakers ultimately choose? What, in the end, does the intelligence debate say about our nation and the purposes behind its policies?

One prominent school of postwar thought knew the answer to such questions even before they were asked. As Hans Morgenthau observed, statesmen "think and act in terms of interest defined as power," where power may be seen as both the means and the end of policy. Nations are compelled to "protect their physical, political, and cultural identity against encroachments by other nations," and the survival and integrity of those identities is the compelling value at the center of the national interest. Once survival is assured – but only then – states may indeed pursue lesser purposes. In the main, however, they can be expected to pursue policies which enable them to keep, increase, or demonstrate power. To assure survival, "states must make the preservation or improvement of their power position a principal objective of their foreign policy."[16]

Though these analyses have been variously criticized, notably on the ground that the idea of national interest is an elusive one at best,[17] some have contended that its concern for power correctly identifies the fundamental dynamic at work behind American decisions.[18] These analysts argue that a power-oriented concept of national interest, based on widely shared beliefs about the competitive nature of the world, about the intentions and capabilities of America's major competitors, and about the consequent behavioral imperatives emerging from those features of the world, is the beginning and end of the American policy calculus.

This thesis still has its followers,[19] but many have been uncomfortable with it. As Paul Seabury observed, the concept of national interest, with its analytical obliteration of prior internal debate about means and ends, points to important truths, but, "to make of the national interest an overarching metaphysic which transcends particular interests risks the danger of ignoring the facts of power and conflict in society by simply not mentioning them." The meaning of the concept becomes clearer, Seabury argued, and more expressive of the realities of decisionmaking, if it is understood that nations have insides as well as outsides, and that the "national interest" is best understood as something which divergent conceptions of societal goals and values compete to define. Moreover, some concept of societal self-image, or rather *competing* concepts composed of different blends of central values, will shape the ends toward which decisions strain.[20] Those societal aims cannot be seen as products of perceived power imperatives only. Nor, similarly, can particular decisions be fully explained by reference to considerations of national power. Analysis must be sensitive to the interplay of national self-image and external imperative, of particularized internal interests and more comprehensive, truly national purposes. Decisions about the use or nonuse of international instruments, and indeed about the composition and maintenance of the state's behavioral repertoire, will reflect some synthesis of these factors.

Samuel Huntington has argued that even those American policies most closely tied to national security and power interests operate in, and result from, the events, interactions, and imperatives of two worlds, the international and the domestic. Policy is not produced by calculations based on a unified concept of national purposes. Nor is its sole concern the maintenance and exercise of national strength. It is, rather,

The product of the competition of purposes within individuals and groups and among individuals and groups. It is the result of politics, not logic, more an arena than a unity. It is where a nation and its government come to grips with fundamental conflicts between those purposes which relate to the achievement of values in the world of international politics – conquest, influence, power, territory, trade, wealth, empire, and security – and those which relate to the achievement of values in the domestic world – economic prosperity, individual freedom and welfare, inexpensive government, low taxation, economic stability and social welfare. The competition between the external goals of the government as a collective entity in a world of other governments and the domestic goals of the government and other groups in society is the heart of military policy.[21]

Competing purposes drawn from two worlds are thus at the heart of foreign policy challenges. Division within society on fundamental beliefs about the world, and about the nation itself, complicate the challenge of decision. Policy decisions orient and activate the instruments of national power, but they also give expression and definition to a collective societal self-image. They serve international interests, to be sure. But they affect internal interests and values, too, by giving them sustained and extended life, on the one hand, or by excluding them from the calculations, on the other. They therefore define the nation by choosing among alternative perspectives on what it must achieve and be.

This is hardly a new phenomenon in the American scheme of things. As Norman Graebner has observed, contention at the level of fundamental national purposes has been the rule rather than the exception in the making of American foreign policy.[22] But it has been a special problem in the years since World War II, when America could not and did not recede from a prominent role on the international scene, and when the nation's leaders could not escape the task of defining that role.

We are thus sensitized to the problem of choice faced by all policymakers, and the outlines and implications of dilemmas of choice become clearer. But what *are* the choices which are likely to compose those dilemmas? What are the tensions, and how are they likely to be resolved? In what direction will policy move, and where will the nation stand thereafter with regard to the values at the center of its self-image? Here analysts have offered different answers.

In his 1951 article "The Pole of Power and the Pole of Indifference," Arnold Wolfers suggested that the making of foreign policy might be understood in terms of contention among three kinds of goals: national "self-extension," national "self-preservation," and national "self-abnegation." These categories, he argued, captured the many "values and purposes for the sake of which policymakers seek to accumulate or use national power." Self-extension, in this view, includes policy objectives which seek to change the status quo to further promote central national interests and values. Self-preservation, where the "self" may refer not only to the nation but also to its perceived extended interests, includes goals seeking maintenance and defense of the nation's present position. Self-abnegation, by contrast, "is meant to include all goals transcending – if not sacrificing – the 'national interest,' in any meaningful sense of the term. It is the goal of those who place a higher value on such ends as international solidarity, lawfulness, rectitude, or peace than even on national security and self-preservation. It is also the goal of individuals who at the expense of the nation as a whole use their influence within the decisionmaking process to promote what might be called subnational interests."[23]

Where there is contention about multiple objectives, self-abnegation goals will likely be pushed aside, Wolfers thought, given the persistence of nationalist sentiment and the ethic of patriotism. Especially in times of stress, self-preservation goals, and even goals of self-extension, will gain the upper hand. But even where security imperatives have been victorious, "idealistic pressures at home in favor of self-denying policies may persist and either delay or reduce the effort to enhance national defensive power." More particularly, the ascendancy of security imperatives

does not preclude the possibility that where influential groups of participants in the decisionmaking process place high value on a universal cause such as peace, pressures exerted by these groups may affect the course of foreign policy. It may lead to a more modest interpretation of the national interest, to more concern for the interests of other nations, to more concessions for the sake of peace, or to more restraint in the use of power and violence. Whether the nation will profit or suffer in the end from the success of such "internationalist," "humanitarian," or pacifist pressures depends upon the circumstances of the case; whichever it does, the abnegation goals will have proved themselves a reality.[24]

Kenneth Waltz's *Theory of International Politics* suggests something different, however. The theory outlined there is avowedly "systemic" in that it focuses on the importance of the anarchic structure of the international system as a determinant of behavior. The presence of other nations, in an international society characterized by the absence of government and a consequent premium on self-help capabilities, acts as an important determinant of behavior: "In any competitive self-help system, units worry about their survival, and the worry conditions their behavior."[25] As a result, each of the units within the system expends a portion of its effort in developing the means to protect itself from others. Each has compelling incentives "to be able to take care of itself since no one else can be counted on to do so."[26] That imperative, derived from the nature of the system in which a state finds itself, will prevail over contrary domestic imperatives.[27] Indeed, states will make internal efforts to strengthen themselves, regardless of how distasteful or difficult that effort might seem for other reasons.[28] Their leaders will see the need for choice and will understand the implications of choice, but their selections among alternatives will serve self-strengthening values before all others. And they will conform to common international practices even though for deeply-valued internal reasons they would prefer not to.[29]

Wolfers and Waltz, in the works summarized here, were speaking about how we should expect nations in general to act, or to equip themselves to act, in the world at large. How *America* resolves the hard cases – chooses between internal and external imperatives – has been seen by Samuel Huntington in his more recent work as a problem of reconciling the normative and existential dimensions of American politics.[30] Widely-shared political values and ideals – liberty, democracy, equality, and individualism – compose an "American Creed" at the heart of the nation's self-image. But these values have always contended with others which tend to pull institutions and behavior in contrary directions, resulting inevitably in a gap between the ideals and the realities of institutional practice. This tension has been particularly acute in the area of foreign policy, for the essence of the Creed is opposition to what international relations seem to require: power and concentration of internal authority. Further, this analysis holds:

In the eyes of most Americans, not only should their foreign policy institutions be structured and function so as to reflect liberal values, but American foreign policy should also be substantively directed to promotion of those values in the external environment. . . . Like Britain and other countries, the United States also has interests, defined in terms of power, wealth, and security, some of which are sufficiently enduring to be thought of as permanent. As a founded society, however, the United States also has distinctive political principles and values that define its national identity. These principles provide a second set of goals and a second set of standards — in addition to those of national interest — by which to shape the goals and judge the success of American foreign policy.[31]

Reconciling the two sets of interests and goals is always an agonizing task. The effort to harmonize them, moreover, does not lead to consistent results. Different blendings of the two have produced very different behaviors. But the important thing is that the conflict persists. The ideals imbedded in internal values and imperatives have not succumbed to the dictates of baser, or simply more pragmatic, motives. They endure, and though they do not always win the policy contests that shape American behavior and capabilities, they win often enough to give the nation a special character revered by its citizens and respected by many abroad. Maintaining that special and distinctive character, in the process of balancing values, is a challenge that figures importantly in decisions about what America should do or prepare to do. In a real sense the political health of American society, its fidelity to fundamental values, can be seen in its alertness to the gap between those values and the behavior and capabilities of its institutions, in its awareness of the disjunction between ideals and reality. It can also be measured by the society's vigilance in seeing that the maintenance of power does not undercut liberal ideals and institutions at home.[32] Other observers, such as Robert Osgood, have argued somewhat differently: unrealistic pursuit of ideals may compromise the strength needed to protect them, and so "the wise conduct of foreign relations must involve a continual series of compromises with perfection." In a dangerous age, Osgood felt, "America's problem of reconciling its ideals with its self-interest comes close to being a life-or-death matter."[33] He was speaking, of course, of the "realities" of international life and what they require of all nations, and he hoped that idealistic visions of international harmony and ineluctable pressures for peace would not obscure those imperatives. But in Huntington's view, one must also understand that those choices about how to respond involve life-or-death struggles for important internal political values whose compromise would strike at the heart of America as a "founded society." The consequences of choice ramify inward as well as outward, and the inner effects are no less important than the outer.

The intelligence debate in America occurred precisely at the intersection of internal ideals and external interests, of domestic political goals and the imperatives of life in the international system. The larger literature suggests that an evaluation of the intelligence rules it produced should provide an important measure of the political health of our nation – the vitality of ideals at the center of its essence – as it strives to cope with the actions and intentions of others. Analysts differ, of course, in their expectations about how these dilemmas might be resolved. Kenneth Waltz would expect the bias toward self-strengthening to be clear and consistently observable over time. Wolfers, too, would expect the emphasis on preparing and exercising tools of power to be clear. But his perspective would also anticipate that in some cases "idealistic" self-denial postures might be taken as a result of policymakers' deliberate choice. And even where self-strengthening postures prevail, influential internal pressures may shape those postures importantly, dampening or delaying the enhancement of power. This perspective, then, envisions possible variance of policies over time, as well as significant curtailment of what an untrammeled will-to-power might otherwise produce.

Huntington, finally, would expect internal pressures for restraint to be lively and vibrant, to be ceaselessly pressing the course of decision toward inhibition of tools of power rather than toward their exhibition and exercise.

These expectations are not necessarily inconsistent, of course. Their divergence is essentially a matter of emphasis and degree: the extent to which they anticipate that internal pressures for control and restraint will be reflected in choices made about the use and maintenance of America's instruments of foreign policy. But that variance is significant, nonetheless. In Wolfers' terms, choices about tools of power are choices about national purposes. In Huntington's terms, those decisions should also be understood as choices about ideals and values central to America's self-image. The inquiry at hand, then, provides an opportunity to monitor and assess the continuing process of nation-creating that is the American policy process.

2

Roles and Rationales
of Intelligence Operations

While intelligence has meant many things to many people,[1] viewed most simply it is a product: evaluated information compiled to apprise and instruct national decisionmakers about situations requiring or likely to require their attention. Intelligence for national security decisions focuses in particular on the capabilities, intentions, and activities of foreign nations, organizations, and persons, and their agents.[2] It covers all aspects of national power belonging to other countries, surveying developments in politics, economics, science and technology, demographics, and other areas in which national strengths or vulnerabilities are grounded.[3] It is produced by a series of activities described by practitioners as an "intelligence cycle," beginning with announcement of information needs by decisionmakers and ending with satisfaction of those needs and declaration of others. The main steps in this process have been described as follows:[4]

(1) Those who use intelligence − policymakers and analysts (the "consumers") − indicate the kind of information they need.[5]

(2) These needs are translated into more concrete "requirements" by senior intelligence managers.

(3) The requirements are used to allocate resources to collectors of information and, when passed to the collectors as operational tasks, serve to guide efforts to respond.

(4) The collectors, using assets and operational techniques available to them, obtain the required information, which at this point is termed "raw intelligence."

(5) The raw intelligence is collated, analyzed, evaluated, interpreted, compared with other knowledge, and turned into "finished" intelligence by analysts.[6]

(6) The finished intelligence is distributed to the consumer, and to the intelligence managers, who state new needs, define new requirements, and make any necessary adjustments in intelligence programs to improve effectiveness and efficiency.

This is, of course, a model − a theory about how the process should work. In practice it may not be at all this systematic. One of the most critical steps, for instance, the establishment of explicit requirements for collectors, has traditionally been the most difficult to carry out.[7] Even when it works in as disciplined a fashion as here described, moreover, the process treats a multitude of intelligence needs simultaneously, with some moving through the system more quickly than others. But the cycle is, nevertheless, an ideal toward which the process strains.[8]

This study of intelligence rules will be concerned, in part, with the operations generated within that process to collect information from which "finished" foreign intelligence is made. This is the first (and many would argue the foremost) aspect of the *operational* meaning of intelligence in America.

The intelligence agencies have also had a second operational role, however, undertaken essentially as an adjunct mission: "to influence the affairs of other nations by secret and unattributable means."[9] A wide range of activities, popularly known as "covert action", has been undertaken to this end. An authoritative if cryptic description of them was provided in President Reagan's 1981 executive order on intelligence, wherein they were termed "Special Activities": "*Special Activities* means activities conducted in support of national foreign policy objectives abroad which are planned and executed so that the role of the United States Government is not apparent or acknowledged publicly, and functions in support of such activities, but which are not intended to influence United States political processes, public opinion, policies, or media and do not include diplomatic activities or the collection and production of intelligence or related support functions."[10]

A third set of activities, known as "counterintelligence," or "CI," is also included in the operational repertoire of the intelligence agencies. These activities protect the product and the process of intelligence from disclosure to unauthorized persons. They also attempt to protect the national policymaking process from unauthorized disclosures and foreign espionage, and they attempt to shield U.S. government installations, property, activities, and officials from foreign espionage, sabotage, or terrorist attacks at home and abroad. President Reagan's executive order defined counterintelligence as "information gathered and activities conducted to protect against espionage, other intelligence activities, sabotage, or assassination conducted for or on behalf of foreign powers, organizations, persons, or international terrorist activities, but not including personnel, physical, document, or communications security programs."[11]

In official parlance, then, intelligence (or, as many prefer, "foreign intelligence"*) has been understood to embrace three kinds of operations:

---

*This term is often used to distinguish activities of the intelligence community from domestic criminal intelligence investigations. The reasons for and significance of that distinction will be explored here shortly.

collection, covert action, and counterintelligence. Since 1947 these functions have been performed by an "intelligence community," which is the official shorthand for the following agencies: The Central Intelligence Agency; the Defense Intelligence Agency; the National Security Agency; offices within the Department of Defense which administer various aircraft and satellite reconnaissance programs; the Bureau of Intelligence and Research of the Department of State; the intelligence elements of the armed forces, the Federal Bureau of Investigation, the Department of the Treasury, and the Department of Energy; and the staff elements of the Director of Central Intelligence, which assist him in his efforts to make the "community" concept a reality.[12] Each of these organizations will be discussed in some detail later. First, however, it is necessary to take a closer look at the three operational disciplines which they, as a community, employ.

The Collection Function

For centuries, in peacetime as well as in wartime, the collection of foreign intelligence has been part of the business of statecraft. More importantly, it has been part of the American scene ever since the nation's birth. The framers of the Constitution knew about and valued the contributions of collection operations[13] and, as Charles Beard noted long ago, their writings laid out a distinct and coherent view of the "national interest" which justified them.[14] The framers understood the world and relations among nations as competitive at best and potentially hostile and dangerous at worst.[15] This gave urgency to the task they set for themselves in the Constitutional Convention: to create a viable governing apparatus for the new American national entity while preserving individual liberties and local governmental authority.

More specifically, this view shaped their ideas about how to equip the national government for its roles in the external world. In their circumstances, and with their world view, prudent nation-creators would be sure to provide the tools necessary to deter the most blatant aggressions and to cope with the more subtle – and more likely – challenges from abroad. Thus it was held that an efficient and effective national government must afford the best security that can be devised. And it was understood that an efficient and effective government in that sense is one whose relative position and capabilities in the international arena do not invite foreign challenges.[16] Attention to national security instruments was, indeed, viewed as wholly natural. In their era and their terms, a national security establishment was conceived primarily as a militia. But they also thought explicitly of another capability: the information-gathering function performed by the national governing authorities.

American government officials in the latter part of the twentieth century have little difficulty understanding these perspectives. The realities of the postwar world – the destructiveness of modern weaponry, the speed with which vast harm can be inflicted upon one nation by another, the shrinking of the world as multifaceted interdependence grows – have only enhanced the role of knowledge in policy calculations, and have thus, in official rationales, reemphasized the criticality of the intelligence community's collection function. As former Senator Frank Church, who headed the Senate's investigation of intelligence abuses in the mid-1970s, put it: "Those nations without a skillful intelligence service must navigate beneath a clouded sky."[17]

In practical effect, moreover, the current utility of knowledge in national security affairs is such that accurate intelligence is considered a "force multiplier" by military planners, enabling a smaller force to counterbalance a larger one and defeat it in combat.[18] It is also viewed as an effective deterrent to attack.[19] As an intelligence professional has noted: "Intelligence monitoring substitutes for full faith and credit between nations . . . The tensions of the nation-state system are, in other words, held in bounds not only by diplomacy and by mutual common sense but by carefully calibrated monitoring systems."[20] Further, the official rationale for collection activity is no longer stated only on the level of the national interest, as protecting the nation as an aggregate. President Reagan has attempted to make it clear to all Americans that in an age of terrorism their personal, individual safety depends in large part on the strength and efficiency of U.S. intelligence-gathering organizations.[21]

What, then, are the operational techniques that have been developed to serve these interests? Collection activities are generally discussed by intelligence professionals in four complementary categories: (1) scrutiny of open, public sources of information, and gathering of information through the normal channels of diplomacy; (2) covert espionage activities using human sources; (3) technical methods of collection which produce various types of imagery – graphic representations of observable phenomena – by photography or by other sensing devices; and (4) technical means of collection which involve interception of communications and other electronic signals emitted by transmitters in countries of interest.[22] Let us take a closer look at the characteristics of each.

We live in an era of exploding communications technology, of expanding worldwide data transmission links that have shrunk time and space in ways that were inconceivable only a quarter-century ago. Detailed information about many of the world's societies, and about the interactions of nations, is publicly available every day in newspapers, journals, and other periodicals, official statements of foreign governments, radio and television broadcasts, and so forth. Further, the normal and open diplomatic activities of American Foreign Service officers stationed abroad generate significant amounts of information about events and personalities in foreign societies. The American intelligence community makes a concerted attempt to use all this data.[23]

Some observers have long believed that nonsecret sources (including effective diplomatic contacts), when combined with scholarly research and analytical techniques, are adequate to satisfy most requirements. Intelligence professionals agree. But they hasten to add that the toughest intelligence targets even for diplomats are the closed societies which are America's major competitors. And they also observe that open sources are not very helpful for the less-developed societies of the world which lack the mature communications services required to transmit large volumes of information to outsiders. Nor do governments or major private organizations in such countries habitually produce significant statistics or other descriptions of their own societies. In these cases, clandestine collection by various techniques must be undertaken to seek key or significant information not obtainable by other means.[24]

To the American public, classic espionage is probably the most familiar of all intelligence operations, thanks to its perhaps inevitable romanticization in novels and motion pictures, and thanks also to the exposé literature that has emerged in the last decade. Public impressions of this collection technique have been shaped by many things, not the least of which is a fascination with the "dark side" of diplomacy and the dark side of human nature it is said to reveal. But these public images more often than not distort or obscure as much as they illuminate. Not all human intelligence involves suborning or entrapping foreign officials or dealing in dangerous circumstances with persons hoping to profit from traitorous activities in their own countries. Much of it, in fact, has to do with legal travellers, businessmen, and others who volunteer what they know, or may someday know, out of a sense of national duty. But in the public eye it is the more dramatic and adventurous activities which hold attention and shape widely shared perceptions. Some observers among a newly attentive public are literally enthralled by them. Others are repelled.

Intelligence professionals know about these public perceptions, and they understand the doubts and uneasiness that can arise from them. Like many concerned Americans, some professionals have wondered about the untoward effects on individual personalities, and on the nation as a whole, of engaging in what appears to be a most unsavory business. They also know that other means of collection — the technical means to be discussed shortly — are now better sources for many kinds of information required by decisionmakers, reducing human intelligence efforts to a rather small corner of the modern profession.[25]

But most intelligence officers, and most government officials who have been responsible for national-level management of the intelligence effort, insist that the human capability makes a uniquely valuable contribution to the process of formulating national policy: it provides information which other sources cannot obtain, particularly about potential opponents' intentions as opposed to their observable capabilities. Human sources are viewed as uniquely capable of finding out what kinds of people make up a country's leadership, what they care about as individuals and as a group, and what they are planning to do.[26] The human espionage rationale also emphasizes its utility in monitoring indicia of strength, such as political cohesion, for which technical means of collection, in their focus on observable data and objects, are unsuited.[27]

Thus, despite some misgivings about the propriety of the discipline, the effort has endured as a valued tool of the nation. Most practitioners and informed observers now argue that America must improve its human espionage capability, though there has been disagreement about how exactly to do that.

The mechanics of this collection technique — how it actually works — have been described in scattered corners of the public record. It involves exploitation of knowledge about foreign areas, personalities, and events that may be acquired by individuals who travel or live in those areas or who are acquainted with persons of interest to American policymakers. Some are witting and willing sources. Some are Americans; many are foreigners. Operational techniques often center around what Frank C. Carlucci, former deputy director of Central Intelligence, has called "essentially a contractual relationship" between American operatives and persons in key positions in foreign governments or societies who might be inaccessible to normal diplomatic contacts. Development of such relationships must usually be accomplished over a rather long period of time, so that mutual trust may be established and so that the source's skills and reliability can be tested and retested. The length of this process is one of its special frustrations, for it may be years before a source is in a position to provide the kind of information needed.[28]

Intelligence agents come in many shapes and sizes, and when "operational" they perform in any number of capacities. On one level there is the agent who is the politician, military leader, or labor union activist creating or participating in the events that the United States desires to learn about or to forecast. At a second level there are sources — mid-level officials — who have access to their leaders' views and plans and who can therefore provide important information about them. A third category includes persons who simply have access to locations where leaders' plans are formulated or announced, or to places (such as military installations) that may be of interest in themselves. And finally, there are many persons who may not be able to obtain substantive information – documents, photos, or authoritative accounts of policy deliberations – but who can serve in support capacities for other agents who do have that kind of access. All these people cooperate with U.S. intelligence efforts for many highly individualized reasons: greed, financial difficulties, ideological antipathies, prospects for personal advancement, and so forth. Assessing these motives is a major concern of American intelligence operatives in the early stages of their relationships with prospective sources.

A survey of the characteristics of human source operations serves also to describe their inherent limitations and to suggest why other techniques have been increasingly important in the postwar era. First, the information produced by each operation is only as reliable as the human source who obtains it. Where the agent is not providing documentary, or "hard," evidence, his reporting is subject to some very familiar human frailties. He can be deceived. He himself may be the deceiver. He may have access to only a small part of the problem or area examined, and he will see that part from only one perspective. His capacities for observation, moreover, may be limited by physical disabilities, by lack of technical qualifications, or simply by unfortunate placement. He has his own personal biases which may infect his reporting. And these considerations aside, he is after all a spy, whose veracity may be viewed by some as questionable in any case.

Secondly, each operation takes a very long time to plan and to put into place, and each requires a good deal of patience and careful management to nurture to maturity. This may call for more endurance than a government bureaucracy, even one devoted to intelligence, can muster. The informational payoff is distant and the operation meanwhile must survive numerous budget reviews, policy and program changes, and wholesale turnovers in administrations and top-level management.

Another limitation is that many of the factors important to the operation's success are well beyond the ability of the parties involved to control, and beyond the ability of the United States itself to affect. Perturbations within certain bounds are tolerable – they can be absorbed without ruining the operation. But wars, the toppling of governments, and political and diplomatic crises may undercut all operations they touch, even the most carefully planned ones.

Even when an agent is in place, ready to report, he seldom can respond immediately to fast-breaking collection needs, nor can he often seize fleeting opportunities and report back quickly on crisis conditions. Specific requirements outside of his normal set of tasks must be transmitted to him, and then he must take action and respond. In crises, and for early warning of attacks or other threats to national interests, most of these operations simply cannot satisfy the most pressing collection needs.

Exposure of these operations, another risk which is always present, is a major embarrassment, since they involve clandestine intrusions into foreign societies. Though technical means of collection may be even more intrusive, they do not as a rule involve the degree of penetration of foreign societies that observers find so objectionable in human source operations. Nor do they involve activities that can so readily be seen as treachery and manipulative cooptation.

An inherent limitation is that the information produced by each human resource operation is unlikely to cover the entirety of the problem addressed. Collection is usually very surgically targeted. It can be very good at what it is designed for but at the same time it may be unidimensional and limited in scope.

Finally, human source collection often simply provides information which confirms or perhaps explains what has been "seen" or "heard" by other sources and techniques. This in itself is a valuable contribution, to be sure. But human source operations are increasingly seen not as sources of truly original data, but as sources of amplifying or explanatory information which can help clarify (or further complicate) the analytical and interpretive task in Washington. This is quite a different justification for the effort than was available years ago, at the beginning of the Cold War, when competing or complementary techniques were not yet fully developed.

At the end of the 1950s intensified Soviet vigilance and countermeasures against human source operations substantially reduced their access to intelligence targets within the borders of the USSR. This placed a premium on new collection methods reliant on technology, especially photoreconnaissance. The U-2 and associated photographic technology had been under development by the CIA since 1954 and had been deployed in "meteorological squadrons" in Europe and Turkey since 1956. The U-2 planes flew photographic missions high over the Soviet Union, eluding interception until the May 1960 incident in which the plane flown by Francis Gary Powers was shot down. The U-2 remains to this day an important reconnaissance asset, along with other, more advanced aircraft and satellites, and the technology associated with these missions has proceeded apace. These techniques have become particularly important tools of early warning for the national defense establishment. They are also essential elements of American capability for verifying Soviet compliance with missile or arms agreements.

The several "imagery-producing" techniques all involve reproducing, electronically or by optical means, a graphic representation of objects on film, on an electronic display device, or on another medium.[29] Photography is of course the oldest of these methods. Cameras and films today provide what many officials consider to be the ultimate intelligence product: a picture of often startling quality and detail taken from high above the earth. Since optical photographic equipment and techniques require daylight or photoflash augmentation to expose the film, the use of infrared film, recording temperature variations on the ground at any time of day or night, substantially augments these capabilities.[30]

Radar imagery, produced by a device that emits a signal and then records it as it is reflected from a target, is also available as a day or night, all-weather collection technique. It requires sophisticated processing and specialized interpretive skills, however, and at present it does not provide specific identification of objects unless it is correlated with data collected simultaneously from other sources.

All imagery depicts only what is observed or sensed, of course, and is often viewed mainly as a valuable, indeed, most reliable, indicator of military-industrial capabilities (as distinct from intentions). Human intelligence specialists are quick to argue that the imagery-producing techniques are not collection panaceas in that regard. But others respond that imagery techniques frequently are the most reliable source of information on intentions, since they provide incontrovertible evidence of actions from which plans can then be inferred.[31]

Signals intelligence as a collection discipline embraces four related but analytically distinct activities: communications intelligence, electronic intelligence, radiation intelligence, and telemetry intelligence.[32] These involve collection of data via intercepting foreign electronic signals emitted, intentionally or unintentionally, in the electromagnetic spectrum. Collection is accomplished in diverse ways: from "airborne platforms," from ground stations, and from specially outfitted ships and submarines at sea. The technology associated with this discipline is highly complex; indeed, it is at the frontiers of communications and electronics technology, using (and depending upon) sophisticated collection equipment and enormous storage, sorting, decryption, and retrieval capacities in massive computer systems. In all cases there are two kinds of information products resulting from these activities: substantive information on national capabilities and intentions, and technical information about the machinery and equipment which emits or transmits the intercepted signals.

Communications intelligence involves intercepting foreign interpersonal communications − transmissions of information by radio or wire. In concept this effort is not a particularly new one. Interception and decoding of all types of messages have been parts of international relations for centuries, and have been integral elements of the American intelligence effort since the Revolutionary War. Today this operational technique is viewed as a primary source of all categories of information about foreign nations, though it is quite susceptible to deception, and though analytical failures can result in harmful misinterpretations, false alarms, or faulty predictions. Additionally, since most governments know that their communications, whether by radio or wire, are subject to interception by a number of other nations, communications security practices frequently diminish the collection "take" appreciably.

Electronics intelligence is technical and substantive information derived from foreign *non*communications electromagnetic radiations. Most modern military-related systems and activities make extensive use of equipment (such as radar) which, when operating, emits distinctive electronic signals that may travel great distances. When collected and analyzed, these signals may facilitate the locating and identifying of a potential enemy's electronic equipment. This requires, of course, a substantial data base concerning the electronic "signatures" of targeted equipment – an electronic order-of-battle, so to speak. Building and maintaining such a data base is an important part of the electronics intelligence mission, and a constant concern of specialists in this discipline.

Closely related to electronics intelligence but requiring uniquely different collection and analysis techniques is the radiation intelligence effort. This concentrates on non-information-bearing energy elements emitted from foreign electronic devices and systems. Certain electronic equipment, even when it is not performing its designed functions, may emit ancillary signals that can be detected and recorded. Analysts may be able to use such information to help identify and define foreign nations' equipment capabilities as well as to determine the electronic "profile" of foreign nations' peacetime defense establishments.

Finally, telemetry intelligence is information derived from the interception and analysis of foreign telemetry, the signals sent, for instance, to control foreign missiles and satellites. If this can be done quickly enough in the case of missiles, it might permit advance determination of flight paths, trajectories, and targets – no small accomplishment in an era in which strategic warfighting remains a substantial concern.

The Counterintelligence Function

The definition of counterintelligence has been a matter of some controversy among professionals and informed observers.[33] All agree, however, that CI as an activity involves a distinctive set of operations which protect the American intelligence apparatus and the national policymaking process from penetration by foreign espionage, human and technical.[34] They also protect the nation and its citizens, activities, and facilities at home and abroad from foreign sabotage or terrorism. CI specialists attempt to identify, and then to neutralize or manipulate, those activities in the U.S. national interest.

Though the words protect and guard often appear in descriptions of these operations, it would be wrong to conclude that they are defensive or reactive in nature. In point of fact, CI specialists are greatly concerned that their operations be both active and aggressive.

Three distinctive features of CI operations warrant mention. The first deals with operational locale and with potential impact on individual Americans. While foreign collection activities and covert action may affect U.S. citizens who happen to be close to the targets of the operations, their domestic impact is likely to be minimal and incidental. But the situation for counterintelligence operations is quite different. Clearly, if foreign "threats" operate in our midst, searching for islands of respite and support and seeking inroads for further infiltration, then the effort to find them and neutralize their activity is likely to impinge significantly upon the lives and activities of Americans, and in many cases upon spheres of individual privacy held by many to be protected from governmental intrusion. As one spokesman for the CI effort has noted, it may, for example, sometimes be necessary to "observe the activities of perfectly loyal citizens in order to learn about the activities of hostile intelligence services."[35] Or, as FBI Director William Webster once put it: "Because of the FBI's counterintelligence mission in the United States, American citizens are sometimes of necessity the objects of inquiry, either as a result of their clandestine relationship with a foreign power, or because of a foreign power's interest in them. Contacts between Americans and foreign intelligence officers are always of concern to us, even though the contact may turn out to be innocent."[36]

A second characteristic is an item of professional dogma among practitioners: that there is an important analytical and practical distinction between CI and law enforcement operations. The asserted distinction centers on the purpose of each kind of activity. Law enforcement operations, as part of the criminal justice system, ulitmately seek the punishment of offenders. Counterintelligence operations do not have this overriding punitive purpose. Their intent, in the end, "is not to prevent crimes and punish criminals but rather to learn about and to neutralize the activities of the nation's enemies."[37] The criminal law assumes an adversary relationship between the government and persons suspected of a crime. But CI specialists insist that their relationship with the targets of their activity is not necessarily adversarial, since deprivation of liberty is not an inevitable prospect and since *all* citizens have an important stake in the national security interests served by those operations.[38] They insist, moveover, that this distinction should make a difference in the regulations and controls applied to CI operations, and they have steadfastly resisted attempts to transport law enforcement rules into the "national security" arena.[39]

A third important characteristic of CI is the result of policies which do recognize some such distinction. The counterintelligence professional has argued, with a good deal of success, that his operations must be initiated, even against Americans, on the basis of fragments of information, with much wider operational focus, and on grounds that cannot be held to criminal-law standards of reasonable suspicion. This reasoning has been widely accepted in official forums outside the intelligence community — even in those, such as the courts, which have been most sensitive to the need to protect citizens from abuse of governmental power.[40]

The result, for CI operators and managers, has been a more expansive sphere of operational permissibility than is the case in law enforcement. Rules have permitted "intrusive" operational techniques to be used earlier without a showing that a crime has been or may be committed and without the judicial warrant required in law enforcement cases. The distinction is controversial, and we shall see that the 1970s regulatory reform movement attacked it directly.

Counterintelligence as an operational discipline rests on a world view which understands the international environment as a constant source of threats to security. The world is seen as an arena in which America's major competitors harbor continuing hostile designs and conduct activities inimical to the interests of American society, even within the nation's borders. Descriptions of "threats" composing this world view are detailed and voluminous, and are taken by CI specialists to be controlling in discussions about operational controls.

Concern about the corrupting influence of foreign nations' actions within and outside of our borders is not new in America. Numerous references in the *Federalist* called attention to those dangers. Alexander Hamilton, for instance, described how the "bribes and intrigues" of other nations might affect the course of policymaking in America. He also spoke of the desire among foreign powers "to gain an improper ascendant in our councils."[41] In 1798, just after the Bill of Rights was added to the Constitution, Congress passed the Alien and Sedition Acts. The Alien Act provided for the deportation of all aliens judged dangerous to the nation's domestic peace and safety, and the Sedition Act prohibited "false, scandalous, and malicious" writing intended to arouse sentiment against the government or to aid a hostile foreign nation.

Today the main foreign antagonists are well known, of course, with the Soviet Union leading the list. Particularly in recent years, intelligence professionals argue that Soviet bloc intelligence activity against the United States has been an important factor in the "rapidly increasing . . . military, economic, and political power" of the Soviet Union and its allies.[42] The Soviets, they say, do not share the Western tendency to treat intelligence capabilities, especially covert action, as "lesser" instruments of foreign policy. Counterpoised instruments must, therefore, be mobilized against them.

Intelligence professionals are not alone in adopting this view. Increasingly the government's entire foreign policy apparatus has been concerned about a wide and global array of Soviet intelligence operations, including efforts to manipulate the press in foreign countries; dissemination of forged documents to mislead foreign governments, media, and public opinion; disinformation activities – circulation of rumors, etc., to discredit the United States and its leaders; political influence operations, which seek to exploit contacts with political, economic, and media figures in other countries to obtain active collaboration with Moscow; use of academics and journalists to pursue Soviet foreign policy objectives in contacts with foreign colleagues; operation of clandestine radio stations; and control of international and local front organizations that serve to advance Soviet aims worldwide.[43]

The CI rationale also takes particular note of the involvement of Soviet intelligence agencies in specific trouble spots affecting U.S. interests. That activity has reportedly included multidimensional campaigns against the modernization of tactical nuclear forces in Europe and against deployment of the "enhanced radiation warhead" there; covert manipulation of leftist insurgents during the civil strife in El Salvador; and attempts to weaken the U.S.-sponsored peace process in the Middle East.[44]

While the Soviet effort is seen as the largest and most capable threat, the activities of other intelligence services in the United States and elsewhere have become part of the operational rationale for American counterintelligence. In fact, after examining the extensive operations of the South Korean Central Intelligence Agency in the United States, the Senate Select Committee admonished the executive branch to establish a special standing requirement for our intelligence agencies to try to discover all such activity. And especially in the 1970s the threat of terrorist activity, whether or not connected to any foreign intelligence agency, was an important element in the world view supporting the American CI effort.[45]

But what *are* the capabilities and activities of the CI discipline, exactly? Practitioners think of them in two analytically distinct categories: defensive operations and practices which are designed to improve security, and more active, offensive measures whose purpose and function is as much exploitative as protective.[46] Security measures are essentially passive, static defenses undertaken to counter what an adversary – a spy, saboteur, or terrorist – is known to do or known to be able to do. They take forms now familiar to anyone who has been associated with the government. Personnel and information security practices include such devices as security clearances, polygraph examinations, procedures and rules for handling classified documents and materials, and encryption techniques. Physical security measures for installations include badge and pass systems, alarms, surveillance and warning devices, and fences and other barriers. Area control measures may include curfews, checkpoints, border control regulations, and so forth.[47]

Active, "offensive" CI seeks first to detect and then to neutralize or manipulate the ongoing activity of foreign intelligence services or terrorist organizations. Detection is of course the first phase, in which foreign operations and the individuals involved in them are identified. When a hostile operation is reported or discovered, a decision might be made simply to permit it to continue, closely monitored. Perhaps a certain amount of information will be released in response to foreign espionage requirements in order to learn the foreign service's interests and modes of operation. Or false or "doctored" information may be provided, perhaps as part of a larger deception plan.

American operatives may also try to turn the discovered operation back upon its initiators via penetration, double agent, or "induced double agent" activities. Penetration is accomplished through inducement of a defection or recruitment of a foreign professional "in place." The operative continues as before in the employ of the foreign service, but in actuality he is secretly working under American direction. Double agent operations arise when an individual is approached for recruitment by a foreign operative and either he reports it to CI personnel or they, having monitored the contact through their own initiative and techniques, persuade him to act in a double agent capacity. The third type of operation involves inducing a foreign espionage approach by "dangling" an ostensibly attractive operational opportunity in hopes that it will lure a foreign service into the trap.

Various kinds of specific investigative techniques are characteristic of CI operations.[48] Surreptitious surveillance methods have been used extensively and have become especially controversial. These include photography, wiretap and eavesdropping devices, and television and film techniques. Physical surveillance, informant infiltration of targeted groups, and extensive data bank systems (dossiers in the era of manual filing systems, now computer files) have been integral to this specialty, as well, and no less alarming to some attentive elements of American society.

The Covert Action Function

Though the general subject of covert action is treated by government officials as quite sensitive, no one denies that we as a nation deliberately undertake, by means of the intelligence agencies (specifically the CIA), actions to influence events and politics abroad without revealing our involvement. In fact, there has been some effort to inform the public about the basic characteristics and objectives of the capability.[49]

All available definitions point to central propositions about the capability, propositions that we must take care to identify here. First, these operations are intended, at least in concept, to support broader national policy goals and to advance specific national interests. They are instruments activated by imperatives emerging from some larger concept of the nation's needs, and they are designed to be consistent with and supportive of American foreign policy more generally. Thus two other propositions about the internal mechanisms of American policymaking are implied: that the impetus to conduct these operations comes from explicit concepts of larger national goals (not, say, from the momentum of existing operations or from a generalized interest in exercising this capability); and that there is sufficient coherence in American foreign policy objectives, and sufficient coordination of goals with instruments, to insure that all these operations are consistent with the national intent, however expressed.

Secondly, on a more general level, these operations are by definition "official" United States government activities, though they are planned and conducted in a manner which hides or disguises official sponsorship. They are national behavior in the same sense as are other external actions, such as the negotiating of commercial agreements or the stationing of troops. They express and reflect the goals America adopts as a nation and the values we adopt as a society. They do this whether they are ultimately revealed to the public or not, and this gives rise in many quarters to concern about conformance with notions of how the United States, as a society, should behave. Such concern quickly takes us beyond assessment of the extent to which the internal mechanisms of decisionmaking can sensibly connect ends and means. We enter instead the troubled arena of conflicting normative predilections, principles, and beliefs about both ends and means.

A third feature of covert action emphasized in the official definitions is its foreignness. The operations themselves are conducted abroad, though certain support functions might well have to be performed in the United States. Given the nature of these activities, it is hardly surprising that those who manage and conduct them wish to make it clear that their domestic impact is minimal and incidental. Arguments about regulating and confining this capability often have roots in fears that it might be turned inward, or that even when directed outward it may affect American society and politics in unintended ways.

Covert action is, additionally, analytically and operationally distinct from other intelligence functions, a point which intelligence professionals will insist upon at the outset of any inquiry such as this. Whatever one may think of covert action, they say, it has little to do with other operational capabilities. Some, in fact, have argued for its organizational separation from other intelligence activities.[50]

But all this tells us little about what these operations may actually involve. They provide action options located somewhere on a spectrum between diplomacy and the use of force, but what exactly are those options? Data accumulated in the public domain over the last decade are helpful here.

We have, for instance, Arthur Schlesinger's survey of major covert action operations undertaken by American presidents in the early days of the Cold War. They include CIA involvement in toppling governments in Iran (1953) and Guatemala (1954), a failed attempt to do the same in Indonesia (1958), successful roles in installing regimes in Egypt (1954) and Laos (1959), and preparation for the expedition which ultimately became known as the Bay of Pigs Invasion (1960-1961). Roger Hilsman discusses many of the same episodes in his own retrospective look at his time in the Kennedy Administration. Henry Kissinger's memoirs focus on more recent activities, perhaps most notably on CIA operations in Chile prior to the death of Salvatore Allende. In that instance, he notes, covert U.S. financing of opposition political factions in Chile had its origins in the Kennedy administration and continued under President Johnson. But in the Nixon years, the president took a personal interest in the CIA as a last-minute tool to engineer the electoral defeat of Allende, even to the point of overruling the agency's own reservations about its ability to accomplish what he desired.[51]

We have, additionally, the views of former covert action operatives and managers who in recent years have attempted to describe the general outlines and purposes of this capability in public. Richard M. Bissell, Jr., who began work on covert action problems in the CIA in 1954 and rose to be deputy director for plans, has noted three traditional purposes of covert action.[52] Some operations were initiated to influence the general climate of opinion in foreign states, so that they might favor American objectives and democratic values more generally. A second type of operation attempted to influence the political balance within foreign countries by strengthening the position of some individuals and institutions and weakening that of others. A third hoped to induce some specific national action serving U.S. objectives. These latter operations were generally one-time, short-term efforts which ended upon success or failure of the immediate objective. The operations conducted to serve these ends included:

(1) Provision of political advice and counsel to leaders and influential individuals in foreign states. Often these advisory relationships began as American collection operations and were broadened when sufficient mutual trust had developed between intelligence personnel and the leaders of the countries in which they were stationed.

(2) Development of contacts and relationships with individuals who, though not in leadership or influential positions at the time, might advance

to leadership positions in the future. These operations might also include actions intended to improve these individuals' prospects for advancement in their own societies.

(3) Provision of financial support or other assistance to foreign political parties. This was particularly important in Europe after World War II. Much covert support went to Socialist parties then in an attempt to provide a reasonable leftist alternative for persons who might otherwise have been drawn to Communist parties.

(4) Provision of support and assistance to private organizations such as labor unions, youth groups, and professional associations.

(5) Covert propaganda undertaken with the assistance of, for example, foreign media organizations and individual journalists.

(6) Relationships with friendly intelligence services to provide technical training and other assistance.

(7) Economic operations by which financial assistance was provided to foreign states for various purposes, but through intermediate sources not overtly connected with the American government.

(8) Paramilitary or counterinsurgency training provided to regimes facing civil strife, where acknowledgment of official United States involvement was not desired.

(9) Development of influential connections inside a particular regime with government departments and factions – particularly, for example, with the military.

(10) Political action and paramilitary operations which attempted to topple foreign regimes and install successors more favorable to U.S. objectives and values. The operations in Iran and Guatemala and the Bay of Pigs invasion were of this genre.

From participants and observers who served at policy levels, then, we have descriptions of operations encompassing large-scale paramilitary campaigns, on the one hand, and secret political maneuvering in foreign electoral processes on the other. Additionally, a number of former intelligence officers have published detailed descriptions of a diverse array of operations worldwide.[53]

There have also been well-documented reports and generally balanced corrective proposals published by the United States Senate after its select investigating committee under Frank Church had inquired into the facts surrounding various allegations of operational excesses. The most startling of these were allegations of CIA participation in assassination plots, a subject treated in the Church Committee's *Interim Report,* published in 1975.[54] Though the inquiry fell short of proving that murderous activities had been undertaken, it did find that some thought had been given to them at operational levels within the CIA. Potential targets included Fidel Castro and Patrice Lumumba. It also found that in those cases and others the CIA had intended to destabilize certain regimes or to bring about coups, and that political violence and possible murders were foreseeable consequences of those actions. The Church Committee's *Final Report,* issued in 1976, contains a comprehensive analysis of the history of our covert action capability, describing both operations and the control procedures governing them.[55]

Even as the era of revelations recedes, the public learns of other activities in diverse ways. Occasionally government officials inadvertently disclose them, or defend operations which might be revealed in "leaks". Former Secretary of State Vance, for instance, speaking on the CBS television program "Face the Nation" in February 1977, defended the payment of secret funds through CIA channels to Jordan's King Hussein. He explained that the United States has "cooperative agreements leading toward common objectives with many countries," and that when intelligence activities are involved, the CIA is America's vehicle of cooperation.[56] Other revelations are generated from time to time by dogged "outside" investigators. John Marks, for instance, published an extensive account of CIA-sponsored research into behavior control via exotic drugs. And soon after the Soviet invasion of Afghanistan the *New York Times* reported that the CIA was providing aid to the Afghan rebels fighting Soviet occupation forces. Reagan administration defenses of covert action to aid rebels opposing the Sandinist regime in Nicaragua have been the most vivid recent example of public postures on such operations, involving extensive media coverage and congressional debate.[57]

We can, then, give some life to the official definitions of covert action by surveying the information already in the public domain concerning past activities. In doing so, we begin to perceive the impressive length and breadth of this capability, at least as it has been exercised in the quarter-century since World War II. It has been, in those years, a policy instrument of worldwide reach, seeking influence in foreign governments, taking sides in foreign electoral processes or other internal political events, supporting political factions and their military forces engaged in violent civil strife, often in places where other great powers were active or interested, and even taking steps to complicate or deepen foreign military adventures of the Soviet Union (as in Afghanistan). It remains a capability which, even in its largest and most ambitious manifestations, intelligence practitioners steadfastly argue must be maintained and exercised as part of a vigorous foreign policy.[58]

Allen Dulles outlined the covert action rationale at some length in his memoirs, describing a Communist blueprint for world domination that made an American response essential to the preservation of freedom. Communist movements around the world, and anticolonial sentiment in many turbulent and strategically important areas of the world, gave the

Soviet Union appreciable advantages and lucrative targets in its competition with the West. America, Dulles believed, had to fight back. And America did indeed fight back during his tenure as director of Central Intelligence in the Eisenhower and Kennedy years. CIA involvement in Iran, Guatemala, Indonesia, and Cuba — which others have since castigated as interventionist — was merely an answer to the real Soviet challenges Dulles saw in each country. And more generally, he argued, in view of the irretrievably adversarial nature of the world, America must be prepared to act early enough to forestall *potential* Soviet advances: "Wherever we can, we must help to shore up both the will to resist and confidence in the ability to resist. . . . Whenever we are given the opportunity to help, we should assist in building up the ability of threatened countries and do it long before the Communist penetration drives a country to the point of no return."[59] The United States, moreover, should not wait for invitations to intervene. Rather, American policymakers should determine unilaterally when, where, and how to act. Nor should they focus only upon those nations not yet under Soviet control. They should actively attempt to unseat any regimes installed by the USSR as a result of covert or overt aggression or manipulation.[60]

There is much resonance between Dulles' perspective and the viewpoints of others who have more recently been involved in directing the tools of American foreign policy. As former Under Secretary of State George Ball, for instance, has noted: "There is still no international police force to deal with thugs, and until we develop one, if we ever do, great nations must retain a capability to intervene in situations that endanger their security." And former Secretary of State Henry Kissinger, in his discussion of the CIA's activity in Chile, emphasized the imperatives of the ideological and political struggle with the Soviet Union. In the context of that international struggle, he felt, "it was neither morally nor politically unjustified for the United States to support those internal political forces seeking to maintain a democratic counterweight to radical dominance. On the contrary no responsible national leader could have done otherwise."[61] Though some observers might disagree with Kissinger concerning what actions the responsibilities of leadership may compel, it is true that a whole galaxy of national leaders supported the covert action function at its birth in the postwar intelligence community, just as many others have supported it in the years since then.[62]

In general, then, covert action advocates have propounded an operating rationale which understands the world as fundamentally competitive, adversarial, and in ascertainable respects hostile and dangerous. For them, protection and pursuit of national security interests become primary values, simply because the very nature and operation of the international system place a premium on tools of statecraft which can help maintain a nation's position vis-a-vis other competing actors. Even more importantly, there are some significant international actors that have genuinely malignant designs and that hope not just to gain competitive advantage but to destroy the major competition. Perception of international danger magnifies the perceived utility of tools which can engage and neutralize intractably aggressive forces wherever they may appear.

An additional, and equally fundamental, proposition can be discerned: when America (or any other power) acts, the consequences of that action can be anticipated – indeed, predicted – and the action and its effects can be controlled and directed always to the appointed ends. The world is in that sense manageable and maleable. Action can be efficacious in predictable ways. Thus, a sense of national confidence and efficacy infuses the world view that has supported covert action as an American tool of policy.

Not everyone, of course, sees either the world or American roles in exactly that way. Nor does everyone share a sense of confidence in American ability to "manage" foreign events. But many who have had serious reservations about covert action have also had to come to terms with the argument about threat. The views of former Senator Frank Church are illustrative here. When he began the Senate's inquiry into alleged intelligence abuses he characterized the CIA as a "rogue elephant," a description which became widely accepted as accurate. Yet at the end of his investigation he decided that America, as a nation that must live among other nations, ought to retain some sort of covert action capability. He recognized the obvious and important costs of using it, but also that the inescapable prospect of danger to America justified maintaining this instrument, carefully controlled, among the many in our national arsenal.[63]

Current international exigencies naturally account in great measure for the potency of this perspective. We live, after all, in the age of the nuclear balance of terror, a modern reality which magnifies the peril otherwise associated with international competition. Ours is an age, furthermore, of instability and internal restiveness in many societies touched by American activities or interests. The juxtaposition of strength and weakness, and growing disparities in the material well-being of nations, combine to increase world tensions and to make the task of resolving them more complex.

But we would be wrong if we viewed the set of perceptions just outlined as a wholly modern phenomenon, leading perhaps to the conclusion that covert action is a transitory product of its age. In fact, America has engaged in covert international activities since her founding. An operation involving the French and later the Spanish secretly provided arms to the American revolutionaries fighting for independence from the British sovereign. And a review of the perspectives of the men who shortly thereafter created our government discovers several themes which recur today in the rationale for covert action. The framers of the Constitution did not, of course, speak directly to that capability, except in oblique references to the influence-seeking predilections of nations. But they shared many of the perceptions of the world, and of America's interests in the world, that support arguments in favor of the covert action capability in our time. In a sense, then, as practitioners and other spokesmen for the capability are quick to note, the modern rationales simply carry forward old perspectives into a new era.[64] Seen in that way, the capability helps America adapt to and influence new realities in order to serve fundamentally traditional goals and values.

The Organizational Context

The definitive organizational history of the American intelligence effort has yet to be written, though several researchers have tried to describe parts of it.[65] For purposes of this study I need only summarize the broad outlines of what is now known about the evolution of the various American intelligence agencies. The ultimate concern here is to provide an overview of the modern "intelligence community" and to give some sense of its institutional history, as well as to delineate the general division of labor among its elements. To this point I have described what intelligence capabilities the United States has chosen to maintain, and why. My interest now is to establish in general who has these capabilities.

I noted earlier that the modern operational capabilities of the intelligence agencies had early antecedents in America. But a formalized institutional structure did not emerge in any operational realm until well into the twentieth century. Instead, for intelligence collection early presidents tended to rely on the normal processes of diplomacy. When there was need for specialized and secret collection missions, or when something akin to covert political action was desired, "special envoys" were used.[66] A counterintelligence capability of sorts was instituted during the Civil War, when Union authorities employed the Pinkerton detective agency for security-oriented purposes, but this wartime effort was later disestablished. No one conceived of "intelligence" as an activity requiring a permanent specialized apparatus to undertake and direct it.

Moreover, such activities were conceived and treated as executive functions. The president's primacy had foundations in his constitutional authority as commander-in-chief and in his preeminence in foreign affairs which was recognized from earliest times. His authority in counterintelligence had further grounding in his obligation (under Article II, section 1) to preserve, protect, and defend the Constitution, and, by implication, to protect the government from those who would subvert or overthrow it by illegal means.[67]

Congress, of course, has its own constitutional powers in foreign affairs, as well as the power of the purse and the regulatory authority conferred by the Necessary and Proper clause. The legislature did play some role, though quite a circumspect one, in intelligence affairs from the beginning. In 1793, for instance, it set up a procedure for financing secret foreign affairs activities: a statute provided for expenses of "intercourse or treaty" with foreign states; the president was required to report all expenditures, but he was permitted to file a certificate in lieu of a detailed report for payments that he wanted to keep secret.[68] But even in matters such as these – legislating on the administrative periphery of operational activities – the congressional role was frequently contentious.[69] For the first 150 years of our national existence, congressional "action" was confined to measures that shaped or sharpened operational tools which remained in the hands of the president.

To be sure, the gradual emergence of intelligence structures, at the hands of the executive, was associated with several legislative grants of authority. But these statutes were so vaguely written that they left much latitude to executive implementers. The Justice Department's investigative powers within the United States stemmed from an appropriations statute, first enacted in 1871, allowing expenditure of funds for detection and prosecution of crimes against the United States.[70] Initially, the attorney general employed several permanent investigators under that authority, supplementing them with either private investigators or Secret Service agents. When Congress prohibited use of the Secret Service for those purposes in 1908, the attorney general created the earliest institutional predecessor of the FBI, the Bureau of Investigation in the Department of Justice. Congress quickly authorized funds for the bureau, and statutes thereafter expanded its investigative jurisdiction. By 1916 it had also expanded in manpower to 300 agents.

The combined efforts of the departments of Justice and State then obtained a major revision of the Justice Department's appropriations statute, permitting the attorney general to appoint officials who would detect and prosecute federal crimes, assist in the protection of the president, and, significantly, "conduct such other investigations regarding official matters under the control of the Department of Justice and the Department of State as may be directed by the Attorney General."[71] That provision opened the way to initiation of unspecified operations beyond the realm of law enforcement. It was immediately put to use against the threat of subversion by aliens in the months preceding U.S. entry into World War I. Half a century later it remained a major element of the FBI's operational authority. In 1972, for instance, J. Edgar Hoover, in testimony before the House of Representatives, cited the statute and described the FBI missions it then embraced. They included diverse investigative activities which monitored the Communist party, "communist front groups," "other totalitarian organizations," and other individuals and groups suspected of trying to overthrow the government.[72]

Though these legislative enactments provided the foundations for what became the nation's major domestic counterintelligence effort, it was, again, presidential directives and imminent wartime exigency which breathed new life into the FBI in the administration of Franklin Roosevelt.[73] Thereafter, evolution of the CI functions and organization of the FBI (and of similar capabilities in the military services) were primarily matters of executive discretion, responding to perceived security needs, particularly in wartime. We shall see that much of the regulatory problem with regard to CI has to do with retrospective reservations on the part of some observers about such deference to essentially unsupervised executive power.

The institutional history of the other two operational capabilities — foreign intelligence collection and covert action — is much the same. Both were associated with broad (or vague) statutory authorizations. And for both, the evolution of operations and organizations was mainly a matter of executive action. From early times until 1947 the president's authority in these spheres was grounded, as we have seen, in the commander-in-chief power during war and the foreign relations authority in time of peace. In the exercise of these powers, presidents experimented fitfully with several kinds of intelligence services or agencies, mainly in the twentieth century. But they did not enter upon the intelligence effort seriously or on any appreciable scale until World War II. At that time the president had at his disposal the as-yet-uncoordinated resources of the State Department's diplomatic reporting, attache and signals intercept reports from the departments of War and Navy, and the FBI under the Department of Justice. The coming war in Europe convinced President Roosevelt of the need for a centralized intelligence function, and this was established by directive in 1941. A year later the Office of Strategic Services, the main operational precursor of the Central Intelligence Agency, was established by executive order.[74]

So it was that the first serious attempt to rationalize the president's management of intelligence functions occurred in the context of wartime exigency and without congressional participation. At the beginning of the modern intelligence effort it was the president's foreign affairs power and his authority as commander-in-chief which combined to provide its legitimizing foundation and rationale. And at the time, both powers were extensive and expanding.

Many observers have believed that the wartime ethos in which the modern intelligence community was born and nurtured had a lingering effect in later years, coloring official and popular attitudes toward all intelligence functions.[75] That may be so, particularly in the arena of covert action. But, just as importantly in many respects, at the time when the centralized intelligence effort was constituted and constructed, when all of its capabilities were being designed and oriented against external threats, it was the president and his executive branch advisors who were in charge, not Congress.

It was not until 1947 that Congress spoke by statute specifically to the "business of intelligence" via the National Security Act of 1947. That statute established the Central Intelligence Agency and charged it with the following responsibilities: (1) to advise the National Security Council (also created by the Act) in matters concerning such intelligence activities of government departments and agencies as relate to national security; (2) to make recommendations to the National Security Council for coordinating such intelligence activities of government departments and agencies as relate to national security; (3) to correlate and evaluate intelligence relating to the national security, and to provide for the appropriate dissemination of such intelligence within the government; (4) to perform, for the benefit of the existing intelligence agencies, such additional services of common concern as the National Security Council determines can be more efficiently accomplished centrally; and (5) to perform such other functions and duties related to intelligence affecting the national security as the National Security Council may from time to time direct.[76] In addition, the director of Central Intelligence was made responsible for protecting intelligence sources and methods from disclosure, and the CIA was prohibited from engaging in internal security functions within the United States.

Insofar as it dealt with the CIA, the National Security Act was mainly an attempt to provide central structure for the then-existing intelligence community and to centralize certain of its functions. It did not explicitly indicate that the CIA as an agency should or would engage in clandestine collection of information. Some observers have thought this significant, later arguing that the CIA was intended mainly to perform analytical functions centrally and that collection duties should be detached from it in order to conform to the original legislative intent. Others have disagreed.[77] It is clear, however, on the face of the act itself, that Congress knew that intelligence collection was occurring in "the existing intelligence agencies" and that the legislature did not by this act attempt to regulate or intrude upon those activities. Thus, the National Security Act of 1947 has since been understood as the institutional foundation of the modern foreign intelligence collection capability. In that sense it was and still is important, representing an attempt by Congress to exercise its own authority in the intelligence arena. But it was a most circumspect enactment, taking executive branch capabilities essentially as given and making some arrangements for coordinating them within an emerging "intelligence community."

The covert action capability has more ambiguous foundations, though it incontestably vested in the CIA immediately after passage of the 1947 act. It was not specified therein as one of the CIA's assigned missions, but the executive quickly found sanction for it in the provision directing the CIA to "perform such other functions and duties related to intelligence affecting the national security as the National Security Council may from time to time direct."[78] Early NSC directives did, in fact, direct the CIA to undertake psychological, political, and paramilitary operations as part of the effort to contain the Soviet Union. And, with the absorption of that function – an old capability to be sure but one which had been most recently a combative instrument in the hands of a wartime president – the peacetime operational repertoire of the modern intelligence community was complete.[79]

In the years since 1947 new intelligence agencies have appeared, new kinds of collection technologies have been incorporated into their capabilities, and the agencies have attempted to respond to new kinds of demands and missions. Several iterations of command and control structures have come and gone, as well. Through all these changes, however, the "community" concept has remained, and several ideas associated with it should be noted.

First, the term "intelligence community" is sometimes used to denote not only the operational agencies but also the national-level policy institutions which supervise their activities both within and outside of the executive branch. Even intelligence professionals have used the term in this sense. In 1975 a letter from the CIA to the House Select Committee on Intelligence responded to a request for description of the "U.S. foreign intelligence community" with a number of charts showing agencies and relationships. One, depicting "organizations involved in decisions concerning policy, programs, and resources," identified the president, the National Security Council, several community-wide staff elements supporting the management functions of the president and NSC, all the civilian and military intelligence agencies, and the several committees in Congress having responsibilities related to intelligence matters – Armed Services, Foreign Affairs, and appropriations (neither house of Congress had yet established permanent intelligence oversight committees).[80] Inclusion of those congressional committees is understandable in the context of that letter, and clearly defensible in terms of the roles Congress can play in supporting and supervising the intelligence effort. But in normal and authoritative usage, even though congressional oversight has now been regularized, the term "intelligence community" refers principally to executive branch agencies.

A second point should also be noted: as a result of the criticisms of intelligence operations in the mid-1970s, the executive intelligence structure now includes, in addition to White-House-level command and control mechanisms, a number of advisory and oversight elements. These include the NSC itself and parts of the NSC which have been charged with responsibility to approve certain operations and to review and evaluate overall performance. They also include advisory and supervisory committees, such as the President's Foreign Intelligence Advisory Board (PFIAB), recently revitalized in the Reagan administration, and the U.S. Intelligence Board, a community-wide coordination forum. In the Ford administration, additionally, an Intelligence Oversight Board was established: three persons from outside the government appointed by the president to review intelligence activities and report to him on problems of propriety or legality. Under the director of Central Intelligence there has grown up a substantial Intelligence Community Staff which assists him in his management of the operational agencies. But even these elements, devoted entirely to intelligence affairs, are sometimes excluded from the formal definition of the intelligence community, which has tended to focus on agencies having operational responsibilities.[81]

As defined by President Reagan, the intelligence community includes the CIA, the National Security Agency, the Defense Intelligence Agency, the offices within the Department of Defense which collect "specialized national foreign intelligence through reconnaissance programs," the Bureau of Intelligence and Research of the Department of State, and the intelligence elements of the Army, Navy, Air Force, Marine Corps, FBI, Department of the Treasury, and Department of Energy.[82] These agencies conduct the intelligence activities "necessary for the conduct of foreign relations and the protection of the national security of the United States," which are specified as:

(a) collection of information needed by the President, the National Security Council, the Secretaries of State and Defense, and other Executive Branch officials for the performance of their duties and responsibilities;
(b) production and dissemination of intelligence;
(c) collection of information concerning, and the conduct of activities to protect against, intelligence activities directed against the United States, international terrorists and international narcotics activities, and other hostile activities directed against the United States by foreign powers, organizations, persons, and their agents;
(d) Special Activities;
(e) administrative and support activities within the United States and abroad necessary for the performance of authorized activities; and
(f) such other intelligence activities as the President may direct from time to time.[83]

These, of course, are cryptic descriptions of operational and associated support functions discussed at some length earlier in this chapter. Activities specified in paragraph 1 constitute the foreign collection effort, and those in paragraph 2 are the follow-on analytical and production actions depicted in the "intelligence cycle." Counterintelligence activities are described in paragraph 3, and the "Special Activities" noted in paragraph 4 refer to covert action.

With respect to the operational missions that concern us, the Central Intelligence Agency collects, produces, and disseminates foreign intelligence and counterintelligence, and it is the only agency in the intelligence community charged with responsibility and authority for "Special Activities."[84] Its collection and CI missions may be performed either abroad or in the United States, provided that in the latter case the operations are coordinated with the FBI, and provided also that any CI activities do not constitute assumption of internal security functions (which belong to the FBI). When operating abroad, the CIA also is given responsibility to coordinate the intelligence and CI activities of other agencies operating there.

The National Security Agency, an element of the Department of Defense, performs the nation's signals intelligence activities, and also is responsible for communications security programs. NSA headquarters is at Fort Meade, Maryland, and it uses a number of operational stations overseas.

The Defense Intelligence Agency, also a Department of Defense element, collects and produces military-related intelligence for the secretary of defense and the Joint Chiefs of Staff. It manages the U.S. military attache system worldwide and coordinates and announces collection requirements for other agencies having operational resources. Headquartered in the Pentagon, it is staffed by both military and civilian personnel who are heavily engaged in analytical, as opposed to operational, functions.

The several armed services each have significant operational capabilities. They attempt to satisfy the service-oriented, tactical intelligence needs of their field commands, but they may also attempt to respond to national-level intelligence requirements. When they do so, they operate in accordance with guidance from the director of Central Intelligence. Outside the United States they must coordinate collection efforts with the CIA, and within the United States they must coordinate them with the FBI. The same is true of CI activities they undertake.

The Department of Defense also has responsibility for national reconnaissance programs and resources, though of course the operation of specific collection resources is delegated to other departments and agencies (e.g., the Air Force). These include the "overhead platforms" discussed earlier (aircraft and satellites), which are especially important in collection of imagery and signals intelligence.

The Federal Bureau of Investigation, as an element of the intelligence community, has primary responsibility for counterintelligence within the

United States. Any such operations conducted by other agencies (e.g., by the armed services in order to protect military installations) must be coordinated with the FBI. The bureau itself may, on occasion, conduct certain CI activities outside the United States after coordination with the CIA. It may also, on request of other intelligence community officials, undertake activities within the United States to collect foreign intelligence or to support the foreign intelligence requirements of other agencies.

The Department of State contributes to the national intelligence effort through overt collection of information, in support of foreign policy concerns, via the normal processes of diplomatic reporting. Its Bureau of Intelligence and Research, as well, produces political and economic analysis meeting departmental needs, and has been the element responsible for coordinating the State Department's relations with other foreign intelligence agencies. The bureau is, additionally, a major participant in the process of producing national intelligence estimates.

The Treasury Department overtly collects foreign financial and monetary information and participates with the State Department in the overt collection of general foreign economic information. With the Secret Service, moreover, it protects the president and other government officials by various security techniques.

The Department of Energy participates with the State Department in overtly collecting information on foreign energy matters. It also makes its expertise available to help refine collection requirements levied on other overt and clandestine collectors in the intelligence community.

Several points are worth further emphasis to summarize this organizational and functional survey, and to provide background for the discussion which is yet to come. First, the "official" descriptions of the community attempt to draw a line between operational responsibilities overseas and operational responsibilities within the United States. The CIA, for instance, is *primus inter pares* for intelligence and counterintelligence overseas. The FBI is *primus inter pares* for counterintelligence within the United States. But in reality it is impossible to separate things so neatly by geography. Collection operations conducted overseas may require support activities within the United States, for instance, so even the mission of the CIA focused on foreign areas must operate at home also. As we shall see, much of the last decade's concern about the CIA and other foreign collection agencies has focused on these kinds of domestic connections, and in some corners of the debate they are still controversial regardless of how the jurisdictional lines may be drawn at any time.

A second point is simply a reminder about control. In surveying the diverse agencies which contribute to the American intelligence effort, and in disaggregating the "community" in order to locate operational capabilities within it, it is possible to lose sight of central mechanisms, including the director of Central Intelligence himself, which give direction to the total effort. The intelligence community is composed in large part of elements that belong to disparate departments and agencies. Many of these agencies, moreover, do not dedicate all their efforts to intelligence. They therefore differ from one another in important ways, but their efforts in the intelligence arena are supposed to serve common goals. It is the responsibility of the director of Central Intelligence to give their efforts coherence, and this is a task which all occupants of that office have taken seriously. It is a large challenge, however, and concern about the ability of any person or institution to control the activities of all these agencies has been an important part of the intelligence debate in America.

In that regard, I must draw attention to one other facet of the history of American intelligence operations: the personalities and backgrounds of the men who led the modern intelligence effort in its formative years. Discussion of the organizational backgound would be impoverished beyond calculation without some treatment of the character and style of its leadership.

Prior to the 1947 National Security Act, the two dominant figures were J. Edgar Hoover, who had already headed the FBI for more than two decades, and William J. Donovan, who had led the Office of Strategic Services (OSS) during World War II. Hoover's vigorous approach to his internal security responsibilities is now legend. It drew substantially upon a deep hatred – it is not too strong a word – of communism and a conviction that America must be ever-vigilant in protecting itself from Communist encroachments.[85] He remained at the helm of the FBI until the 1970s, maintaining to the end his aggressive operational outlook and defending it with increasing resoluteness against those who wished to confine it.

Donovan is an equally legendary character whose forceful, dominating personality and imaginative, activist approach to the business of intelligence (OSS missions embraced both foreign intelligence collection and covert action) left it indelibly imprinted with an operational energy that was passed on to successor agencies in peacetime. As Anthony Cave Brown's biography has recently shown, he not only presided over the founding of a secret intelligence and special operations service, but he made it work, and he made a generation of America's "best and brightest" believe in the necessity for and efficacy of such clandestine activities.[86]

The men who followed Donovan were not of that distinctive stature, nor were they as flamboyantly adventurous. But they were beneficiaries of the legacy, nonetheless. With only two exceptions in the next thirty years, the director of Central Intelligence was either a military officer or an intelligence official who had spent most of his professional life in the clandestine services. The first four DCI's were prominent military men: Rear Admiral Sidney Souers (to June 1946); Lieutenant General Hoyt Vandenberg (to May 1947); Rear Admiral Roscoe Hillenkoetter (to October

1950); and General Walter Bedell Smith (to February 1953). Smith was succeeded by Allen Dulles, brother of the secretary of state, who had been an OSS operative in World War II and whose interests and expertise still lay mainly in the operational arena (as opposed to the arena of analysis and estimates). In November 1961 he was replaced by John A. McCone, a businessman who was the first true "outsider" to become DCI. He left in April 1965 and was followed by Admiral William F. Raborn, who served only one year. Richard Helms, a veteran of twenty years in clandestine operations, followed Raborn in 1966 and remained until February 1973. James Schlesinger succeeded Helms, only to depart in July of that year, and William Colby, another OSS veteran and clandestine operations specialist, took charge until December 1975, by which time the intelligence debate had begun in earnest.

It is not my intent here to argue that such men were incapable of controlling the intelligence agencies in ways that served nonoperational interests. Indeed, William Colby, for one, seems to have had just such an impact. And James Schlesinger also, in his abbreviated tenure, sought to rationalize management of the CIA in ways that were very painful for many of the agency's old hands. But it is nevertheless of interest to us that most of those who administered the community from atop its central superstructure throughout the period of operational abuses and well into the decade of debate about intelligence controls, had themselves been brought up in the Donovan tradition, surrounded by the energetic operational spirit he left behind.

3

The Public Critique
of Intelligence Operations

By 1960 each of the operational capabilities discussed in the previous chapter had acquired standing as a distinctive discipline in the intelligence profession. Organizations had grown up around them, efforts had been made to delimit operational spheres and responsibilities, and routines had been developed for coordinating activities at agreed jurisdictional boundaries.[1] A number of community-wide directives issued by the National Security Council stated national needs, assigned tasks, set priorities, and performed other internal guidance and management functions.[2] But there was no effort during this time to define the outer perimeter of intelligence activity, to specify the boundaries beyond which operations should not go. In fact, it was not until 1976 that an attempt was made to specify, in a community-wide presidential directive, the boundaries of operational permissibility and to fix – as a matter of public record – responsibilities for control and oversight of the intelligence agencies. When that first directive was issued by President Ford, many regarded it as long overdue. But the executive branch did not take up that task readily, even then. Only after an explosion of criticism and extended inquiry into alleged abuses did President Ford and his advisors decide to address emerging concerns via a public executive order.

The intent of this chapter is to survey the rulemaking problem faced by the Ford administration. There was, unfortunately, no comprehensive and coherent reform agenda, no synthesis of claims into a single bill of particulars. There was only an accumulation of major themes of criticism and pressures for reform: for constraining operations many viewed as suspect or overused, for eliminating capabilities some viewed as dangerous or abhorrent, and for specifying the locus of control for such operational capabilities as the nation might choose to retain.

At the time, to be sure, the "allegations" were in the headlines nearly every day.[3] But it was only a very generalized sensing of a still-emerging

critique – and a desire to address and control it within executive channels – that activated rulemakers in the Ford administration.

The intelligence critique actually began long before the 1970s, however, and in much quieter times. The rhetorical pyrotechnics of the 1970s
brought important problems into the limelight as never before. But long
before the most inflamed stories about operational excesses were published,
the work of a few observers in academia had pointed to a number of
enduring issues that the revelations now served to illustrate.

The Scholars

In the early postwar years those academics who chose to study the
business of intelligence focused mainly on strategic intelligence (information on the capabilities, vulnerabilities, and intentions of potential adversaries) and its role in policymaking.[4] They surveyed the organization,
practices, and products of the intelligence agencies and offered a number of
important criticisms of their performance.[5] Such analyses identified major
problems that still bedevil the community in the 1980s. But they did not
direct attention to the problems that were to develop later concerning how
to confine intelligence operations sensibly without disabling the nation. It
took about a decade after the war for that kind of concern to appear, in part
because intelligence operations were then shrouded in the sanctity of the
Cold War ethos and protected from public view by secrecy practices about
which all concerned were deadly serious. But starting in the late 1950s a few
studies began to reflect upon new kinds of issues. ·

The work of three men stands out in retrospect: Harry Howe Ransom,
Paul Blackstock, and Roger Hilsman. There was, additionally, one intelligence practitioner turned scholar, Lyman Kirkpatrick, whose insights
about the source of our policy dilemmas have proved especially prescient.

Ransom's book *Central Intelligence and National Security* dealt, inter alia,
with issues of operational rationale, controls and constraints, and oversight
within the executive branch, as well as with the problem of surveillance of
intelligence activities by Congress. Ransom knew, of course, that his
analysis was a rarity at that time. Few Americans knew anything about the
intelligence agencies beyond what appeared in magazine or newspaper
stories.[6] This meant that in public consciousness there had developed no
raison d'être supporting specific intelligence activities and functions.[7] There
was no general understanding of functions and of proper boundaries for
functions, no thought-through set of purposes and expectations for intelligence activities. To be sure, the widely shared assumptions and beliefs
which composed the prevailing Cold War mindset would have influenced
public attitudes about those things in important ways. But the questions

had not yet been asked that would have forced these perspectives to coalesce and to be made explicit. One of the great ironies of the intelligence debate that would occur years later is that it did force discussion of operational rationales at a time when the silent, Cold War consensus about the world and about the imperatives which ought to shape American behavior had come unraveled. At that time there was no foundation of public belief, understanding, trust, and confidence to support the activities then conducted by the mature intelligence community.

The "softness" of unstated operational rationales was in part attributable to the cryptic, uninformative language used in legislative authorizations. The 1947 act creating the CIA had defined the agency's functions and responsibilities in only a very general and indeed incomplete way. While the statute was an important benchmark in the history of the American intelligence community, it hardly was intended to promote public education and understanding about intelligence activities. And the job of authorizing more specific functions was left to secret, or at least nonpublic, executive regulations and directives.[8]

The secrecy surrounding operational authorizations, combined with the practice of including the CIA's director as a major functionary on the NSC, which was supposed to oversee intelligence activity, led Ransom to question the efficacy of executive branch controls on operations. The director, it seemed could – and almost certainly would – importantly affect the National Security Council's perceptions and decisions about operational needs.[9] He had control, after all, of the methods by which information supporting decisions could be collected. He also controlled certain means of implementing decisions. He might be tempted in NSC deliberations to work toward expanded operational authorizations in both spheres. To note that this might occur is not to impute to the intelligence community's leaders any venality of purpose. It is simply to observe, as Ransom did elsewhere, that it is important sometimes to think of the director of Central Intelligence as essentially a bureaucrat possessed of great political resources and influence, and seeking to use both.[10]

Indeed, when he surveyed the length and breadth of the intelligence power base within the executive, Ransom found reason to wonder whether *any* internal oversight mechanisms could be adequate to contain the intelligence agencies. If knowledge is the foundation of policymaking, then knowledge confers political power. As the collector and custodian of knowledge, the intelligence community must inevitably have a major role in the formation of national security policy and foreign policy – a role which political science theories did not then seem to address adequately.[11] Further, the CIA might well be tempted to become an advocate for particular goals and tools of policy, not just a provider of information.

Other factors, as well, were likely to favor the CIA and its brethren in competition with the rest of the national security and foreign policy community. The pressures of the Cold War were likely to continue, Ransom believed, and perhaps even to intensify, thus magnifying the need for the intelligence agencies' major product – information. And, just as importantly, the CIA in particular had the advantage of a vastly talented personnel pool: great expertise kept in place over many years, not rotated from place to place or job to job, as was the constant practice in competitor agencies within the foreign policy apparatus. [12]

Ransom was also troubled by an issue of specifically constitutional import, the extent to which Congress ought to participate in the authorization and monitoring of secret intelligence activities. Congressional supervision of intelligence activity was then desultory at best. The budget for the intelligence effort was secret, hidden even from Congress in the appropriations of other executive agencies. Actual operations were secret and as a rule reported only to a few executive officers outside the intelligence community. A proposal to rationalize and regularize congressional oversight via creation of a joint intelligence committee had just been defeated in Congress, but Ransom knew that it touched upon central political values of shared and limited governmental power. For that reason he knew the issue would rise again someday. [13]

In the end, Ransom argued for more rigorous and clearer controls and for more vigilant application of the checks-and-balances mechanisms central to the American version of democratic government. He was a firm believer in the intelligence community and in its ability to serve the American national interest. But he also believed that the intelligence agencies must be made to operate within the framework of distinctively American political values, particularly those pertaining to constrained governmental power and protection of individual liberties. [14]

Paul Blackstock's 1964 study of the covert action capability had similar concerns. He noted early that intervention to influence policies and political events in other states was an ancient diplomatic practice, and that Communist regimes in particular had developed a systematic doctrine of revolution and intervention. But, in contrast, modern Western societies had not devised any comparable set of principles. [15] There was no operational "manifesto" for covert action which specified expectations, purposes, or practical rules and guidelines. Nor had there been any attempt explicitly to locate and legitimize the activity, however delimited, in the wider repertoire of the American nation-state.

This, for Blackstock, had important ramifications on two levels. Among the public (and among most political scientists) in the first instance, there was little understanding of intelligence functions and their rationale, and there was no attempt on the part of government officials to correct that. Indeed, the intelligence agencies seemed to revel in the romantic mystique associated with their carefully cultivated public image as a highly effective but invisible arm of government.[16]

Secondly, within the government itself, there was an inflated sense of confidence in the efficacy of covert action, by itself, to solve important Cold War problems, to address major international challenges, and to resolve them reliably in America's favor. This stemmed, at bottom, from an exaggerated sense of national efficacy and from an oversimplified view of the nature of international challenges.[17] In Blackstock's view, secret intervention in the political affairs of another nation might be a necessary expedient at times, but it could never provide a panacea for all Cold War challenges. It had to be fitted into and correlated with some larger policy context, alongside other policy tools, and subordinated to a controlling vision of long-term policy purposes. But progress toward that end was only barely perceptible.

One prescription emerging from this analysis was to lift the veil of secrecy surrounding this policy instrument and to study its inherent limitations and the principles which ought to govern its use.[18] To illustrate the kind of inquiry needed, Blackstock offered an extended analysis of "lessons learned" from the Bay of Pigs invasion. He worried, as well, about certain "policy sabotage" ramifications of covert action. Even when the capability is not used, it can nevertheless present significant problems for the nation's foreign policy establishment, which must deal with a world suspicious of its exercise. The Central Intelligence Agency, and America as a nation, could thus find itself blamed for a whole range of events with which it had no association at all. The policymaking apparatus would be required periodically – and without advance notice – to pay attention to these charges and perhaps to react to them by adjusting current policies and programs.[19]

A second aspect of the "policy sabotage" problem involves the effects of compromised or "blown" operations, cases in which the covert interventionary capability is in fact exercised and things go awry, resulting in discovery of the activity itself and possibly of American sponsorship. In some such cases the United States government might appear to have said one thing in public (and perhaps in confidential communications to other states) while its secret agents abroad were acting in direct contravention of those postures. The result, of course, would be serious national embarrassment as well as tarnishing of the nation's reputation.[20]

A third problem, Blackstock observed, arises from successful covert action operations. It is the nature of such activities to shape or influence foreign events, and in that sense they can structure other situations which American foreign policy must confront, both at the time they are conducted and afterward. They have palpable, observable consequences, some of which can be foreseen while others cannot. Inevitably, then, they help to create wider foreign policy challenges with which American leaders must cope. [21]

These three sets of observations led Blackstock to worry about problems of intra-executive control and coordination. In the extreme, he observed, there was the unpleasant prospect of an emergent *staat-im-staat* should the activities of a secret organization be left unsupervised and untrammeled within the apparatus of government. That was, surely, only a remote prospect, not a fact, in the American polity. But in the case of the CIA, he felt that the problems inherent in controlling a large and unwieldy foreign policy bureaucracy, combined with the secrecy of intelligence operations and the inclination of other agencies to avoid learning about potentially chancy endeavors, left room for uncoordinated, poorly conceived exercise of the interventionary capability at the behest of the agency possessing it. [22]

Like Ransom, Blackstock wondered about the ultimate effect of combining an action arm with an information arm in one intelligence agency (the CIA). Possession of an action arm inevitably involves the agency, and its reputation and bureaucratic interests, in policy deliberations, since for some situations CIA covert action might be considered a viable option. This interest in certain policy outcomes could affect the way the agency performs its informational functions. [23]

But beyond these questions of internal executive organization and controls, Blackstock worried about external supervision, congressional oversight. He noted that Congress had been inactive, even reluctant and recalcitrant, in that regard. He also wondered whether, given the secrecy accorded intelligence activities and the natural deviousness of the operational culture, the intelligence agencies *could* be scrutinized from the outside in any meaningful way. He was sure, however, that congressional interest in intelligence activities would grow as it became clear that those activities reflect international commitments, engagements, and behavior of the kind that, arguably, Congress should know about and even authorize and approve. [24]

Roger Hilsman's observations about intelligence in his retrospective assessment of the Kennedy Administration combined the perspectives of insider and ousider, of policymaker, practitioner, and scholar. [25] He helped to sharpen focus on several major facets of the intelligence operational "problem" and to introduce (by making it explicit in the intelligence context) the relevance of moral or ethical judgments about national behavior.

On the basis of his own experience in government Hilsman expressly put to rest the *staat-im-staat* specter evoked by part of Blackstock's analysis. The intelligence agencies clearly did not present that kind of threat to the American system of government. But there *was* a related point requiring attention: that the CIA and its brethren do present significant, but manageable, problems of power in our political process of national decisionmaking. [26] As a player in that process, the CIA had extraordinary resources and important advantages. It had large numbers of employees with superior qualifications and abilities. It had worldwide presence and functions. It had money, lots of it, and in amounts known only to a very few. It had information, the indispensable ingredient of intelligent policymaking, and it had facilities enabling instantaneous communication of that information around the world. It operated in secret, functioning actively as a combatant for a nation which, at that time, felt in need of combative capabilities. Even the information it possessed was secret, handled so carefully in the decision-making process that the number of persons having access to it, and able to participate in decisionmaking, could be quite small. In functional alliances with other actors at home (e.g., the Department of Defense) and abroad (e.g., foreign intelligence services and even heads of state), it had acquired significant political leverage. All these resources could amount, in the aggregate, to significant competitive advantages in the policy formulation process. And this, for Hilsman, was the central observation to be made about CIA power.

A major prescription emerging from that analysis was, of course, to create rules and mechanisms for coordinating intelligence operations with other foreign policy instruments, both in Washington and at the operational level in foreign countries where diplomats and intelligence agents work side-by-side on their own compartmented pursuits. The Kennedy Administration took steps to do just that,[27] but the issue remained for subsequent administrations to address, as well.

Hilsman also felt that America's leaders in the 1950s and 1960s had lost sight of the proper place of covert action in America's more diverse international arsenal. It was a simple fact of international life that covert interventionary tactics must sometimes be used to serve or advance national purposes. But important limits had to be observed, reflecting the inherent limitations of America's ability to control foreign events. Such limits should reflect the dictates of good sense concerning what can actually work, as well as abiding principles of decency.[28] Operational controls should be conceived not just in procedural terms — approval mechanisms, coordination routines, and the like — though these were certainly important. They should also include substantive declarations about what kinds of things could not or should not be done. Practical judgments about priorities in national interests and instruments, and also about probabilities of success, would be one source of these substantive constraints. But equally important were normative convictions about the possibly corrupting effects of these operations on central ideals at home and on America's image abroad. Covert action could be a useful supplement to other policy tools, an instrument of last resort. But it had been overused, needlessly and at times foolishly, at great cost to the nation's international reputation. That reputation – for openness, respect for others, and idealism – was an important but fragile political asset which had been undercut by too-eager resort to instruments of secret manipulation and intrigue.

In *The Real CIA*, Lyman Kirkpatrick highlighted a theme which had emerged from the work of the earlier studies: because Americans knew very little about intelligence, public support for it was exceedingly precarious. Intelligence agencies and operations were instruments of governmental power, and the distinctive precepts of American political culture had always held all governmental power in suspicion. By failing to explain their *raison d'être* to the American public, even in the most general terms, and to familiarize the citizenry with their functions, the intelligence agencies had neglected to build public trust in their purposes and activities. They were therefore vulnerable to future challenges derived not from a distaste for intelligence activity per se but from a traditional and quintessentially American fear of abuses of power. Unfortunately, Kirkpatrick observed, the intelligence community did not seem at all to be aware of this, continuing to operate unexplained and in secret, trading essentially on the assumed endurance of a strong, silent, supportive consensus.[29]

Kirkpatrick believed America must maintain all the operational capabilities – collection, counterintelligence, and covert action – that had emerged to that point, but he was sensitive to the need for controls, both within and outside of the executive branch. He approved of high-level executive oversight boards, and he believed as well that more attentive congressional surveillance of the intelligence community was needed. With regard to covert action he, like Hilsman, thought it had been overused and that the rules governing its employment ought to make clear that it is a tool of last resort, available only in times of the most serious national emergency.[30] As a nation, in his view, we need to think through the consequences of having such a capability and to devise some explicit formula for regulating its use.

The National Debate

By 1970, events outside academic circles were beginning to give more concrete meaning to the intelligence "problem." Certain activities had come to light which many thought clearly objectionable. Perhaps the most widely publicized were those involving CIA payment of financial subsidies, through intermediaries, to the nation's largest student group, the National Student Association. The subsidies and other forms of assistance were provided in return for information on foreign student leaders. Their disclosure led to other revelations which seemed to some observers to indicate that the CIA had been involved with nearly every segment of American society – business, women's groups, labor, news media, teachers, and so forth.[31]

A surprised American public looked on while an extended and articulate challenge was mounted by critics who deplored the "police-state" implications of secret and potentially manipulative governmental activities undertaken at home in the name of national security. Society's most important civil institutions seemed in danger of official subvention and cooptation. An official inquiry into the NSA contacts agreed, recommending that the United States government should not provide "covert financial assistance or support, direct or indirect, to any of the nation's educational or private voluntary associations."[32]

But at another level of the nation's experience in the late 1960s and early 1970s, domestic political events and the prolonged effort in Vietnam provided both cause and context for growing challenges to the exercise of governmental power. The mid- and late 1960s saw an outbreak of violence and rioting associated with the civil rights movement. Local government authorities and their police forces were sometimes hard pressed to maintain order. The federal government watched each eruption nervously, frequently stepping in with military troops at the request of state authorities. As later revelations made clear, these missions were also accompanied by intelligence activities conducted by local, federal, and military authorities.

Revelations about army intelligence activities were especially important, channeling growing suspicion and resentment in the direction of the intelligence agencies. National concern about military surveillance of civilian politics resulted in substantial and self-imposed curtailment of the army's domestic intelligence activities, as well as in an extended and well-publicized congressional investigation.[33] But public interest in intelligence issues had been aroused irrevocably. Relevations were to continue, and indeed to gain momentum, as congressional inquiries, lawsuits, and journalistic investigations all focused almost passionately on the intelligence agencies. By 1976, one critic of the intelligence community charged, on the basis of the public record as it then stood, that U.S. intelligence agencies wielded a "frightening degree of secret, sometimes illegal, and often uncontrollable power." They were, he argued, a "corrupt force in American society," and therefore a justifiable and overdue focus of aroused and widespread public concern.[34]

Many had come to agree with him. In just ten years after the National Student Association revelations, the undergirding of support for the intelligence community, so essential but so taken for granted earlier, had collapsed, eroded by a generalized mistrust of government and subverted also by a lively questioning of the rationales for specific intelligence activities. Three forums of debate were particularly important: the public media, the courts and Congress.

The Media

By the mid-1970s coverage of various accusations and charges about operational excesses had become front-page news in print and broadcast media across the nation. There were a number of ways in which previously secret information about intelligence activities came to light. Investigative journalism was of course important. Requests for information under the Freedom of Information Act and the Privacy Act of 1974 also forced documents and data out of government files and into the open. Lawsuits aired suspicions and grievances and generated other disclosures. "Whistle blowers" within the intelligence community also had an important role to play. The product of all this was an outpouring of information about intelligence activities and capabilities, and increasing concern about them.

There were two major themes of criticism: objection to intelligence activities conducted within the United States, and objection to certain ativities allegedly conducted, contemplated, or simply existing within the realm of operational capability, abroad. The word "objection" is used here advisedly, for that was the orientation of many commentators. Knowledgeable, but admittedly embittered or disillusioned, former intelligence operatives[35] and others who claimed high level expertise in the intelligence community[36] published detailed indictments that sold briskly. Outsiders wrote strident protests based upon officially-released government documents which were used to illustrate runaway official intrusiveness.[37] Studies more supportive of the intelligence agencies appeared somewhat later,[38] but not in time or in sufficient volume to balance the earlier public discussion.

Attacks on domestic information-gathering focused mostly on the FBI and CIA. Revelations of FBI operations went beyond security-related information collection activities to its now-celebrated COINTELPRO, a program of clandestine manipulative activity against selected targets (covert action at home). There was, not surprisingly, widespread concern about abuse of constitutional rights, as well as fear that the FBI might become a political agency instead of a police agency. Later examination of FBI activities by Congress added fuel to this fire with revelations about FBI activities against such individuals as Dr. Martin Luther King and others involved in domestic political agitation.[39]

CIA activities at home were attacked when allegations were made about various kinds of operations: wiretaps, break-ins and mail intercepts whose targets included national political figures, technical assistance to the infamous "White House Plumbers" associated with the Watergate affair, training in clandestine techniques for domestic police officers, and involvement in the academic world through subsidies, research contracts, and, on at least one occasion, publication of research without notation of CIA sponsorship.[40] These allegations and others raised the same issues (and hackles) as the FBI's domestic operations. There was the same concern for the individual rights of Americans and the independence of institutions whose freedom from governmental control was believed indispensable to a democratic society. But such activities were criticized as violations of the agency's foreign intelligence charter. Even the super-secret National Security Agency was not immune from these concerns. Fear of its collection capability turned inward was fueled by reports that its immense apparatus had been used to intercept telephone communications in which Americans had participated.[41]

The public scrutiny also reached CIA activities conducted within the United States to support its foreign collection mission. These had not been examined on the public record before, and surprise and curiosity surrounded CIA programs "aimed against foreign students and other visitors to the United States," contracts for development and procurement of "esoteric espionage equipment," programs for exploitation of Americans traveling abroad, and organizations providing CIA operational cover.[42]

The public debate also addressed overseas operations, and here it was CIA covert action that drew the most fire. Alleged assassination plots, in particular, were reported as evidence of government betrayal of basic American ideals, or as the senseless schemes of foolish, ignorant (and therefore dangerous) men.[43] Other operations were criticized because they supported repressive, undemocratic regimes or movements, or simply because the critics felt America had no business trying to influence political events in other societies. Some persons, additionally, were concerned that the covert action capability gave the American government power to affect the attitudes of its own citizenry by influencing events, media, and people abroad. Activities of concern included funding of groups that were friendly to U.S. governmental interests, training for foreign workers, propaganda schemes which hid U.S. authorship or attributed authorship to someone else, support for irregular or guerrilla forces opposing foreign governments, and penetration of foreign political parties.[44]

Public outrage and more reasoned public opposition to domestic and foreign activities drew strength from initial impressions publicized by members of Congress and others that the intelligence agencies, especially the CIA, had been operating in large measure on their own.[45] Abuses of existing restrictions and of less definitive notions of propriety were thought to have resulted largely from the runaway, uncontrolled initiative of the agencies, many of whose activities were not sufficiently supervised (were perhaps even unknown) at high levels.

Viewed in retrospect, at least three policy recommendations could be distilled from the charges and counter claims that had been aired in the media by 1975:

(1) Create comprehensive, public charters for the intelligence community, both to improve control over the agencies and to allay the critics' suspicion and fear. Even the intelligence community's friends recommended some rearrangement of control procedures, and many others seemed to believe that a clear description, on the public record, of functions, authorizations, and prohibitions would go far to restore citizens' faith in the intelligence agencies.

(2) Insure that proposed operations are carefully evaluated – and approved or disapproved – by persons who have more than narrowly operational perspectives and responsibilities. There was palpable pressure, in other words, to move ultimate decisionmaking authority away from the intelligence professionals. This would permit larger policy considerations to control operations, and it would also avoid the problems that are created when control of secret operations is left to the "clandestine clan" whose inclination is, after all, to be active and aggressive.

(3) As approval authority moves into other hands, move it also upward and establish a clear chain of accountability from individual operators to the highest policymaking levels. This would insure that the national leadership, including the president, must take responsibility for the actions undertaken by the intelligence agencies.

The Courts

Judicial involvement in the intelligence problem has centered on one particularly troubling issue: the distinction between criminal investigations and counterintelligence operations. Traditionally, different rules and different standards of permissibility have been applied to each. By 1970, criminal investigative activities were comparatively tightly circumscribed by constitutional (and other) proscriptions against governmental intrusion on individual rights. But for intelligence activities, which used many of the same operational techniques, government decisionmakers and operators were permitted more discretion and wider operational latitude. Increasingly, civil libertarians brought judicial pressures to bear against this distinction, fearing that relatively untrammeled "national security" operations appreciably increased the danger of political surveillance and retribution inimical to the exercise of constitutional freedoms. "Political surveillance," one wrote, "has a long and troubled history in the United States as an indirect method of controlling and repressing controversial political expression through techniques traditionally associated with law enforcement."[46] In congressional testimony he added that in current litigations there was much evidence that domestic operations had become in essence discretionary within the executive, undertaken without judicial or legislative control.[47] Action in the courts was meant to challenge that.

The judiciary's impact is best illustrated by developments in the law on "electronic surveillance" – wiretaps and eavesdropping. Civil liberties activists considered this area the most important of all, the most in need of reform, because it represented "the most intensive form of investigation" possible.[48]

For many years, federal courts addressing domestic wiretap cases adhered to the principle, announced in *Olmstead* v. *United States*, that government wiretapping was not a "search and seizure" subject to the Fourth Amendment's limitations.[49] This meant, essentially, that it could be done without a judicial warrant based upon probable cause to believe that a crime had been or was about to be committed. The theory used to distinguish wiretapping from Fourth Amendment situations held that the wiretap involved no "trespass" into the victim's home or office, and that spoken words themselves could not be "seized," thus there was no infringement of rights protected by the Fourth Amendment. This doctrine was subsequently applied in "bugging" (eavesdropping by electronic devices) cases, too.[50] In 1967, however, two Supreme Court decisions, *Katz* v. *United States* and *Berger* v. *New York*,[51] held that electronic surveillance was a search and seizure within the meaning of the Fourth Amendment and that the fruits of domestic electronic surveillance activities were therefore subject to exclusion from criminal proceedings if the probable cause and warrant requirements of the Fourth Amendment had not been satisfied.

These decisions, however, involved investigations into crimes, not "intelligence" or "national security" operations, and two justices took explicit note of that distinction. In a footnote to the majority opinion in the *Katz* case, Justice Stewart observed that the court was not addressing a case in which national security was involved. Justice White's concurring opinion expressly approved of a "national security" exception to the Fourth Amendment's warrant standard.[52] Thus, although intelligence activities were not then before the court, there were indications of support for the view that different rules should apply to them.

Prevailing sentiment in Congress agreed. One year later the Omnibus Crime Control and Safe Streets Act of 1968 announced that judicial warrants were required for electronic surveillance by government authorities, except for such surveillance undertaken for "national security" purposes. The exception was couched in language indicating deference to executive authority and responsibility in this field.

Nothing contained in this Chapter or in Section 605 of the Communications Act of 1934 . . . shall limit the constitutional power of the President to take such measures as he deems necessary to protect the Nation against actual or potential attack or other hostile acts of a foreign power, to obtain foreign intelligence information deemed essential to the security of the United States, or to protect national security information against foreign intelligence activities. Nor shall anything contained in this Chapter be deemed to limit the constitutional power of the President to take such measures as he deems necessary to protect the United States against the overthrow of the government by force or other unlawful means, or against other clear and present danger to the structure or existence of the Government.[53]

In the courts, however, recognition of presidential authority was carefully bifurcated into "foreign" and "domestic" categories. The Supreme Court in *United States* v. *United States District Court*, a case involving electronic surveillance of domestic dissident groups, refused to accept the national security justification as a basis for exception to the warrant requirement.[54] While the court did not consider the need for prior judicial authorization in foreign cases (i. e., where the surveillance was for "foreign intelligence" purposes), that question was addressed in *United States* v. *Butenko*, a Court of Appeals decision which the Supreme Court later declined to review.[55] There the defendant had been convicted of giving national defense information to foreign agents. Earlier he had been the subject of electronic surveillance authorized by the president (upon advice of the attorney general). The parties to the lawsuit stipulated that the surveillance had been conducted solely to obtain information for intelligence purposes (i.e., prosecution was not the objective). The court held that the warrantless surveillance was not illegal.

The *Butenko* court did not, however, accept the intelligence rationale on its face as concluding the argument. In the past, the judiciary had been reluctant to evaluate the "reasonableness" of investigative activity once the government had made the requisite assertion about national security needs.[56] In *Butenko*, however, the court weighed competing interests and concluded that the purposes supporting the surveillance justified disposing with the warrant requirement. On the side of the government, the court recognized a strong public interest in the free flow of this kind of information to executive branch decisionmakers. The need in general for effective intelligence gathering was a matter of significant concern, and the court saw a limited role for the judiciary where, as in this case, the president's foreign affairs authority was implicated. Noting the clandestine, highly unstructured nature of the intelligence effort, the court was reluctant to interpose prior judicial review requirements and was satisfied with a showing of necessity based upon effective policymaking. In the end, then, the executive won this case, but the court made the contest somewhat more difficult than had others in the past.

All these cases had involved operations conducted within the United States. In 1974, however, a lawsuit was filed in the District of Columbia which challenged activities carried out abroad. In it a number of individuals claimed that the U.S. Army intelligence units overseas had violated their constitutional rights by surveillance activities directed against them over a period of years. This lawsuit – *Berlin Democratic Club, et al.* v. *Brown* – became perhaps the most visible of all the mid-1970s litigations. It was founded on a former army counterintelligence agent's disclosures about various operations – wiretaps, mail openings, covert penetration of civilian groups, and personal surveillance – directed against American citizens and others in Europe who were thought to be active in inducing desertions and promoting indiscipline within the ranks of army units. Scrutiny of these operations in court, and simultaneously in congressional investigations, told attentive segments of the public a great deal about their government's intelligence and counterintelligence effort abroad, and about the effects of those operations on the rights of Americans.[57]

The lawsuit was stalled by prolonged delaying tactics and procedural infighting for six years, never reaching a decision on the constitutional issues. It was finally settled out of court in 1980. But there was one early pronouncement by the court which had far-reaching implications and effects. In a ruling on preliminary matters the federal district court judge stated his view that U.S.-instituted electronic surveillance of American civilians in Germany must be subjected to the domestic rules of the Fourth Amendment. This, he held, was so even though the actual surveillance may have been conducted, after U.S. request, by German authorities under German law (unless the Germans had exercised enough independent discretion on U.S. requests to make approved operations effectively German).[58] This view, had it become recognized as authoritative, would have called for a substantial extension of constitutional constraints, and it caused a considerable stir even though it was not necessarily representative of other courts' positions.

This, then, was the climate of legal activity and opinion in which the other institutional players, Congress and the president, began to act out their own regulatory roles. The president faced a judiciary which no longer would allow citation of "national security" rationales to confer absolute protection for the exercise of executive powers either at home or abroad. The domestic intelligence arena was, naturally, a matter of prime concern, but even in the foreign intelligence field, the fact of foreignness did not itself mean that U.S. intelligence activities, and the executive judgments supporting them, were exempt from potential judicial scrutiny.

The impact of judicial activity was felt in another, very practical realm, too. The *Berlin Democratic Club* case is one of several litigations which attempted to affix personal liability on intelligence operators and their superiors for unconstitutional actions they were alleged to have taken in performing their duties. These lawsuits sprang from an earlier Supreme Court ruling which was construed to recognize a cause of action for money damages against government officials whose official actions were later found to have been unconstitutional.[59] Application of this ruling to intelligence activities was one of the hotly contested issues in the *Berlin Democratic Club* case and others in which plaintiffs sought enormous sums in compensation for alleged unconstitutional activities directed against them. The government response was that the traditional rule granting absolute immunity to officials for actions within the scope of their duties ought to apply in these cases, if anywhere. Otherwise, intelligence officals must subject themselves to potential judicial second-guessing and the chilling prospect of adverse damage judgments with every decision they make. Where rules concerning constitutionality are clear, it may make sense to enforce them that way. But where those rules are constantly evolving, as in the arena of individual privacy rights, the government contended that fairness and good sense demanded protection for official actions taken within legal constraints applicable at the time. The courts had agreed with this general proposition,[60] but they also had occasionally made exceptions to it. Whether the intelligence arena ought to be treated as such an exception was a most controversial issue which still has not been resolved.

Those who watched these developments in the courts could not but find in them cause to insure that, where intelligence operators wanted to use collection techniques to which judicial sensitivity had increasingly been shown, their recommendations would be reviewed at levels where awareness of legal implications could figure in the decision. This, of course, relates directly to the thrust of many public arguments for reform of the intelligence community – establishment of an identifiable chain of approval and responsibility at the highest levels. The legal factor now indicated that the chain should make provision for consideration of the applicable (or, perhaps more importantly, the *arguably* applicable) law.

Congress

Some exasperated observers of the foreign policy scene in the early 1970s lost patience with the helplessness of Congress in the face of executive fiat. Protests over U.S. involvement in the Indochina War had found frequently eloquent expression, but little action, in Congress. And revelations or allegations about intelligence activities provided further evidence of congressional helplessness and even delinquency. One critic's views are illustrative:

The Cold War not only emphasized diplomacy by arms race, but diplomacy by political intelligence, subversion, and counter-insurgency. The CIA has become a major arm of our foreign policy in some parts of the world. Yet Congressmen agreed that they should not supervise the CIA in the way they do other agencies, due to the need for secrecy. Even the CIA's budget is broken up and hidden among those of other agencies. More important than the fear that Congressmen who knew too much might compromise the Agency's security was the feeling that the Agency was engaged in a necessary but very dirty business that it might compromise Congressmen to know about.[61]

Not all members of Congress felt this way, to be sure. As Congress's awareness of its own impotence in foreign policy grew, it began to see the emerging intelligence problem as part and parcel of the larger problem of controlling U.S. behavior abroad. Alleged intelligence abuses had of course to be investigated and their causes found and corrected. But, in addition, some better arrangement had to be provided for congressional participation in the intelligence business as a whole.[62]

In 1974 Congress took a significant step forward in that regard via the Hughes-Ryan Amendment to the Foreign Assistance Act of 1961.[63] Using its appropriation lever, Congress announced that no funds could be spent for CIA covert action operations "unless and until the President finds that each such operation is important to the national security of the United States and reports, in timely fashion, a description of the scope of such operation to the appropriate committees of the Congress, including the Committee on Foreign Relations of the United States Senate and the Committee on Foreign Affairs of the United States House of Representatives." The statute did not insert Congress into the approval channels for covert action, requiring only "timely" notification of presidential decisions to conduct those operations.[64] And it specifically exempted collection operations from its reach. But it did require the president himself to be involved in the approvals, and it stated a standard against which approval authorities must measure any proposals: important service to national security. Thus Congress asserted its regulatory authority to arrange and order the channels for management of covert action, and to draw some boundaries around operational activity. Boundaries based on "national security" interests might indeed prove elastic, and the elasticity might be a function of executive judgments about the demands of national security. But this statement of standards by Congress was precedent-setting nonetheless. Twenty-five years earlier, in the provision of the 1947 National Security Act which became the "justification" for covert action, Congress had said only that the CIA would do those things which might be directed by the National Security Council. It did not specify even "national security" standards, in any degree of importance, for those directives.

The next important step taken by Congress was to investigate the charges about operational excesses. Inquiries in both the House and the Senate gave further impetus to the critique of intelligence operations and pointed the way for remedial efforts which were to follow in the next few years. The much-publicized 1975-1976 House and Senate investigations focused on and publicized criticism of a number of operations at home and abroad. Especially in the Senate, moreover, there was much dissatisfaction with the status of the intelligence community as an instrument of unilateral executive power.

In the House, the special investigating committee headed by Congressman Otis Pike focused mainly on the costs and risks of the intelligence effort and on the quality of its product. This reflected Pike's own strongly-held view that the intelligence community as a whole had strayed so far into irrelevant and wasteful pursuits that it could not be relied upon to perform its most important function: to provide warning of an impending attack. [65] Though in the end a clear majority of the House (246 members) voted to suppress publication of the committee's report, fearing that it contained information that would harm U.S. intelligence activities, a brief summary of the committee's recommendations was published as a committee print. [66] Additionally, a copy of one of the drafts of the full report was leaked to news reporter Daniel Schorr, who then had parts of it published in a New York newspaper, the *Village Voice* (on February 16 and 23, 1976). The House Committee's work thus ended in great controversy, and at the time it seemed to some that its most lasting effect would be a backlash reaction against congressional involvement in such matters. [67]

The Senate investigation, chaired by Senator Frank Church, examined the "abuses" and searched for ways to improve Congress's participation in intelligence controls. Senator Church, like Congressman Pike, began his inquiry with certain skeptical views concerning the intelligence community. His characterization of the CIA as a "rogue elephant" was widely publicized. [68] At the same time, however, he publicly acknowledged that there was legitimate work to be done by the intelligence and security agencies, even in the area of covert action operations. [69]

The committee's investigatory charter was broad and open-ended, instructing the members to measure any and all intelligence activities against standards of legality and propriety. [70] It is important here to notice this explicit license to challenge lawful (i.e., not illegal) activities on the ground of impropriety. This would ultimately play a large part in the committee's findings and recommendations.

In November 1975 the committee issued a report on alleged assassination plots, after listening to more than 100 witnesses and deciding that the evidence established U.S. implication in several schemes. Potential targets included Fidel Castro, Patrice Lumumba, and Rafael Trujillo. While the evidence was admittedly ambiguous and fell short of proving that murderous activities had been sanctioned at the highest levels of national policymaking, the committee felt it had nevertheless identified sufficiently a problem worth addressing: operational authorization procedures seemed so deliberately compartmented and secretive that it would have been possible to set in motion a plan to kill a foreign leader without explicit presidential approval. Further, in the committee's view, CIA officers clearly perceived that assassination was within the range of permissible agency activity. [71] And while no high-level and specific authorization for assassination could be found, the committee argued that administration officials over a period of years had failed to be sufficiently precise in their directions to the intelligence community concerning "troublesome" foreign leaders, and that their attitude toward the possibility of assassinations was ambiguous in the context of other violent activities that they *did* authorize, such as covert actions against Cuba intended to discredit and overthrow the Castro regime.

The committee was particularly confounded by the "plausible denial" concept, familiar to intelligence professionals as a planning guideline to protect the United States from the aftereffects of compromised operations. Throughout its hearings, however, and in its report on assassinations, the committee viewed that concept as a device for shielding the president personally and his senior advisors from responsibility for unsavory covert action operations. [72] The committee further noted that in the intelligence "subculture," where watchfulness and quick wits are prized, subordinates may find unintended operational proposals (or even directives) in general remarks made by the president or those close to him.

The committee's recommendations, in its "assassinations" report, aimed at correcting that weakness by specifying openly the locus, within the executive branch, of responsibility for approval of covert action operations, all along the chain of command and particularly at its highest echelons. [73] The committee's final report, issued in 1976, echoed this concern. In executive branch records the committee had discovered that between 1949 and 1968 several thousand covert action projects had been undertaken, but only 600 or so had been formally elevated in proposal stages to approval authorities outside the intelligence community via National Security Council coordination procedures. [74] Over time, more projects had been submitted for that approval, and approval procedures were significantly tightened (telephonic coordination had been common practice in the early days). But particularly low-risk, low-cost covert action projects, such as routine press announcements placed in foreign news media, did not receive that attention. And the CIA itself acknowledged that those approval channels and practices did not apply to collection or counterintelligence operations or to decisions about overt activities. [75] Moreover, the committee took particular note of the CIA admission that, even by 1972, NSC-level approval and coordination were obtained in only about one-quarter of the CIA's covert action projects. In many cases the practice was to obtain approval for broad program guidelines, but individual projects then generated in accordance with those guidelines were not reviewed outside operational channels for further, individual approvals. The committee's final report, not surprisingly, pointed to the need for meaningful oversight of the executive approval process as it operated in specific individual cases.

Perhaps as an indicator of what congressional oversight would look for, the committee's 1975 report on assassination plots had argued that "traditional American notions of fair play" should guide all American activities on the international scene, even with respect to nations whose ideals and standards are known to be less than generously disposed toward ours.[76] The final report reemphasized that concern for adherence to "fair play" ideals. A pervading theme was that in the "national security" arena, where intelligence and security activities had not been subjected to the restraints applicable in domestic criminal proceedings, the looseness of rules and the wide operational discretion vested in the executive branch had led to operations sometimes resembling those of our totalitarian enemies.[77] Remedies suggested by the committee included clear legislative delineation of the scope of permissible activities, and better procedures for supervising intelligence operations (including more rigorous congressional oversight).[78] Specific recommendations included:

(1) A provision in a statutory charter which enumerated the authorized CIA functions as collection of foreign intelligence, conduct of foreign counterintelligence activities, covert action, and production of finished intelligence.

(2) A statutory requirement that the attorney general must report to the president and to relevant congressional committees any activities which he believed might have violated the constitutional rights of American citizens or other provisions of law.

(3) Establishment within the executive of a special committee, chaired by the secretary of state, to review all human espionage activities, and to make recommendations on the choice between overt and covert methods of collection.

(4) Congressional review of collection activities to make sure that clandestine means are used only when the information sought is sufficiently important and such means are indeed necessary.

(5) Specific limitation of covert action by charter legislation, including prohibition of all political assassination, all efforts to subvert democratic governments, and all support for foreign police or other internal security forces which engaged in systematic violation of human rights. The commit-

tee also argued that the legislation must require the participation and accountability of the highest level policymakers in controlling covert action as a tool of last resort.

(6) Statutory prohibition of the use of certain categories of persons in intelligence operations, including recipients of grants through educational or cultural programs sponsored by the U.S. government, U.S. journalists and foreign journalists accredited to U.S. media organizations, and American clergy and missionaries.[79]

In the aggregate, then, the committee's recommendations clearly signalled to all observers a profound dissatisfaction with past and current control practices, with the mechanisms for congressional participation in those controls, and with the framework of rules, statutory and otherwise, then governing the business of intelligence. The next few years saw concerted attempts by deeply committed members of Congress to institute new rules, procedures, and practices that would remedy these deficiencies.

In the Senate, a Select Committee on Intelligence was quickly established in May 1976, with Senator Inouye of Hawaii as chairman. Senate Resolution 400, the committee's charter, appointed it the Senate's agent for intelligence oversight and declared that the committee should be fully informed of each intelligence agency's activities, including anticipated activities. Early indications were that it was, in fact, fully informed. [80] In the House of Representatives, meanwhile, establishment of a companion committee was delayed until 1977, and its oversight role and impact early in the new regime were accordingly diminished.

A major early hope in Congress was that it would pass a statutory charter for the intelligence agencies which would make public and clear prohibitions, authorizations, and lines of responsibility, and establish structures and rules which the executive could not change merely by issuing internal directives, and in which the Congress would participate. Work on such a charter began almost immediately in the Senate committee. It proved to be an extraordinarily difficult endeavor, however, particularly as presidents issued their own charters, via executive orders, and as executive-legislative coordination and consultation about the emerging rules became intricate and regularized. [81] The story of this effort will appear later in this study.

In the House, although for some time there was no substantive committee for intelligence, individual congressmen nevertheless seized the initiative and introduced charter legislation. Several sought sweeping changes, even to the point of prohibiting covert action and clandestine collection operations except in time of war *declared by Congress* – thus making a congressional decision the device activating certain intelligence capabilities abroad. [82]

There was, additionally, growing insistence that Congress should re-

quire the intelligence agencies to provide it the information needed to
exercise effective oversight and to make the constitutional design of checks
and balances work in foreign affairs more generally.[83]

In 1976-1977 the Senate Intelligence Committee quickly seized the
lead in asserting congressional influence over the intelligence agencies and
in attempting to remedy control deficiencies. In doing so, the committee
sought to serve congressional and constitutional interests in the following
areas:[84]

(1) Obtaining information needed for Congress to participate in foreign
policy decisions. The committee had been instructed by the Senate to do
this[85] in an attempt to diminish that significant information advantage of
the executive which had been recognized early in our constitutional history
and which had lately been identified as a critical issue for Congress to
address and resolve.

(2) Controlling through the Budget process. The committee began to
examine appropriations proposals exhaustively, and it made classified reports (including project-by-project reviews of covert action) available to the
entire Senate, so that voting on intelligence funds could, theoretically,
represent informed decisions.[86] Because of the secrecy which had previously
surrounded intelligence appropriations, the Committee felt that any disciplined review would exert more congressional influence than had been felt
in the past. It also believed that the full effect of congressional power would
not be felt without some more focused activity in that realm.

(3) Controlling by investigatory power. In its first year the committee
investigated 100 indications or allegations of operational improprieties. Its
inquiries relied in large part on reports provided by the intelligence agencies
themselves, but it also conducted independent investigations where that
seemed advisable. The role of Congress as an institutional inquisitor is of
course a well-established one, and the committee was convinced that it
would be an especially valuable tool in discharging congressional oversight
responsibilities.

(4) Supervising approvals. The committee hoped to make even more
significant advances, however, by supervising approvals for operations. The
oversight procedure that had been worked out with the executive for covert
action worked this way: Once the president approved a proposal, the
committee was immediately informed and briefed about the operation, and
it was also briefed at regular intervals thereafter. If it should disapprove of
the operation, and if the executive still wished to conduct it, a closed session
vote of the full Senate could authorize disclosure of details concerning the
operation, effectively destroying it. The concept was that a disagreement
over the advisability of a particular operation would probably not escalate to
disclosure. The executive, confronted with the resolute opposition of a
majority of the committee, would almost surely abandon a plan before

risking disclosure (which could come through a vote of the Senate to disclose, or through "leaks" generated by opponents).

(5) Stating of congressional roles. The Senate committee was convinced that congressional roles ought to be stated in detail as a matter of law, not left to executive condescension. To that end, the charter proposal introduced in 1978 (S. 2525, the National Intelligence Reorganization and Reform Act) provided that the "Director of National Intelligence" (the renamed DCI) must insure that all intelligence activities provide "the executive and legislative branches with the information and analysis that those branches need to fulfill their responsibilities under the Constitution and laws of the United States." The charter proposal also attempted to solidify the current oversight procedure, with its operational approval aspects, in statute, and would have established greatly detailed operational restrictions reflecting many of the Church Committee's recommendations.[87] Some thought was given to congressional control of paramilitary operations by procedures similar to those of the War Powers Act.[88] Nothing ever came of that, but the proposal brings immediately to the forefront an issue which is implicit in all congressional-executive interaction on intelligence activities — the inherent powers of the presidency. Interestingly, the Senate committee observed that although the Ford administration had insisted that intelligence-related legislation give due recognition to such presidential authority, the Carter administration did not.[89]

The Carter view was reflected in other legislation, as we shall see in some detail later. An early Carter Administration proposal on electronic surveillance, a core issue of presidential prerogative, was signed into law in 1978 as the Foreign Intelligence Surveillance Act after much work in Congress led by the Senate Intelligence Committee. It required judicial warrants for all electronic surveillance for foreign intelligence or counterintelligence purposes in the United States when communications of "United States persons" might be intercepted. Although some critics deplored the limitation of this legislation to activities conducted in the United States, [90] it was nevertheless a major — perhaps a historic — executive concession. Not only did the president submit to congressional rulemaking power in a field long held to be within his protected sanctuary of prerogative, but he also submitted to a system of judicial review of specific operational proposals. This was unprecedented in the area of national security affairs. Legislators were quick to notice this and to take encouragement from it.[91]

The Central Themes of Debate

For many participants in the intelligence debate, placing limits on presidential power vis-a-vis Congress was surely important. But there were other values at stake, too. By 1976-1977, in fact, the major perspectives about operational restrictions had coalesced into four "camps," according to the main principles each emphasized. Rulemakers in all forums, in dealing with these perspectives, confronted truly fundamental dilemmas of choice.

For many persons, the most important considerations collected around some notion of national security. Some, indeed, insisted that there can be no other test of the intelligence community's value and performance, and no other guidelines for rulemaking, than service to the nation's security needs. Security was the primary societal value, assuring all others. The first duty of government was to see that the society could defend itself and its interests from its enemies, or from those who would seek to bring it down. And this required great national strength and the resolve to use it, covertly if necessary.[92] Many thought the logic of this position self-evident, and that the American public would readily close ranks behind it. [93] But several difficulties considerably reduced the effect of the national security formula as guidance for policy and as an argument in the intelligence debate.

First, and most generally, that formula rested on a world view which many simply did not accept. Individuals who had served in policymaking or operational positions, and who had used intelligence products or conducted intelligence activities as instruments of national policy, tended to see the world in terms of threats to America and, by extension, to American national interest in the world at large. For them, international politics was understood as fundamentally competitive, if not always threatening. Events worldwide were evaluated in terms of their pertinence to defense of American interests. The specter of a monolithic Communist menace was no longer current, but images of the Soviet Union as expansionist, or at least as aggressively opportunist, were usually at the center of this perspective.

No one disagreed with the proposition that American society ought to be in some sense secure. But on the other hand not everyone understood the world solely through that prism. Some saw international events as reflections of forces and pressures which were not centrally instigated or managed by the USSR, and which were not so much threatening as insistent on their own independent outcomes. America should seek to align itself with those forces, some argued, for they carried within them the seeds of an inexorable future. To resist them, with the CIA or any other tools of the national self-interest in security, was to place the nation on the wrong side of history.[94]

Others saw pursuit of American self-interest as fundamentally destructive of all hope for international harmony. They argued for dramatic changes in national outlook, policy process, and behavior. [95] Still others, though sharing the view that security interests were important, argued that those imperatives did not compel the kinds of manipulative activities contemplated by the CIA's covert action capability.[96]

Inevitably this divergence in underlying world views produced contrasting approaches on intelligence issues. Those, for instance, who did not
perceive the world as naturally hostile or threatening, or who believed that
international harmony will emerge if our institutions and practices will
only permit it, were unlikely to be persuaded of the need for intelligence
capabilities that might be perceived elsewhere as combative (e.g., covert
action). On the other hand, those who understood international behavior as
concerted pursuit of national self-interest were reluctant to cast aside any
tool of foreign policy, including the capability to influence events abroad by
secret means.

But even when participants in the debate agreed on the general characteristics of the external environment and could turn attention to identifying
and understanding specific external threats, there was disagreement on the
nature of those threats and on their implications for America. One who
believes that America's most challenging military competitor, the Soviet
Union, is basically more fearful or suspicious than aggressive, will not easily
be convinced that our national interests demand intelligence capabilities
that might be considered threatening. On the other hand, if it is thought
that the Soviet Union is an expansionist power, the prudent policymaker is
likely to resist all attempts to confine significantly the capabilities entrusted to the intelligence community.

Because the national security formula failed to recognize and reach this
deeper conflict of perspectives, it failed to satisfy many critics of intelligence operations. National security arguments had difficulty, in summary, because they did not convince critics that aggressive capabilities, or
relatively permissive rules, were valuable to America. Other perspectives
resisted submersion in any larger concept of national security. Where some
considered information-gathering activities essential to informed decisionmaking, others feared potentially intrusive spying techniques turned inward on American society. Where some viewed covert action as just another
instrument in America's foreign policy repertoire, others saw in it the
potential for mischievous, if not malevolent, manipulation of other societies. Where some saw intelligence as an important tool in the arsenal of
defense and therefore peace, others saw it as a clandestine tool of presidential
prerogative subversive of basic principles of limited and balanced governmental power. Competing values, then, entered the debate claiming equal
stature. And it was their claims for attention in the regulatory process which
made visible the most fundamental contention.

For many attentive observers, a second goal-value was protection of
citizens from intrusive government. Intelligence operations seemed to
threaten unacceptable incursions across the boundaries established in the
Constitution to preserve civil liberties. [97] The oft-cited history of arguable

"abuses" — mail openings, domestic political surveillances, wiretaps, and break-ins — only deepened their concern about expansive and abusive governmental power.

Though fearful of governmental interference or intrusion, those who viewed intelligence issues from this perspective did not necessarily demand cessation of all potentially worrisome operations. They, too, wanted to make our society secure.[98] But they did argue for operational rules which recognize and protect individual rights and freedoms at home and for Americans abroad. From their viewpoint, an overarching purpose of our government is to preserve and protect a free society, not to subvert it in the name of defense against assumed or vaguely defined external threats. Like our Founding Fathers, these critics were suspicious of governmental power regardless of its rationale. They were not willing to presume that any government is by nature benevolent. They feared, with some cause in the aftermath of Watergate, the retributive tendencies of those in power. Government can be venal and misguided, they argued, and all of its instruments must be carefully and clearly constrained. As the Senate Select Committee's final report asserted: "The natural tendency of Government is toward abuse of power."[99] Not surprisingly, then, the tendency of intelligence activities to expand to unacceptable proportions was viewed as a phenomenon which rulemakers must consciously try to curb.[100] And, as we shall see in more detail shortly, adherents of this perspective believed that the restrictive rules already protecting the citizenry from abusive acts of law enforcement authorities ought to be applied as well to protect against similar capabilities installed in the national security establishment.

Other critics of intelligence operations used yet another standard to judge the acceptability of government actions, even beyond arguments about protecting citizens' rights. They argued, as did the Senate's investigating committee in 1976,[101] that traditional American norms of "justice and fair play" must govern all our foreign behavior. Not surprisingly, the covert action capability drew most of their concern, often transforming latent suspicions about government into explicit distress over the prospect of American meddling in foreign societies. Others argued, on a more practical level, that covert action too often degenerates into useless or counterproductive folly. And still others shared those concerns but recognized a need to retain some such capability, properly constrained.[102]

Although some commentators cautioned against careless application of ethical codes as operational limitations,[103] we shall see that various rules announced within the intelligence community did try to respond to these points of view. But even so, the issue of executive branch control over covert action remained a fertile ground for debate.[104] Most fundamentally, there was uneasiness about the very idea of executive self-regulation. Any constraints it announced were self-imposed, after all, and could be changed whenever the "self" changed. For many, they lacked the reassuring constancy and the abiding underpinning of legitimacy which would be provided by statutory or judicial pronouncements.

Not everyone, furthermore, agreed that decisions about intelligence operations should – constitutionally – be left to the president or to his most senior advisors in the White House or executive branch. Many now understood the intelligence problem as part and parcel of an ongoing institutional struggle within the national government. From that standpoint, the relevant issues were framed quite differently. Should other governmental institutions outside the executive participate in decision-making about intelligence operations? If so, how? And should they take part in supervising those operations? How?

Such questions touched upon yet another major value concept underlying the intelligence debate in any form: our Constitution's design of shared and balanced governmental powers. The struggle over control and content of American foreign policy is an old one in America, quite familiar to those who have studied the constitutional blueprint (or, more appropriately, the lack of a constitutional blueprint) for the conduct of our foreign affairs. The problem, simply stated, is that the formulas for distribution of functions and responsibilities within the national government – "separation of powers" and "checks and balances" – found no comprehensive expression in the Constitution's treatment of foreign affairs powers. The Constitution is largely silent on many important issues of power distribution, and, in the words of one scholar, where lines of demarcation do exist between the branches of our government, powers are "not so much separated as fissured, along jagged lines indifferent to classical categories of governmental power."[105] As the law, and procedures and practices, evolved over time, some foreign affairs authority clearly belonged to the president and some clearly belonged to Congress. But much was combined, too, in anticipation of (and dependence on) joint and collaborative activity. Perhaps most importantly, there were (and are) many issues yet to be resolved.

In this context of irregular and often disputable division of authority and much occasion for challengeable assertion of authority, where does the intelligence community belong? Who owns it, who should control it, and how?

Throughout World War II and the Cold War years, the intelligence community and its aggregate capabilities were essentially tools of unilateral presidential prerogative. In World War II the Office of Strategic Services, forerunner of the CIA, operated as one of the many warfighting instruments at the disposal of the president as commander-in-chief. [106] Later, in peacetime, the intelligence agencies were held securely within the president's own domain of discretion, operating secretly in the foreign affairs "silences" of the Constitution. By the mid-1970s many observers agreed with former Under Secretary of State George Ball, who gracefully summarized many concerns by describing the domestic and foreign capabilities of the intelligence community as an "enormous temptation" to the president.[107]

But the problem was more than unilateral executive branch control of covert action. It also involved presidential control of a vast array of information-gathering capabilities – a monopoly which conferred significant advantages in the competition for management of our foreign relations.[108]

In time, as criticism of swollen presidential prerogative grew within and outside of the government, Congress became more active and aggressive in a number of foreign affairs arenas. As we have seen, oversight of intelligence operations and regular access to their information products became prominent institutional goals. By the mid-1970s, the Senate investigation of alleged intelligence abuses would find three main departures from its concept of the Constitution's design:[109]

(1) Excessive presidential power. For too long, the committee believed, Congress, the courts, the press, and the public at large had left the business of controlling intelligence activities solely to presidential prerogative and discretion. The concept and reality of inherent presidential power had accordingly expanded to unconstitutional proportions.

(2) Excessive secrecy. The committee believed that the shield of secrecy had unduly and unnecessarily inhibited outside scrutiny of intelligence programs and practices. To restore the constitutional plan of balanced power, secrecy, as a means of protecting a sanctuary of presidential prerogative, had to be severely curtailed. The problem was not seen as one of publicizing intelligence operations but of establishing arrangements for outside supervision.

(3) Avoidance of the rule of law. Intelligence operations had too often been insulated by national security rationales from some Bill of Rights-derived restraints and from specific prohibitions applicable to other governmental activities (such as law enforcement). This may have contributed, the committee believed, to sentiment within the intelligence community that this arm of unilateral presidential power was above the law as well as beyond the reach of other governmental institutions.

Given such concern, the obvious policy recommendation was to improve congressional participation in control and direction of intelligence operations. The Hughes-Ryan Amendment's requirement that the executive must notify congressional committees of covert action operations, the oversight routines thereafter worked out informally between Congress and the intelligence agencies, and the effort to produce a statutory charter, all derived from that basic perspective.

These modes of interaction had expanded the spheres of collaborative activity between Congress and the intelligence agencies even by 1975-1976. Critics of presidential prerogative, however, were anxious to assess the sufficiency of those coordination routines over time and to express them in statutory form. Their participation in further regulatory inquiries reflected a central and enduring concern – adherence to constitutional design – which they fully expected others in the debate to respect and accommodate.

4

The Ford Administration's Response

By late 1974 President Ford himself was being called to account for intelligence activities now widely publicized in the emerging debate. In the midst of controversy about the pardon he had granted former President Nixon in the Watergate affair, Ford was again and again forced to respond to queries about the ways in which the intelligence agencies had been used and were being used. An exchange in a September 16 news conference is illustrative:

Q.   Mr. President, recent congressional testimony has indicated that the CIA, under the direction of a committee headed by Dr. Kissinger, attempted to destabilize the Government of Chile under former President Allende.

Is it the policy of your administration to attempt to destabilize the governments of other democracies?

THE PRESIDENT.   Let me answer in general. I think this is a very important question.

Our government, like other governments, does take certain actions in the intelligence field to help implement foreign policy and protect national security. I am informed reliably that Communist nations spend vastly more money than we do for the same kinds of purposes.

Now in this particular case, as I understand it – and there is no doubt in my mind – our government had no involvement whatsoever in the Allende coup. To my knowledge, nobody has charged that. The facts are we had no involvement in any way whatsoever in the coup itself.

In a period of time, three or four years ago, there was an effort being made by the Allende government to destroy opposition news media, both the writing press as well as the electronic press, and to destroy opposition political parties.

The effort was made to help and assist the preservation of opposition newspapers and electronic media and to preserve opposition political parties.

I think this is in the best interest of the people in Chile and, certainly, in our best interest.[1]

So that no one would think that such activities had been undertaken lightly, the president added that a National Security Council committee (then called the "Forty Committee") had watched over them since 1948, and that currently it reviewed "every covert operation" and informed relevant House and Senate committees about them. He also indicated that he hoped to establish other collaborative and oversight mechanisms in the future. But critics were persistent. In the September 1974 news conference just cited, another reporter challenged the authority under which such operations were conducted. The president responded by saying, essentially, that the rationale for these activities rested on the very nature of international politics: other nations conduct them and have conducted them, pursuing their interests in a competitive world. So the sensible, rational course for the United States is to adopt the same practices, or at least to maintain the capability to employ them.[2]

But the challenge was not deflected that easily, and the public critique of intelligence gathered momentum. Finally, just as Congress was beginning its own investigations into alleged operational abuses, President Ford established (on January 4, 1975) a blue-ribbon panel headed by Vice-President Rockefeller to investigate CIA activities within the United States.[3]

This was not the first time that a special, high-level, and high-visibility commission had been instituted to study intelligence affairs. Indeed, by the Rockefeller Commission's own count it was the eleventh such major study conducted since the founding of the CIA in 1947. But the panel took care to point out that these earlier investigations had been preoccupied with organizational, not operational, issues, and that in its specific concern with CIA operational activities the Ford Administration's initiative was truly unique.[4]

The Rockefeller Commission's report – 300 pages of findings and recommendations produced within six months – articulates important perspectives of the mid-1970s debate in some detail, and I will explore those perspectives shortly. First, however, we should note some significant characteristics of the panel itself.

The most basic observation has to do with the scope of its investigative mission, which was limited to examination of CIA activities within the United States and to determination of whether any had exceeded the Agency's statutory authority (the 1947 National Security Act). The panel adhered to this restriction scrupulously even though this meant it had to set aside many of the most contentious issues in the public debate. Allegations concerning plots to assassinate foreign leaders, for example, were not pursued, though in the course of the investigation some information about such activities was discovered and turned over to the president.[5] This became a matter of some public concern; President Ford was repeatedly asked to explain why the commission would not pursue the matter. In response, he assured the American public that he personally was examining all assassination charges.[6] In the end the materials discovered about them were given to the House and Senate investigating committees, which were interested in exploring them in detail.[7]

But even beyond the assassination issue, the commission did not delve at all into the foreign intelligence, counterintelligence, and covert action capabilities unless domestic ramifications were discovered or apparent, and unless there were indications that such activities had exceeded authorizations.

It was clear to all concerned, of course, that the public debate was already larger in scope than the commission's inquiry. But the president hardly intended to launch a "zero-based" review of the CIA and its operations. Instead, the authorizations and prohibitions of the 1947 National Security Act were posited as the controlling investigative parameters. The validity of activities conducted in compliance with (i.e., not in violation of) the act was assumed at the start. But since the 1947 statute did not even identify the activities and capabilities that later emerged in the CIA, on what grounds could the commission declare any to be either authorized or unauthorized? President Ford himself supplied the answer: the CIA's operational capabilities which had been developed over the years were to be considered "authorized," though the statute itself was silent about them.[8] "Unauthorized" actions were those which transgressed the explicit statutory prohibition of CIA involvement in domestic security affairs. *That* prohibition was the firm legislative pronouncement which determined the mission of the president's special investigating panel.

Many objected to the taking of refuge in an inarticulate statute, and pressed for more precise identification of the executive's concepts of "authority" and "limits." In one news conference, for instance, the president was queried specifically about reports of CIA stockpiles of poison dart guns, cobra venom, and shellfish toxin. What limits ought to be placed on activities that might make use of such things? The president responded that the "basic limitations come from the law," and then he outlined various mechanisms and procedures designed to guard against violation of law.[9] In another interview the president was pursued tenaciously by Eric Sevareid on the issue of whether to expand legal controls on covert action to embrace a wider range of "propriety" concerns than the law then seemed to reflect:

MR. SEVAREID.   Mr. President, wouldn't the whole thing be safer and clearer and cleaner if it was simply the law that the CIA gather intelligence only and engage in no covert political operations abroad?

THE PRESIDENT.   If we lived in a different world . . .

MR. SEVAREID.   It might help to make the world different.

THE PRESIDENT.   Well, I can't imagine the United States saying we would not undertake any covert activities, and knowing at the same time that friends, as well as foes, are undertaking covert activity, not only in the United States but elsewhere. That would be like tying the President's hands behind his back in the planning and execution of foreign policy. . . .

Now, we cannot compete in this very real world if you are just going to tie the United States with one hand behind its back and everybody else has got two good hands to carry out their operations.[10]

Accordingly, the president was careful not to invite adoption of new regulatory theories that might significantly confine intelligence operations. He thus limited the Rockefeller Commission's charter to the one operational limit specified in the 1947 statute: proscription of CIA involvement in internal security matters. And more generally, he specified legality (or avoidance of illegality), not propriety, as the standard against which all scrutinized activities were to be measured. In effect, he indicated that value judgments about intelligence activity were relevant to the regulatory effort only insofar as they had been made visible in the law. This was, even in initial concept, an essentially conservative response to growing public, legislative, and judicial concern about the intelligence agencies.[11]

Presidential perspectives governing the panel's effort were evidenced in other ways, too. In his public statement accompanying appointment of the commission, Ford outlined the classic national security rationale for intelligence activities – activities not specified in the 1947 National Security Act but developed thereafter to cope with national security challenges.[12] He further suggested that by protecting the nation these activities serve important societal vales, such as protection of "fundamental freedoms," which might seem in the abstract to be threatened or compromised by them. In essence he argued that the asserted dichotomy between intelligence capabilities and domestic liberties that seemed to preoccupy some critics was in actuality false. Safeguards for civil liberties and tools of national security are devices protecting the same core values. They are of equal stature in that effort, moreover. Their purposes can and must be harmonized, based on the underlying commonality of values. Radical prescriptions favoring either do great disservice to the nation.

Just as importantly, Ford also noted that the CIA had in fact been an important protector of democratic values in an unfriendly world, though the requirements of secrecy prevented elaborate public demonstration of that fact. Excesses there may well have been,[13] as well as errors of operational judgment reflecting overzealous pursuit of a major and unarguable national value, security. These mistakes, he asserted, would be discovered and revealed. Corrections would be made. But the great bulk of countervailing evidence about useful and successful operations must necessarily remain secret. The public, not having access to that information, must be careful about judging intelligence operations and controls based upon scrutiny of only a few aberrational cases.

Two final points about the commission help to place its work, and the public reaction to it, in perspective. First, in focusing its effort the commission was concerned with "public charges" and "allegations" about various activities. Penetration of domestic dissident groups by government informers, mail intercepts, electronic eavesdropping, and "break-ins" (forced entry and search of homes and offices) were among the most controversial of these. The sources of these charges and allegations were never specified (though of course the public debate was in the headlines recurrently). In effect, the commission itself, in taking notice of particular criticisms to focus its effort, decided which charges to investigate and which not to investigate. This was hardly enough to satisfy those in the debate who were suspicious of executive power and motives.

While the focus on unauthorized and domestic activities significantly circumscribed the investigation, there is no evidence that the commission avoided difficult issues encountered within the bounds of its charter. It is true, however, that in tone and substance its final report is kinder to the intelligence community than the parallel congressional investigations which delved into the length and breadth of all operational capabilities and which took none as definitively sanctioned by largely unarticulated national security rationales.

We must also take note of the panel's composition. Three characteristics of the group stand out in retrospect and suggest that these people may have brought to the inquiry a distinctive set of interpretive lenses, even apart from the presidential perspectives imbedded in their mission, which gave their work a certain cant at the outset. The most obvious shared trait was government service; five of the seven members had long and high-level experience in government. Most were familiar with the operational instruments the national government had developed and had come to rely on in international affairs, and they had been sensitized to the general rationales supporting them. These were people, in short, who would not have been shocked about intelligence functions or uncomfortable with the rationales offered in support of "authorized" activities. Unlike much of the larger public in the 1970s, they would not be immediately suspicious of "national security" arguments. In fact, they were likely to understand their rightful place in the inquiry. For that reason, they were less likely than many to draw the line between authorized and unauthorized activity in a way which undercut important governmental and societal security interests.

Another factor was their age. All were a generation removed from many of those who were protesting so rancorously in public about the excessive use of governmental power in Vietnam and Watergate. They knew that power in itself was not the central problem. In their time it had rescued European democracies in their hour of greatest need, and at home it had been used to uplift the needy and to vindicate the rights of groups formerly excluded from meaningful participation in our society. The real focus of concern was how power was used. It was specific activities, not just the capability to act, which needed close scrutiny and perhaps criticism and limitation.

Finally, we should note that all the commission's principal members had been top-level officials in large bureaucratic organizations. They knew that errors of omission and commission can be made at lower levels in such organizations, even though detailed, comprehensive guidance may have been given about performance expectations. They knew how things at the operational level can go awry in unexpected ways, and how both written rules and unspoken (but well-understood) expectations can be thwarted by the dynamics of bureaucratic reality. They knew the difference, in short, between organizational clumsiness and institutional malevolence. They would recognize mistakes quickly, but they would not be surprised, and they would listen to explanations that less-experienced observers might dismiss out of hand as unacceptable. In this way, too, they differed from many participants in the larger public debate.

The Rockefeller Commission's Report

The commission began its work with a statement of the problem. Three interrelated propositions were set out to frame the central issues:

(1) The Constitution recognizes and protects a "high degree" of individual privacy for members of our society, and the proscription of internal security functions for the agency served that value.

(2) Individual liberties depend on government observance of the law. The executive must observe the limits of authorities delegated by Congress, and, importantly, must also stay within authorities inherent in the office of the President.

(3) The need to protect individual liberties does not argue only for *limits* on government power. It argues also for *competent* government suitably equipped to preserve internal order and defend against external threats.[14]

The regulatory dilemma, as seen by the commission, was clear: to draw "reasonable lines − where legitimate intelligence needs end and erosion of Constitutional government begins."[15] It is important to note the most fundamental premise of this statement of the problem: that in the final analysis the dilemma can be resolved in a way that preserves central values on both sides. Intelligence activities and individual liberties are not incompatible. In fact, "public safety and individual liberty sustain each other," reflecting their orientation on common societal values. It is also important to emphasize that even in its statement of the basic issues the commission made ample room for "inherent" presidential power and for tools that enable the government to deal with perceived threats.

Since the commission was directed to search out unauthorized activity, and since CIA operational authorizations in general had not been made explicit as a matter of law, the commission's report took pains to outline a concept of the legal grounds and scope of CIA authority. Not surprisingly, given the president's earlier public remarks, the commission held that all the operational capabilities developed within the CIA were within the bounds of applicable authorities. It was the exercise of those capabilities which may occasionally have exceeded proper bounds. This was, then, a highly visible, unmistakable rejoinder to those critics who had argued that part (or all) of the intelligence effort ought to be disestablished.

When the 1947 National Security Act was passed, the commission argued, Congress had indeed contemplated (though it did not explicitly say) that the CIA would be involved in "all aspects of foreign intelligence, including collection," and that the agency would also engage in some activities within the United States. [16] Members of Congress in fact expected the National Security Council to direct the CIA to engage in clandestine espionage activity. And further, the commission observed, no one in Congress attempted to restrict NSC power to assign other functions to the CIA. Indeed, it seemed clear that Congress meant to leave room for responses to unforeseen contingencies, by statutory language which could be used as authority for other directives (such as covert action). [17]

It was of course true that Congress had wanted limits on CIA activity. Domestic police and security functions were, after all, prohibited, as properly within the province of other agencies. But this was best understood as a way to coordinate and delimit complementary governmental functions assigned to separate agencies. The problem, to the extent that one existed, was in that sense a jurisdictional one, not one of reining in an obstreperous foreign intelligence agency.

Commission perspectives on CIA authority were notable also for three themes. The first was the need to clarify, not diminish, authority. In an introductory assertion characteristic of the rest of its argument, the commission noted that "Congress vested broad powers in the CIA." [18] Other observers might have substituted "vague" or "ambiguous" for the word "broad." Indeed, the commission itself might better have chosen that phraseology, since the report then observed that reasonable men can (and do) disagree on the extent of those powers. Clear, precise, definitive lines of authority, and thus of legality and illegality, had not been drawn either on the public record or in guidelines published within the executive. This was true at two levels: general operational capabilities were undefined in basic authorities, and for specific activities there were no hard-and-fast guidelines for operators showing where the lines of prohibition might be drawn. If, then, there had been errors, the Rockefeller panel seemed to suggest that it was not surprising.

The second theme was that "extralegal" policy considerations argued against diminishing authority. Rules, when clarified, can be either expanded or contracted to suit underlying policy needs. President Ford had earlier made clear that his inclination was not to curtail activity by adoption of extralegal notions about constraints. His preference was to defend most operations as necessitated by international realities, perhaps making some adjustments at the margins but retaining all basic capabilities. Accordingly, the commission used policy considerations to support much existing operational practice and to argue for clarification of the legal authority to engage in it.[19] Indeed, it argued for clear specification of rules which would recognize operational necessity (and national security) as a major determinant of the outer reaches of permissibility.

A related point is important here, too. The distinction between illegalities (violation of specific provisions of law) and improprieties (violation of extralegal "policy" notions about ethics and morality) was not recognized by many critics of the intelligence agencies. Frequently they mixed the two, seeking more rigorous controls and more confining limitations grounded in normative judgments. In arguing that current capabilities need not be constricted (and might, in fact, be expanded) by extralegal policy considerations, the commission sent clear signals to these attentive audiences about its status quo orientation.

Finally, the commission upheld the distinction between "law enforcement" rules and "national security" rules. Earlier I described the emerging challenge, in the courts and before Congress, to the relatively permissive operational rules governing intelligence operations. Because of the special deference accorded national security purposes, intelligence operations had been insulated from important constraints applied in law enforcement. Now, however, that distinction was controversial. The commission entered that contentious arena when it tried to decide what kinds of domestic operations the CIA could properly undertake without intruding on authority that belonged to the FBI. The test, the panel finally decided, was not the nature of the activity undertaken nor its effect on Americans, but its operational purpose: "If the principal purpose of the activity is the prosecution of crimes or protection against civil disorder or domestic insurrection, then the activity is prohibited. On the other hand, if the principal purpose relates to foreign intelligence or to protection of the security of the agency, the activity is permissible, within limits, even though it might also be performed by a law enforcement agency."[20] The commission here adopted the intelligence professional's classic − but now contested − distinction between national security concerns and law enforcement, as well as the rationale for the larger operational scope of intelligence operations serving national security purposes. In siding with the professionals, the commission also rendered its report vulnerable to all the criticism leveled against that distinction and against the special status of national security rationales.

The Rockefeller Commission evaluated operational safeguards in two arenas: controls external to the CIA and controls internal to the agency. Among the external controls, the report described a multitude of agencies at least nominally involved in supervising CIA activities. But as a result of its investigation the commission believed that official oversight mechanisms had to be improved in both Congress and the executive, and its recommendations were in large part designed to do that. It spoke mainly to controls over domestic activities, but its findings were such that by implication they raised larger questions about control and direction of operations abroad.

At the highest level, executive control over CIA activities was exercised by the National Security Council. But for the purposes in which the commission was interested, control by the full NSC was mainly peripheral.[21] That body pronounced upon large issues and set the directions in which existing capabilities would be exercised. But the NSC was not a forum for debate and reflection about details, or about why and how to exercise or confine operations.

Two committees of the NSC had intelligence duties. The Intelligence Committee was a subcabinet level group representing users of intelligence products. It met infrequently, mainly to evaluate the quality of intelligence analysis. The Forty Committee, on the other hand, was involved in operational approvals. It reviewed covert action proposals and activities as well as collection operations involving high risk and sensitivity.[22] The Rockefeller Commission found, however, that it had never passed upon any CIA domestic activities, even those which the CIA considered sensitive, because none had ever been submitted to it for approval.

The President's Foreign Intelligence Advisory Board (PFIAB) was first established in 1956 by executive order as a means to provide the president "outside" advice on the objectives and management of the national intelligence effort. Composed of prominent Americans named by the president, the PFIAB had met for twelve days each year (two days every two months), generally to hear briefings given by the intelligence agencies and policymakers. Since those briefings were its main source of information, the commission concluded that the board could not in any manner be considered to have functioned as a meaningful control device.

The NSC had established several other bodies which acted as coordination mechanisms at the top of the intelligence community's hierarchy. In a general sense each provided a measure of direction and control. The director of Central Intelligence chaired them all, however, so they could hardly be counted as truly "external" institutions. The Intelligence Community Staff then consisted of about fifty persons drawn from agencies throughout the community, supporting the director in his supervisory and coordination roles. The Intelligence Resources Advisory Committee advised the director on preparation of the intelligence budget, and the United States Intelligence Board advised him on such matters as intelligence collection and production needs and priorities. The USIB was composed of the heads of the principal foreign intelligence agencies and was broken down into eleven standing committees specializing in review of specific functional areas. It was expert in what it did, but it was not an operational control device.

The Office of Management and Budget exercised control over resources allocated to the CIA, but mainly on the basis of information supplied by the agency, and to do even that it employed only one budget examiner and his supervisor. When approved at OMB and presented to Congress, budget requests for the agency were hidden in proposals for other executive departments (though the congressional oversight committees knew, or could find out, where the CIA allocations were). Once the budget was approved, the single OMB analyst then transferred the funds to the CIA's accounts. OMB had no operational oversight role, however, nor did it have a voice in intelligence policy. It was generally aware of large-scale agency programs, activities, and functions, but specific operations and policies were planned and approved elsewhere. [23]

The Rockefeller Commission had relatively harsh words for the performance of the Department of Justice in intelligence oversight. In theory, as the president's strong right arm in insuring that the laws are faithfully executed by government officials, the Justice Department possessed the most drastic form of external control of misconduct: criminal prosecution. Yet since 1954, in deference to the perceived needs of secrecy, the Department of Justice had ceded to the CIA the initial and most important investigatory functions in cases of suspected operational illegalities. The practice worked as follows: if the CIA, after its initial inquiry, believed that any prosecution would require release of sensitive information it preferred to withhold, the agency was not required to refer a case of possible violation of law to the Justice Department for further action. It was a classic illustration of the special status accorded the national security perspective: operational necessity — the need to protect CIA activities from disclosure — had been given precedence over public pursuit of violations of law. In acceding to this practice, the commission argued, a succession of attorneys general had abdicated their statutory duties to the president and to the country, a situation which was not corrected until January 1975, just as the Rockefeller Commission began its work.

Outside the executive, other control devices surveyed by the commission included congressional oversight committees, the Government Accounting Office, the courts, the press, and various special commissions and panels.

Within Congress, the armed services committees had exclusive jurisdiction over nonappropriations bills related to intelligence. They were, at least in theory, primary instruments by which congressional influence could be exerted over the CIA. Each had subcommittees designated for intelligence matters, but no substantive legislation for the CIA had been proposed since the 1940s, so there had been little work to do. Their influence, accordingly, had been limited. The appropriations committees also had subcommittees appointed to handle intelligence affairs. These subcommittees reviewed CIA budget requests in secret, examining information not made available to the full membership of the committees or to Congress as a whole. But overall, the commission concluded, little real control had been exercised.[24]

To be sure, there was some highly visible recent evidence of more assertive congressional interest and activity in intelligence: the 1974 Hughes-Ryan reporting requirement for covert action operations and the special investigating committees just established in both houses. But the Rockefeller panel saw those actions against the background of Congress's historical disinterest in supervising intelligence activities. The fact that a reporting channel existed was not, in itself, evidence that meaningful oversight was being exercised. And the charters for the special inquisitions were temporary. Whether either initiative would endure, once the public furor about intelligence issues had subsided, seemed an open question.

The Government Accounting Office, the commission found, had not conducted any review of CIA activity since 1962, and in any event it had no voice in matters of operational control and policy. In assessing the impact of the courts, the commission noted that since 1947 only seven judicial decisions had involved the CIA directly, and by mid-1975 none had resulted in substantial checks on operations.[25] With regard to the media, which everyone knew had become more vigilant and knowledgeable about intelligence operations, the commission believed that even the most dogged investigative journalism could not be relied upon to police the intelligence agencies effectively. Reporters depended upon leaked, and often inaccurate and incomplete, information. Their public revelations, moreover, had unexpected and often harmful ramifications for other, unquestionably legitimate, activities.

Finally, special commissions and panels had not been used to inquire specifically into operational issues, and so they had had little effect in areas that concerned the Rockefeller panel most.

In the realm of controls within the CIA, the commission evaluated seven major control mechanisms: the chain of command; "lateral" coordination routines between offices; written regulations; "watchdogs" within the agency (e.g., the inspector general); various controllers of resources (money, property, and personnel); training courses; and more informal means of communication outside the official chain of command. Overall, the commission found that two impediments had limited the utility of these devices. In the first place, "compartmentation" of knowledge about operational activities significantly limited the number of persons who were in a position to evaluate them against nonoperational values.[26] And secondly, the ethos and practices of secrecy which individual operatives had internalized so deeply could conceivably lead them to use their professional skills to avoid or deceive close scrutiny, even by authorities who were well-informed.

Nevertheless, the commission found that "virtually all of the Agency activities criticized in this Report were known to top management, sometimes as a result of complaints of impropriety from lower-ranking employees."[27] This, it was concluded, seemed to validate the effectiveness of these internal channels for communication purposes, though the adequacy of the controls exercised through them was a different matter.

In the final analysis the commission concluded that the best assurance against abuse of CIA capabilities lay in the character of the person appointed to be the director of Central Intelligence – in his ability to resist improper pressures from within or outside of the agency. The panel recommended that the search for such individuals include consideration of nonprofessionals of proven management and administrative skills. It further recommended that the quality of the agency's legal and inspector general staffs be strengthened and that the scope of their functions be increased. In the past, the panel found, both offices had been insufficiently involved in examination of CIA operations, partly as a result of the compartmentation practice.[28]

Because CIA directives did not spell out in detail which activities could or could not be undertaken, the Report recommended issuance of internal agency guidelines specifying those domestic activities, by general type, which are permitted and those on the other hand which are prohibited by statute, executive order, or other regulations. Not surprisingly, the phrasing of this recommendation echoed the Ford administration's focus on compliance with law as the standard for defining operational permissibility. The report held that the agency guidelines should specify that "unlawful methods are prohibited,"[29] as if that proposition could not be taken for granted.

In considering particular operations conducted by the CIA, the commission did uncover some activities which led its members to believe that the agency had occasionally – and, more importantly, knowingly – trespassed over the line any reasonable person would draw between intelligence operations and law enforcement activities. Mail intercept operations conducted at various times in the 1950s, 1960s, and early 1970s in New York, San Francisco, Hawaii, and New Orleans were a major concern. The New York operation had lasted for twenty years, while the others were short-lived or intermittent, but all involved the intercepting and opening of mail to examine the contents. The hope was to gain insight into the activities and interests of foreign intelligence services, and to discover possible operational leads. Three postmasters general and one attorney general had known of the projects in varying degrees. And the CIA "was aware of the law making mail openings illegal, but apparently considered the intelligence value of the mail operations to be paramount."[30]

Inquiry into the CIA's so-called "Operation CHAOS" touched another sore point. In 1967 a Special Operations Group had been established within the CIA's counterintelligence staff to collect, coordinate, evaluate, and report information on the foreign contacts of American dissidents. Over a period of six years, this group compiled 13,000 files about those contacts, including dossiers on 7,200 U.S. citizens, with all documents and data cross-indexed and retrievable by computer. From the start, in anyone's estimation, this initiative brought the agency perilously close to the internal security arena. Yet just as importantly, insistent demands from the White House by two presidents and their staffs, seeking more and better information to cope with domestic civil strife, had led to expansion of the project and to pressures within the agency for activity that ultimately transgressed the statutory prohibition of internal security functions. To further compound matters, the operation was removed from the normal chain of command and was isolated within the CIA even beyond the normal requirements of secrecy and compartmentation. There was no supervision of the project by persons not involved in it or dependent on its product.

The commission concluded that the declared mission which generated Operation CHAOS — collecting intelligence abroad concerning foreign influences on domestic dissident activity — was proper, but that later, when the CIA became a repository for voluminous data on the domestic activities of Americans, derived principally from FBI reports and not directly related to foreign connections, the agency's statutory authority had been exceeded. Stated in another way, legal proscriptions had been violated.[31]

The commission also examined certain activities the agency had undertaken in order to protect its own security, including assistance to CIA recruiters visiting college campuses (determining in advance the level of dissidence there); infiltration of Washington, D.C., dissident groups; and more general research and analysis on domestic dissidence. The panel found the testing of campus "protest" waters a legitimate exercise of the agency's responsibility to protect its personnel and operations. But it also held that security-oriented domestic infiltration operations should be conducted by the CIA only when support from law enforcement agencies was unavailable, and then only on approval by the DCI.

All these activities, and others not mentioned here,[32] were of interest to the commission because of the substantial invasions of privacy they threatened. The commission, quite clearly (if at times cryptically) outlined their import and criticized them in just those terms. Yet the panel also observed in a separate chapter, entitled "The Need for Intelligence," that the operations conducted within the United States by agencies of foreign governments presented a threat to American privacy which seemed at least as intrusive, and certainly as great a cause of concern, as any CIA activities.[33] In their silent war on the United States, other nations employed all conceivable techniques of surveillance and monitoring. At the outset, then, even before addressing the CIA activities just described, the Rockefeller Commission seemed to say that there were more important problems for civil libertarians to worry about than the CIA's occasional errors of judgment. Or, stated in another way, there were other factors the civil libertarians had not introduced into the calculations that produced their positions on operational constraints.[34]

Though the commission did discover legally objectionable activities, it also determined that the great majority of the CIA's domestic activities fell clearly within existing statutory authorizations, or, more accurately, that such operations did not trespass into operational arenas forbidden by law.[35] Though in some respects operational limitations were ill defined, and though control mechanisms had occasionally been lax or unsuited to purposes now highly valued, the record of protection of individual liberties had been quite good. The CIA had been no abusive renegade or rogue, as some segments of the public feared. It was an instrument of national security charged with an important mission. From time to time, in a context of regulatory ambiguity and perceived operational need, it had misjudged the limits of its authority. Such mistakes, however, were aberrations, not evidence of any repeated patterns of illegal practices. Most activities undertaken by the agency had been eminently defensible as necessary for national security and as not transgressing applicable legal proscriptions.

In effect, then, the Rockefeller Commission's report ratified the thrust of existing rules and the agency's understanding of those rules by refusing to challenge most activities that had been undertaken pursuant to them. But because some of the operations examined were held to have been unlawful, the commission made a number of specific recommendations designed "to clarify areas of doubt . . ., to strengthen the Agency's structure, and to guard against recurrence." These included:

(1) Amendment of the agency's charter (section 403 of the 1947 Nation-

al Security Act) to make it clear that the CIA's activities must be "related to foreign intelligence."[36] The wording of this recommendation is significant. It is not a prohibition of domestic activities, nor even by its terms a curtailment of them. Indeed, its companion provisions state several examples of permissible domestic activity.[37] Further, the commission's parallel recommendation that an executive order prohibit CIA collection, processing, and storage of information on domestic activities of Americans, is qualified by language that seems to extend CIA investigative authority into the FBI's preserve. The agency, said the commission, should be empowered to monitor the actions of "persons suspected of espionage or other illegal activities relating to foreign intelligence, provided that proper coordination with the FBI is effected."[38] The commission also noted that the collection of foreign intelligence from open sources should continue, even though done at home. These provisions reflected the commission's view that much of the widely-perceived CIA "problem" in the United States could be traced to vagueness in charter provisions. Thus, the remedy was to make authority and permissibility clear for domestic functions that seemed eminently defensible, even necessary. Clarification and public education were much of the answer, not change for the sake of change.

(2) Division of regulatory labor between the president and Congress. As just indicated, the regulatory framework envisioned by the commission included on the one hand a revised statutory charter that would be more explicit about general authorizations and prohibitions, and, on the other hand, an executive order which would place on the public record certain more specific rules.[39] That executive order would take special care to clarify what kinds of information the CIA could collect about the domestic activities of American citizens. It would be issued "after consultation with the National Security Council, the Attorney General, and the Director of Central Intelligence," and it would be modified thereafter only through published amendments. While a certain amount of legislative activity was necessary, and indeed was invited, at least at the level of broad grants and limitations of authority, the development of particular operational rules was to be left to the executive. Further, insofar as the commission believed that even more detailed guidelines were needed, it thought that they should be issued by the Central Intelligence Agency itself.[40] I shall have much occasion later to examine other views about the appropriate division of labor in the effort to regulate the intelligence agencies, especially with respect to the proper content of the rules to be announced by Congress. For present purposes, however, we need only note that President Ford's special investigating panel clearly believed that the executive should maintain control of the bulk of the regulatory process via issuance of an executive order and subordinate implementing directives.

(3) Revitalization of both executive and legislative oversight. To dis-

charge congressional oversight responsibilities, the commission recommended establishment of a Joint Committee on Intelligence, modeled after the Joint Committee on Atomic Energy, and also recommended that the president take the lead in urging Congress to establish it. Within the executive, the commission believed that the PFIAB should be made into a meaningful, full-time oversight body, with responsibility for evaluating the quality of the CIA's performance as well as its compliance with statutory authority.

The commission was concerned, as well, with checks against misuse of the CIA by the president and others, recommending establishment of a single channel, through a designated NSC official, for transmission of White House requests to the CIA.[41] The panel also sought to clarify operational rules, specifying the locus of responsibility and accountability for operational decisions, and streamlining channels for making internal objections and complaints visible at high levels. The agency was, further, admonished to take more care that the traditional concept of compartmentation not be used to shield possibly objectionable activities from view.

(4) Constraints on "intrusive" techniques. The report also suggested certain rules for particularly controversial investigations. First, the commission recommended adoption of instructions designed to prohibit any CIA domestic mail intercept (opening mail and reading its contents) in peacetime. Mail cover operations (examining the envelope but not the contents), however, were deemed permissible when in compliance with postal regulations and "in furtherance of the CIA's legitimate activities" – another domestic activity allowable when supportive of the foreign collection mission.

The commission believed that infiltration of "dissident" elements at home should not be undertaken without a written determination, by the director of Central Intelligence, that a threat to CIA interests exists which cannot be sufficiently countered by law enforcement authorities. The CIA's Operation CHAOS, in which it had collected and stored information on Americans gathered by the FBI and by its own stations abroad, was singled out for strong criticism.

Physical surveillance of even CIA employees, the commission believed, should not be undertaken without written approval from the director of Central Intelligence. The commission also felt that under current constitutional law, electronic eavesdropping required at least the written approval of the attorney general based on a finding that national security was involved and that the case had significant foreign connections. It further held that in the United States and its possessions, such activities fell within the province of the FBI, not the CIA. For the commission, the warrantless "national security" wiretap problem was really a matter of allocating authority and jurisdiction more than a problem of constraining intrusive activity.

(5) Limitations on experimentation. The commission held that domestic science and technology activities should not include testing of drugs or of eavesdropping equipment, except on willing subjects.

In addition to those prohibitions, the Rockefeller Commission addressed controversial areas of CIA activity which it found unobjectionable. It specifically approved of CIA activities at home designed to provide and control cover arrangements for CIA operatives. It had no objection to ongoing CIA "proprietary" operations – enterprises that provided cover and performed administrative tasks for the CIA with no visible connection to the agency. Development of contacts with foreign nationals in support of the foreign collection mission was found unobjectionable. Solicitation of voluntary assistance by Americans in that effort was also held to be within the agency's authority.

In sum, the commission's report accepted the legitimacy of CIA activity within the United States where that activity was clearly supportive of the agency's own security interests or its foreign missions. Many of the report's recommendations were meant to make public and clear the lines of responsibility and the boundaries of legitimate authority so that public fear and confusion concerning the CIA might be alleviated and any future abuses might be recognized and halted quickly, mainly by internal review and control mechanisms. Its suggested "restrictions" were not far-reaching and in effect simply elaborated upon existing rules. There is little doubt that the commission's report was influenced by the realization that most of the activities found objectionable had ceased before the inquiry began. Significantly, there were no objections to activities that were permissible under existing law. This orientation, the taking of refuge in existing law, was later to be reflected in the approach taken by the draftsmen of EO 11905 and was to be the source of much dissatisfaction in the wider public debate about the scope of intelligence powers. [42]

The Public Reaction

When the Rockefeller Commission's report was released, President Ford hailed it publicly as a fair, frank, and balanced assessment of a problem which needed exactly that kind of treatment. [43] He anticipated that it would be a major factor in restoring the CIA's credibility in the eyes of the American public. For similar reasons he also spoke generously of the parallel inquiries in Congress and of their progress toward ultimate legislative enactment of corrective proposals.

But in mid-1975 another, more detached observer might have reached a quite different conclusion about the likely place of the Rockefeller Commission and its report in the larger public debate. As just noted, in its narrowed inquiry the commission found most of the CIA activities it examined unobjectionable, clearly within the law, and where legal issues were raised they were understood to argue simply for transfer of specific activities or functions from the CIA's operational jurisdiction to the FBI's. The commission's report was a jurisdiction-clarifying document much more than a manifesto for operational constraints.

This provided little comfort to those among a very attentive public who were concerned not simply about which agencies had authority to conduct domestic intelligence activities, but also about the scope of the authority that government as a whole had arrogated to itself in that realm. As one law professor told a committee of Congress just as the Rockefeller inquiry got underway, the FBI was no more skillful or careful about judging what ought to be the limits of its power than was the CIA or any other government instrument. Persons trained in and devoted to the investigative discipline and its associated national security imperatives naturally found it extremely difficult to distinguish legitimate political activity from criminal conduct.[44] This fundamental suspicion of the ability of intelligence officials to delimit their operational spheres in a way that serves nonoperational values figured prominently in subsequent congressional investigations and their proposed remedies.

When the Rockefeller Commission began its work, an American Civil Liberties Union spokesman told Congress:

As a result of our litigation we have reached two general conclusions about the kinds of legislative controls which should be imposed on investigative and intelligence-gathering agencies in order to dismantle the surveillance apparatus which has been assembled over the last decade. First, the warrant procedure must be strengthened and broadened so that no intrusive surveillance is conducted over American citizens outside of the judicial supervision required by the Fourth Amendment and in the absence of probable cause that a crime had been or is about to be committed. Second, the law must develop a variety of flat statutory prohibitions, including (a) a ban against the conduct of any form of surveillance over persons because of or in order to determine the nature of their political views and activities, in violation of their First Amendment rights; and (b) a bar against use or dissemination of the fruits of any lawful investigation beyond the purpose for which it was conducted. Both legislative approaches should be backed up by strong criminal and civil remedies.[45]

These themes and others were now taken up in diverse forums – the media, the courts, and Congress. Pressures for reform were beginning to converge, encircling executive positions in the domestic intelligence arena heretofore steadfastly defended as belonging to the sphere of inherent presidential power.[46] Civil liberties activists especially were now finding receptive forums in which to air their grievances about the special status of "national security" rationales and the more permissive rules that were applied to intelligence operations. The Ford administration's position, in response, was at first to resist substantial intrusion by either the legislature or the judiciary. It had much support, of course, in the Rockefeller Commission's report. But by mid-1975 there were indications of movement. In June, when called to testify before Congress on whether judicial warrants should be required for certain "national security" investigations, Deputy Assistant Attorney General Kevin T. Maroney observed that the Department of Justice had long taken the position that the president had unilateral constitutional authority to use electronic surveillance (for an example) to protect important security interests. And beyond what the law allowed, he said, reasons of practicality argued forcefully against the courts' involvement in supervising those techniques when used in intelligence operations. Such cases involved special kinds of political and diplomatic considerations with which judges might not be familiar. The Courts' interposition in the operational approval process, by means of a warrant requirement, might therefore impair the functioning of vital intelligence capabilities. And since the president's claims of authority rested on constitutional foundations, legislative tampering with his powers raised profound issues concerning Congress's own proper spheres of activity. In other words, the rationale for executive activity was so strong that a challenge to it might in the end only expose the relative weakness of contrary arguments.

But, Maroney added, administration officials responsible for making such operational decisions would not oppose a sharing of that burden with other branches of government if certain important executive postures could be accommodated. These included, not surprisingly, preservation of the distinction between intelligence and law enforcement operations, based on the special purposes of each, and assurance that the new extra-executive review channels would protect operational information from unauthorized disclosure.[47] Executive postures had moved, then, from resistance to all sharing of authority to receptivity to some sharing.

A growing number of observers now began to ask Congress to intercede and establish both substantive limits and procedural mechanisms for control. Former Secretary of State Dean Rusk, for instance, told the House Judiciary Committee that government officials should be required to seek judicial warrants for wiretap and eavesdropping operations even in national security cases.[48] The practice at that time for FBI wiretaps required only the personal approval of the attorney general when he determined that the operation was necessary to serve national security or foreign intelligence purposes.[49] In Rusk's view, the procedural requirement to seek judicial warrants, if superimposed on that process, would not impede collection of information needed by government officials. He was not concerned, as some were, about placing such decisions in the hands of judges. It seemed likely that they, like other officials, would be as concerned about national security as about protecting individual privacy, and they could weigh the competing interests at least as well as anyone else.[50]

But, significantly, although Rusk (and others) had no objection to the warrant procedure, nor to legislative specification of the appropriate mechanisms by statute, he was unwilling to retreat entirely from the line drawn by the time-honored substantive distinction between national security and law-enforcement operations. He argued that, because of the special security-related imperatives to which intelligence operations respond, they need more permissive rules than the criminal standard — "probable cause" to believe a crime has been or will be committed.[51] Imposition of criminal standards would simply be too confining, though there was certainly room for some kind of judicial scrutiny of operational proposals.

This new, more modest argument for the special status of the national security rationale gained a good deal of currency. Supporters of the intelligence agencies, sensing the strength of the emerging critique, began to offer alternative formulas designed to strike the balance among competing values in ways that would not endanger operational capabilities they considered vital. There was also increasing recognition that this is an appropriate sphere for legislative (i.e., statutory) activity, defining the judicial review process and the criteria which must govern judges' decisions.

But this moving of the battlelines in the "national security" camp was not enough for many critics of executive prerogative. They continued to demand imposition of "probable cause" requirements, or the "criminal standard," on all intrusive government activity, even in the face of arguments that this would disable the nation in its effort to deal with the exigencies of international life.[52]

At about this time, publication of the Church Committee's report on assassination plots evidenced still other pressures on the executive. Appearing in November 1975, that report called not only for cessation of any U.S. involvement in assassination schemes, but also for intervention by Congress to proscribe it as a matter of law.[53] Here the basic objection was not only constitutional, or legal, in nature. It also dealt expressly with considerations of morality and of conformance of American behavior abroad with American principles and ideals.[54] Rules governing intelligence operations must reflect those standards, even though that might result in constraints not adopted by other nations.

Also by late 1975 the congressional hearings on the full length and breadth of the intelligence activities were proceeding apace. The House Select Committee headed by Congressman Pike completed its report in January 1976. It was leaked to the press just as President Ford was preparing to issue his long-awaited response to the intelligence problem: an executive order announcing operational restrictions and clarifying controls. Publication of the House Report served only to agitate the debate among watchful, and increasingly knowledgeable, observers.

One other event of some significance occurred just as the Ford Administration prepared to act. William Colby, who had borne the brunt of public, media, and congressional criticism as director of Central Intelligence, left that post in late 1975. The president, cognizant of the Rockefeller Commission's suggestion that a nonprofessional might bring to that office useful perspectives as well as the ability to resist improper pressures, appointed former United Nations ambassador George Bush to that position, a well-known "outsider" with considerable foreign and domestic political experience, but certainly not a participant in the emerging intelligence critique.

Executive Order 11905

On February 18, 1976, President Ford issued Executive Order 11905, *United States Foreign Intelligence Activities.*[55] In a statement issued at a news conference the previous day, he described it as a comprehensive public charter which provided a new, recognized command structure for foreign intelligence agencies and set stringent protections for citizens' rights, and which forbade the worst of the alleged overseas abuses, peacetime assassination activities.[56] The attorney general, he further indicated, was then in the process of writing strict guidelines which would apply more specifically to the FBI. He also promised that his administration would soon begin to meet with leaders of Congress to devise legislation that would provide judicial checks on electronic surveillance and mail openings, two kinds of investigative activity that had been of special concern to the Rockefeller Commission and many others. The president said he would support legislation that prohibited assassination in peacetime, and that he looked forward to institution of regular congressional oversight of the intelligence community.

The executive order was truly unprecedented in its scope and was clearly intended to be the open, public charter that many critics had been advocating for some time. Outside the four corners of the order itself, the president's parallel initiatives in support of congressional legislation to regulate certain operations and in favor of some prior judicial review of "intrusive" investigative proposals were also unprecedented. In them he was responding at last to the pressures that had been building for reform.

Though his administration was attempting to respond to the critics of the intelligence agencies, and though he indicated some receptivity to congressional regulation and judicial scrutiny of intelligence operations, President Ford also stated his firm intention to retain the nation's collection,

CI, and covert action tools substantially unimpaired.[57] He was not going to render the nation more vulnerable to its enemies by disabling it in any of those operational arenas.

There was, additionally, further evidence that the executive was by no stretch of the imagination falling back in disarray from positions no longer thought tenable. In the statement accompanying issuance of the executive order, the president also announced that he would seek from Congress new legislation that would stiffen the rules and strengthen the punishments applied to unauthorized disclosure of critical intelligence secrets. Just as his administration believed, and affirmed, that the age of operational abuses had passed, so also it believed that the age of tolerating promiscuous leakage of intelligence secrets had passed. When he was asked whether this action might not deter the kind of internal "whistle-blowing" needed to uncover operational excesses, Ford deflected the question almost indignantly as misunderstanding the purpose of the legislation.[58]

The first feature of the executive order to be considered is its stated purpose. The order was by no means an act of executive contrition. Much of it reads, in fact, as if the major national concern in 1976 was to strengthen, rather than to constrain, our intelligence capabilities. By its own terms it was intended to establish policies which "improve the quality of intelligence needed for national security, to clarify the authority and responsibilities of the intelligence departments and agencies, and to establish effective over-sight to assure compliance with law."[59] Beyond this, no attempt was made in the order itself to describe the particular problems it was meant to address. In the provisions which announce "restrictions" there is an oblique reference to the ongoing debate about alleged excesses, but this is coupled with a statement affirming the need for competent information gathering.[60]

Balancing of values, then, is the basic regulatory exercise required. Recitation of criticisms, however valid, does not amount to a compelling case that operational capabilities must be dismantled or even, necessarily, significantly curtailed. Activities which execute those capabilities may be confined by rules, but arguments about confining them do not defeat the basic capabilities.

This balancing of values must, furthermore, weigh manifest governmental needs against established (i.e., generally recognized) views about civil liberties. Radical, out-of-perspective arguments, or hopes for new departures in the ever-evolving constitutional law, have no place in the calculation, no role in the shaping of executive regulations. Aggressive changes in the law were for other institutions to accomplish, not for the executive, and certainly not in the sensitive arena of securing the nation against real threats.

The next thing to be noted about the order is its emphasis on procedural mechanisms. Though one part of the directive (section 5) contains a number of provisions purporting to restrict operational techniques, the main burden of the order lies in the procedural and organizational realm: establishing intra-executive control and oversight mechanisms and defining the duties assigned to each element of the intelligence community. For the watchful public, now equipped with more knowledge, impressions, and suspicions of intelligence than ever before, the president hoped that this explicit delineation of functions and responsibilities, and specification of operational approval/review channels, would restore confidence that the intelligence agencies were well controlled and accountable for their actions. Three innovations are especially noteworthy, dealing with what the Rockefeller Commission had earlier termed "external" controls.

First, the order established a Committee on Foreign Intelligence (CFI) chaired by the director of Central Intelligence and including the deputy secretary of defense for intelligence and the deputy assistant to the president for national security affairs. Working directly under the NSC, the CFI was given responsibility for controlling the preparation of the intelligence budget, for allocating resources, and for establishing collection priorities. It was, in President Ford's words, "a single new committee" charged with "management of intelligence."[61] For some observers this no doubt appeared to be a substantial control-related innovation. In actuality, however, it mainly consolidated functions previously performed by other committees. The supervisory role of the NSC remained, and the president said that it was the NSC that would provide overall policy direction for the intelligence community.[62]

But some have since argued that this initiative's major contribution was to enhance the position of the DCI. His chairmanship of the CFI in effect gave him a new, formally-elevated, and more visible policymaking position in the national intelligence effort.[63] He was not simply one attendee or observer among others in the major management institution atop the intelligence hierarchy (the NSC). He was now chairman of a single body charged with management duties. Since it was clearly the imperative of the times to specify openly the locus of authority and responsibility for intelligence policy and activity, this part of EO 11905 went far to make explicit the DCI's primary role and responsibility.

But the CFI was not charged with responsibility for approving or disapproving operations. For that purpose the executive order established a second institution, an Operations Advisory Group (OAG) composed of the assistant to the president for national security affairs, the secretaries of state and defense, the chairman of the JCS, and the DCI. The attorney general and the director of the Office of Management and Budget were designated observers. This body was to review proposals for covert action and sensitive collection operations. Under previous practice, officials at the under-secretary level, in the so-called Forty Committee and its predecessors, had passed on such proposals. Now, in the OAG, Cabinet principals would exercise that authority in the case of sensitive or risky collection operations. For covert action proposals, which the president was required by the Hughes-Ryan Amendment to approve, the OAG would develop recommendations which (along with any dissents) would be forwarded to the president for a final decision.[64]

Here, then, was an effort to specify clearly, for all to see, the places where approval authority resided, in the interest of public accountability. Although the executive order added little to the existing control framework beyond the publicizing of its approval mechanisms and some elevation of approval authority to higher-ranking officials, it did attempt also to assure the public that decisions would be taken after hearing all views of responsible officials, especially including all dissenting views. Indeed, in the case of covert action, it was now a matter of record and regulation that objections to specific operations would survive the national-level review process and would be considered by the president if the dissenter(s) could not otherwise be satisfied.

The third institutional innovation dealt with oversight procedures. One of the Rockefeller Commission's recommendations had pointed to the need for reenergized oversight by the PFIAB, the board of "outside" advisors to the president. The commission had also recommended that the internal review mechanisms of the CIA – the inspector general and the agency's legal office – be upgraded and become involved in the internal oversight process. The executive order responded to both those suggestions. It required the inspectors general and the general counsels of the various intelligence agencies to monitor internal practices, procedures, and operations to identify any that might raise questions of legality or propriety. It also created an Intelligence Oversight Board (IOB), composed of three persons appointed from outside the government (concurrent membership on the PFIAB was permitted), to review reports from those authorities. The IOB, in turn, would report serious questions about legality to the attorney general and important issues of propriety to the president.[65] Significantly, the IOB had no charter to review ongoing or proposed operations on its own initiative. Its authority was limited to periodic reviews of subordinate oversight channels. The president named its first three members immediately: former Ambassador Robert Murphy; Leo Cherne, an economist known also for his commitment to civil liberties; and former Secretary of the Army Stephen Ailes.[66] This new board was clearly an attempt to accommodate suggestions that "outside" perspectives be considered in the shaping of intelligence policies. But it is important also to note that the perspectives of the IOB, by its charter, would be called into play not for broad reviews of intelligence purposes or capabilities, but only to collect and pass on to others specific problems raised from within the intelligence community itself. In effect, only those activities which offended the operational mentality would be brought before the IOB, and the IOB would not itself dispose of the issues raised by those objections. Though its establishment reflected some sensitivity to pressures for stricter oversight, for many critics it was bound to fall short of full assurance that perspectives outside the national security rationale would shape the government's behavior.

An emphasis on "legality" also characterized EO 11905. Except with respect to reports forwarded to the IOB, which could raise objections based on notions of "propriety," conformance with law was the main standard against which operational behavior was to be measured. When the order prohibited the use of certain techniques, the restrictions were phrased in such a way as to prohibit what was already illegal. They were, undeniably, constraints of a sort, but they amounted merely to executive codification of its own understanding of the existing list of illegalities. They were not substantive concessions on matters debated widely outside the government, and they provided little comfort to those who were already unhappy with the relative generosity of the law concerning intelligence activities.

Moreover, these restrictions contained explicit exceptions which assumed or asserted authorization to engage in the excepted category of activity. Such assumed authorizations might well have been narrowly-conceived, and might well only have reflected existing practice, but they had not been a matter of public record to that point. Thus, the new "restrictions" served two important purposes in the administration's "public information" program: they focused attention on clear operational limits announced by the president on his own initiative, and they also carved out spheres of permissible behavior and made those plain on the public record.

A few illustrations may make these points clearer. In restrictions on "collection," several provisions declared that intelligence agencies were prohibited from engaging in the following (emphasis is added to highlight newly-visible permissions):

(1) Physical surveillance of a "U.S. Person" (generally, a citizen or permanent resident alien) "*unless* it is a *lawful* surveillance conducted pursuant to procedures approved by the head of the foreign intelligence agency" and directed against (1) a present or former employee in order to protect intelligence sources; (2) a U.S. person who is in contact with either a former agency employee or a non-U.S. person targeted in a counterintelligence or intelligence inquiry; or (3) a U.S. person outside the United States "who is reasonably believed to be acting on behalf of a foreign power or engaging in international terrorist or narcotics activities or activities threatening the national security."

(2) Electronic surveillance to intercept a communication which is made from, or is intended by the sender to be received in the United States, or is

directed against U.S. persons abroad, *except lawful* electronic surveillance conducted under procedures approved by the attorney general.

(3) Unconsented physical searches within the United States; or unconsented physical searches directed against U.S. persons abroad, *except lawful* searches under procedures approved by the attorney general.

(4) Opening of mail or examination of envelopes of mail in the United States *"except in accordance with* applicable statutes and regulations."[67]

From one point of view, of course, it was entirely appropriate for the executive to seek refuge in the operational permissions thought to be contained in existing law. But the boundaries of these permissions were not clear or self-evident. Many were contentious even where the courts or Congress had addressed them. And it was not at all certain, given the nature of our political system, what kinds of activities might in the future be declared lawful if challenged in the courts or addressed in legislation. Thus, though the restrictions sounded, as announced, as if they designated clear standards of behavior, in fact they did not. Two kinds of observers were especially concerned about this: those who desired definitive limits on the intrusive and potentially abusive powers of government, and, within the intelligence community, those officials and operators who wanted clear guidance about permissible activities and clear assurance that the activities they undertook would be upheld, if challenged.

These considerations naturally focused attention on the role of legal advice in the operational approval and review process. The executive order did provide for participation by the attorney general and other legal advisors in those procedures. The attorney general, as we have seen, was given a prominent position in the OAG's deliberations on operational approvals. Though his status was that of an "observer," in that role he could advise the other participants about the legal implications of proposals laid before them. And since OAG was charged with responsibility for conducting periodic reviews of ongoing sensitive collection operations, the attorney general's views could be applied from time to time to those operations as they were actually carried out. He was also to review certain oversight reports passed to him by the IOB as possibly involving illegalities. But this latter function, again, was one which depended upon internal "whistle-blowing": the attorney general examined problems identifiied by persons within the intelligence community and passed to him through the IOB. He was not given authority to conduct operational reviews on his own initiative.

The executive order refers to the attorney general most prominently, however, and most often, in his capacity as reviewer of operational procedures in special categories of activity and in his capacity as supervisor of the FBI. An example of the former was provided earlier: the attorney general was required to approve the procedures under which foreign intelligence agencies engaged in electronic surveillance. And in the latter capacity he was to issue special regulations for FBI intelligence and counterintelligence operations – a subject to which we shall return in a moment.

We can see, overall, an attempt by the Ford Administration to respond to a concern evidenced earlier in the Rockefeller Report: If the law is the sole source of operational constraints, the sole standard for evaluating behavior, then it makes no sense to exclude legal advice from the operational review and approval process. Though EO 11905 did not go far enough in this direction to satisfy all critics, there is no question but that it provided the attorney general a more visible role than had been the case in the past.

The order's focus on domestic interests and activity also requires comment. The section of the directive which announced operational restrictions stated that its provisions would apply both within and outside of the United States. But as noted in my discussion of the order's purpose statement, to the extent that EO 11905 acknowledged values counterpoised to the need for aggressive intelligence operations, it was domestic civil liberties interests that were so recognized. Accordingly, most of the operational limitations dealt with "intrusive" investigative techniques long challenged by civil liberties activists: electronic surveillance, physical surveillance, physical searches, mail openings and mail covers, examination of tax records, domestic infiltration of groups and organizations, and collection of information about the domestic activities of United States persons.[68] Several of the restrictions were written so as to apply mainly, perhaps even exclusively, to operations within the United States. In some cases there were provisos which exempted overseas activities. The only provision which announced a substantive restriction on the foreign covert action capability was the prohibition of political assassination.

One more observation should be made here concerning the president's directive: any intrusion upon arenas of inherent presidential power was left to subsequent bargaining between the executive and Congress. I noted earlier that the tone of the order was hardly one of contrition for past abuses. Though the president was sensitive to the need for clarification of operational limits, he was not going to draw them as if the curbing of operational excesses were his only purpose. Similarly, he was not going to surrender any of his own rulemaking authority to the other branches of government, at least not in his own executive order. EO 11905 was as much (and perhaps more) an attempt to maintain executive control of the reform movement as it was an attempt to accommodate reform pressures. Indeed, the order had very little to say with respect to participation by Congress or the courts in intelligence controls. It made only one reference to Congress, in a provision designating the DCI as the primary spokesman for the executive on intelligence matters.[69] And it never mentioned the judiciary, nor any standards the courts might apply should they become involved in reviewing investigative proposals associated with national security operations. Its provisions outlining control and oversight procedures addressed only executive mechanisms.

Soon after issuance of EO 11905, however, President Ford sent a message to Congress proposing legislative reforms going beyond that directive. He said that he hoped executive-congressional consultations in the near future would develop a "special procedure" for electronic surveillance activities undertaken in the United States for foreign intelligence purposes. This would involve, he suggested, a requirement that government operatives obtain a judicial warrant authorizing such activity. This was a clear step beyond the position the Justice Department had stated before Congress eight months earlier. But even as outlined in concept, the proposal had two important caveats: it would apply to activities within the United States but not to those abroad, and it anticipated enactment of a "special" warrant procedure, not necessarily one that looked like the practice in criminal cases involving the classic "probable cause" standard.[70]

A related proposal "to expand judicial supervision of mail openings" in intelligence cases sheds further light on what kind of procedure the president had in mind: "This would require a showing that there is probable cause to believe that the sender or recipient is an agent of a foreign power who is engaged in spying, sabotage, or terrorism. As is now the case . . . [in] criminal investigations, those seeking authority to examine mail for foreign intelligence purposes will have to . . . accept the limitations upon their authorization to examine the mail provided in the order of the court."[71]

Though couched in language acceding to a new role for the courts in "national security" cases, this proposal was equally an effort to establish new authority where before there was none on the public record. But an even more subtle point has to do with the nature of the restriction this procedure would represent. Though the president indicated receptivity to some kind of judicial review, and though he took note of the judicial review practice in criminal cases, he did not propose that the standard in intelligence cases would be the criminal standard. He said only that the courts would determine whether there was probable cause to believe that spying, sabotage, or terrorist activities were involved.

There is, of course, a wide spectrum of activity that might be associated with espionage, sabotage, or terrorism, ranging from very tenuous, unwitting, and decidedly noncriminal contacts with foreign agents to the actual unauthorized transmission of classified information or commission of violent acts (which are crimes). National security arguments had long supported surveillance of those activities at a very early stage, triggered, for instance, by knowledge that one of the parties was associated with a foreign intelligence agency and that his observable behavior aligned with what was already known about normal espionage modus operandi. It was exactly that early activation of intrusive investigative techniques that concerned civil liberties activists. They argued for application of law enforcement standards, requiring more evidence or expectation of actual wrongdoing before the government's intrusive apparatus could be activated. The standard of judgment here advocated by the president, however, fell short of that. Again, there was a conscious effort to preserve a larger field of operational permissibility in intelligence affairs than in criminal matters.

The president also outlined several principles which he thought central to proper and productive congressional oversight. First, the purpose of such oversight should be to provide assurance to the public that "the foreign intelligence agencies are adhering to the law in all of their activities."[72] In the context of the times, this was not simply a restatement of the executive position about conformance to law as the standard for judging operations. It was a response to a quite different point of view then developing in Congress. A few months earlier (in November 1975), at the end of its report on assassination plots, the Church Committee had argued that, regardless of any perceived international imperatives and practices, America must not adopt the tactics of her foreign enemies. The means by which we pursue foreign policy goals, the committee urged, must align with and be constrained by our national ideals. Once again the president took special care to state his own contrasting view, that only those ideals that had been made visible in the law should shape operational rules and behavior, not some more evanescent and contestable set of subjective principles said to be derived from American political culture.

In line with the earlier recommendations of the Rockefeller Commission, the president also urged that congressional oversight responsibility be consolidated and centralized, preferably in a single, joint intelligence committee. He also wanted both houses of Congress to establish effective measures to protect secrets and deal with unauthorized disclosures. The leaking to the press of the Pike Committee report a few weeks earlier was the most egregious example of delinquency in this regard, but President Ford himself had complained publicly for months about other, smaller incidents of mishandling of sensitive and classified information.[73] He had also indicated in public that in his view too many members of Congress knew far too much about intelligence activities. When he was in Congress, he asserted, perhaps ten or twelve members were regularly informed of such matters. Over time, however, the number had expanded far in excess of any institutional need, to perhaps fifty or even seventy-five.[74] Now, though the president would encourage rationalized and more energetic congressional oversight, he clearly meant also to work for reduction in the number of persons involved in it, as well as for more responsible exercise of that authority, as conditions of continued executive cooperation.

Ford noted further that respect for constitutional precepts of shared and balanced governmental power, which were at the heart of many arguments for confining executive prerogative, also required a vigorous defense against excessive intrusions by other branches on executive authority. He was prepared to make room in executive practices for some measure of congressional oversight. But members of Congress, in return, must recognize that they could not on their own motion overrule or disregard the president's postures on secrecy. If anything was to be achieved by collaborative interaction, each branch must recognize and respect the rights of the other. Otherwise, future dialogue about the mechanics of their relationship would be fruitless.

FBI Postscript

On May 28, 1976, Attorney General Edward Levi promulgated two sets of operational guidelines for the FBI, one for domestic security operations and the other for foreign intelligence and counterintelligence activities. These were the rules which EO 11905 had directed the attorney general to produce, and the ones also referred to by President Ford in several earlier public statements. They remained in force until 1983, when the Reagan Administration revised them substantially.[75]

The Justice Department had been working on the guidelines for a number of months, even prior to the issuance of the executive order, and had discussed them in some detail with the Church and Pike committees. In the drafting process there had been close scrutiny of several central control issues. Of special interest and difficulty were the level of justification to be required for initiation of the most intrusive techniques of investigation (the "criminal standard" versus the "national security standard") and the question of whether an impartial "outside" agency, especially the courts, ought to participate somehow in reviewing operational proposals.

The rules for domestic security investigations were devised fairly early in the process, governing a special category of operations dealing with acts of violence within the United States.[76] Under these new rules, information on domestic groups and individuals could be collected on executive branch initiative only where there was a "likelihood" that they would use force in violation of law, and in certain other clearly specified instances.[77] The kinds of techniques to be used in the initial stages of such operations were also limited, and authorizations were only to last for designated periods of time (ninety days) with the possibility of renewal upon reapplication. The attorney general told the Church Committee that these kinds of safeguards approached "as close as is feasible" the criminal standard demanded by critics of the intelligence agencies. He wondered at the time if this formula was too restrictive (others have since argued that it was[78]), but on balance he felt, and the administration felt, that it was tolerable.

Though the investigative standard for these specified domestic operations did thus attempt to respond to outside pressures, there was no
requirement that proposals be reviewed by persons or agencies outside the
Department of Justice. In fact, there was no requirement even that the
attorney general approve such operations beforehand (except in the case of
wiretaps and eavesdropping), though he had to be informed of them all and
could terminate any he found lacking in justification. Critics who wanted
the executive to submit to external review were not likely to be impressed by
these new guidelines.

In the December 1975 Church Committee hearings, Attorney General
Levi had been queried about the efficacy of such outside review and approval
mechanisms.[79] He acknowledged that reporting of FBI activities to Congress would be an appropriate supervisory tool. Even more broadly, he
favored an effort to legislate a clarified charter for the FBI, so that the bureau
would no longer have to rely on outdated and incomplete statutory language. But he also observed that, regardless of the rules ultimately adopted,
the control structure will always depend in some measure on faithful
performance of duty by the leadership of the FBI. Trust in the director, in
particular, must inevitably be part of any control system. Any manner of
outside review could not eliminate that central fact. As we shall see,
however, the effort in Congress to erect an elaborate external control
framework by statute proceeded nevertheless, and it certainly did not reflect
any inclination to trust the practitioners of intelligence.

The separate guidelines for foreign intelligence and counterintelligence
were classified, but it is known that they permitted earlier activation of
more intensive investigative techniques than did the domestic rules. Although they established no "external" approval mechanisms for operational
proposals, they did describe internal executive rules about controls and
constraints.[80]

Despite all this public clarification of what had previously been secret,
and despite all the careful thought about devising real restrictions that left
room for the perceived needs of national security, many observers, including
some deeply involved in the process of developing rules, were not satisfied.
In challenging FBI and Justice Department thinking about the bureau's
operational guidelines, then-Senator Walter Mondale, a member of the
Church Committee, voiced his dissatisfaction in language which would be
echoed later in the Carter Administration, when he became vice-president.
His remarks help prepare the way for that part of this study:

> When I look at these vaguely defined guidelines, I have to ask, would they
> stand up under the direct orders to the contrary from a President of the United
> States? Would they stand up in the face of a willful Director who is angry or hostile
> or suspicious about some of these political ideas, or about the next Martin Luther
> King? My feeling is that based upon what we have learned, without any doubt,

they would be swept away, as quickly as a sand castle being overrun by a hurricane, they would mean nothing. . . . The question now is once we know what has happened, and we know the abuse that arises when people have this unlimited, ill-defined power, what do we do, if possible, to try to prevent its recurrence? That is the issue that faces you. That is the issue that faces me, and I am convinced that guidelines written by the executive can be rewritten by the executive, and if not by you, by those who follow. And they will mean absolutely nothing against the will of a willing president, or a willing Director – absolutely nothing, because they do not have the force of law.[81]

By the end of its tenure in office, the Ford Administration had shown some degree of movement on the "touchstones" of debate, the central barometers used by critics to evaluate policies and rules. For civil liberties activists it had acknowledged the sensitivity of the distinction between "criminal" and "national security" rationales, and it had tried to accommodate arguments for extension of the "criminal standard" to policies and procedures for initiating certain intelligence operations likely to affect Americans. Similarly, it had shown receptivity to arguments for larger congressional and judicial roles in monitoring intelligence. And it attempted to assuage concerns about the morality of government behavior by prohibiting assassination and insisting upon the rectitude of values then reflected in the law.

But in all cases, administration policy was conditioned by an explicit desire – indeed, determination – to protect inherent presidential powers and to be sure that the government was well-equipped to protect national security interests in an uncertain world. For many, that response was not enough. Critics of all persuasions pushed on, in other forums, hoping to limit the intelligence agencies and the president more severely by law, and to watch over operations more closely to be sure that the rights of individuals and the ideals at the center of our society were not abused.

5

The Carter Administration's Response

As the presidential campaign gained momentum in the summer and fall of 1976, the findings of the Church Committee's multivolume final report were widely discussed, and the work of the new standing committee for intelligence in the Senate kept the search for operational abuses in the headlines.[1] Persistent investigative journalists keyed on the Senate committee's proceedings, or on the earlier work of the Church Committee, and dug deeper into disclosures emanating from lawsuits.[2] Challenges to executive postures became increasingly well informed and tenacious, at times even ferocious. The Democratic candidates for president were running in part on an intelligence reform platform, and after the election a vigilant watch began, both within and outside of government, for indications of how the new administration would deal with the major issues that had been raised.[3]

All this occurred in the context of keen disappointment felt by many after issuance of EO 11905. President Ford's public rhetoric had promised an open, public charter stating clear restrictions and accountability procedures. But the order was seen, perhaps predictably, as prohibiting only what was already against the law, and therefore as an affirmation of authority and "legal" activity that many still questioned.[4] President Ford had not made concessions on what many now saw as the central issue, inherent presidential power. Further, announcement of a chain of accountability by executive order did not satisfy those who argued that we must put our trust in laws (meaning statutes), not in men or in directives which might be changed at any time by the individuals who hold executive power. Members of Congress were of course in the forefront of this critique.[5] But even if operational capabilities were to be confined by legislation, there still remained the problem of which branches of government ought to participate in the policing of those boundaries.[6] More extensive involvement by the judicial and legislative branches seemed necessary to many observers, yet there was much disagreement about the proper nature and extent of that involvement. Proposals ranged from micro-management of intelligence activities by Congress and the courts – challenged by many as unwise and unworkable – to arms-length supervision and after-the-fact reviews of activities already undertaken – challenged by others as insufficient.[7] Not even members of the Senate intelligence committee, who had spent a year and a half thinking about the problem, could agree on when and how the legislature should be involved in the operational approval process.[8]

In some corners, moreover, the inquiry had reached an even deeper level. As two scholars observed in 1976, at that moment in its history the nation had essentially to "rethink what it wants from intelligence and how to get it."[9] In the national breast-beating and agonizing about operational excesses and deficiencies of control and oversight, and in the back-and-forth of diverse proposals for reform and defenses of the status quo, it would be easy to focus principally on the more observable but smaller problem of which words to use in a scattering of remedial rules. But the more difficult challenge was to specify the principles from which a regulatory framework should take its bearings.

It was not only scholars who attempted to draw attention to this task. When he was director of Central Intelligence, William Colby argued that government officials, even intelligence officials, have an obligation to explain to the American people the functions and activities of their organizations.[10] Colby himself went before audiences of all sorts attempting to do that, and he continued the effort after he left office. Given such explanations, he believed, informed Americans might be able to come to terms with the existence and exercise of intelligence capabilities. The job of explanation faltered, however, and controversy about basic issues persisted, as did the vulnerability of the intelligence community to renewed attacks based on objections resurrected again and again from the revelations of the past.

Those who were looking for indicators of how a Carter Administration might view the intelligence problem at this level of analysis could have found much food for thought in an essay published by Senator Walter Mondale early in the presidential race.[11] He reviewed the history of excesses and the various remedial proposals: tighter restrictions, better accountability, more rigorous oversight. All were fine, except that none got to the heart of the matter – aligning intelligence activities and policies with the more modest post-Vietnam view of America's role in the world. It was to that task, Mondale argued, that the nation's leadership must turn.

For its part, however, the Ford Administration in its last months staunchly defended EO 11905 and the balance of values it had struck. While the Ford Administration was receptive to proposals for legislation updating the 1947 National Security Act, its spokesmen counseled against using such a charter to state restrictions that might bind the executive inflexibly in foreign affairs. [12] And, in response to continuing concerns about preserving civil liberties at home, the administration insisted that the protections for American citizens contained in the executive order and associated directives were sufficient in themselves to prevent abuses. Clearly Congress could act if it wanted to, said the administration, on these and other matters. But such action would be unnecessary, thanks to executive self-regulation, and possibly quite harmful to the national interest.

In some respects Jimmy Carter's views on intelligence issues, at least as expressed in the first weeks of his administration, sounded much like Gerald Ford's. He of course intended to prevent operational abuses and also to keep the public as informed as possible about intelligence affairs. But at the same time he knew he had to protect intelligence functions from the kind of erosion of effectiveness that might incapacitate the nation in international affairs. He had reviewed, he said, the work of the Intelligence Oversight Board, and he had independently detected no instance of impropriety or illegality in the activities it had been called upon to examine. [13] He would welcome active congressional oversight of the intelligence community, just as President Ford had. But he, like Ford, felt that too many people in Congress were then involved in that effort, and he hoped that the procedures would be streamlined in a joint oversight committee with limited membership.

But it was clear also that Jimmy Carter brought importantly different perspectives to the intelligence problem. To some intelligence professionals watching the Ford-Carter transition arrangements, in fact, this was clear even before the Carter Administration took office. [14] The views of his vice-president, Walter Mondale, already noted above, were well known by this time, of course, and these alone helped to identify the incoming administration as seriously reformist in inclination. But there was little doubt that Jimmy Carter had his own convictions about intelligence controls and that he intended to act on those views quickly.

The most visible of his initial actions was to nominate Theodore Sorensen to be his director of Central Intelligence. A "nonprofessional" known for his service in the Kennedy Administration and for his dedication to civil liberties, Sorensen had recently published a book arguing for the kind of presidential accountability that would keep the nation's leadership within ethical and constitutional bounds. [15] His nomination, however, was criticized heavily in Congress and elsewhere. The controversy focused on affidavits he had provided several years earlier in support of Daniel Ellsberg's defense against charges of disclosing government secrets. In those affidavits he had said that overclassification of information was an accepted norm in the government, and that deliberate, selective abuse of secrets through manipulative "leaks" thought helpful to executive policies or harmful to executive opponents was also common practice.[16] These observations were seized upon by opponents of his nomination as indicating unfitness for leadership of America's intelligence community. For that position, it was held, the nation needed a person whom intelligence professionals would respect and follow, who would (at a minimum) keep secrets and enforce the practices which protect them, and who could be trusted by Congress as well as by the leaders of other nations.[17] Though Sorensen had much support, particularly from persons who admired his conviction that moral and legal standards must govern national security decisions,[18] he surprised Congress and the nation by appearing at his confirmation hearings only to decline his nomination. He was unwilling, in the end, to be forced to respond to "baseless personal accusations" by those who he felt were anxious to suppress his point of view and to exclude it from the intelligence community's leadership.[19]

President Carter quickly chose another nominee: Admiral Stansfield Turner, his classmate at Annapolis years earlier. Turner's nomination was approved without difficulty, and in his confirmation hearings he told the Senate that the intelligence agencies would do their work within the boundaries set by law and American values.[20] The reference to "values" was not accidental – Turner himself stated most strongly that the intelligence agencies must live up to the ideals reflected in "our moral dedication to the rights of the individual."[21]

This was, of course, in part a restatement of a familiar formula: the government must respect constitutional protections and precepts. But it was more than that, too, in its incorporation of even wider, value-based principles outside any specific provisions of law. This posture, already characteristic of President Carter's views on foreign policy in general, was to be central to his administration's approach to the intelligence regulatory problem.[22]

The legislators were also interested in learning the Carter Administration's attitudes on congressional roles. Turner indicated that "within the limits of the Constitutional prerogatives of the executive branch," he hoped to contribute to continued cooperation with Congress. Speaking for the administration, he did not oppose enactment of a revised statutory charter for the intelligence agencies, and in fact he supported an effort to make operational authority explicit by statute. He was not quite sure where the line should be drawn between matters to be addressed in statutes and matters best left to executive orders, but interbranch discussion could work out an appropriate division of labor.[23]

On one issue then of great interest to legislators, covert action controls, Turner indicated that wherever possible he would provide the notifications required by the Hughes-Ryan Amendment *before* implementation of operations approved by the president. Though no statute required it, he indicated that the Carter Administration was also amenable to establishing notification requirements, similar to those of Hughes-Ryan, for collection operations which carried high political risks.[24] Such mechanisms did not, in the administration's view, intrude too much on the constitutional prerogatives of the executive.

Turner was pressed hard by some members of the committee on the thorny subject of standards and procedures for "intrusive" investigative techniques. How much executive authority would the Carter Administration defend? Would it follow the lead of the Ford Administration, or would it accede to substantial participation and supervision by the legislature and judiciary? Senator Birch Bayh asked specifically whether Turner would support legislation requiring criminal law standards for initiating electronic surveillance in intelligence – or "national security" – operations. Turner replied that he could support some kind of legislation on authorization procedures, but he did foresee certain difficulties with requiring judicial warrants. That might, he thought, encumber the process unwisely, with adverse effects on national security, and any such proposal would have to be carefully considered from that perspective.[25]

May 1977 Initiatives

An initiative on electronic surveillance gave President Carter himself an opportunity to address the intelligence problem in the context of "human rights" goals he had already set for the nation in foreign policy.[26] In May 1977 he sent to Congress a proposal for legislation on electronic surveillance activities conducted for foreign intelligence purposes, the details of which will be examined later. For present purposes, we need to note the context of national objectives in which the president placed his proposal. He felt it would at last resolve the conflict between the need to obtain adequate intelligence to protect national security and the desire to preserve "basic human rights" at home and abroad.[27] Carter recognized the national security imperative at the center of the intelligence regulatory problem, and he knew it demanded a strong intelligence service. But he also recognized the need to set boundaries beyond which the actions of government may not go. In expressing the constraint rationale in human rights terms, however, he went a step beyond many critics of the intelligence community, whose main concerns stemmed from fear of domestic civil liberties abuses, on the one hand, or from fear of foreign misadventures on the other. In his mind those criticisms converged into a desire to regulate government actions, wherever they take place, by a set of principles not fully expressed in law and not yet fully articulated in any definition of America's self-interest, but based on an overarching concept of human dignity and entitlement.

Whatever else may be said about this human rights formula, it was a new way of thinking about operational controls. In the past, arguments for constraints had generally proceeded from precepts of American constitutional law or from notions about American values and ideals. These arguments were in that sense inward-looking and introspective, springing mainly from a concept of American self-image. On the other side of the debate, however, "national security" arguments against constraints looked outward to the international environment, with a more or less defined theory of international politics that emphasized the realities of life in an uncertain and unsafe world. In doing so they addressed external factors that other, competing views did not reach, in effect taking important argumentative ground without contest.

The Carter approach, however, supplied the critics of intelligence operations with a contrasting theory of international politics and behavior, and one of equivalent scope if elaborated beyond the cryptic rudiments of "human rights" rhetoric. An enduring element of the external environment – human nature and the rising (or perceived to be rising) aspirations for fundamental freedoms around the globe – became the centerpiece of rationales for regulating American actions in the world.[28] With this perspective, reformist analyses and prescriptions had their own world view. They faced outward as well as inward, just as did the national security argument. What had previously been an unbalanced debate between perspectives of unequal scope became at last a full-blown confrontation of differing visions of the world and of the nation. And ironically, it was the president himself who laid the groundwork for enhancement of the critics' arguments in that manner.

The president's proposal for legislation on electronic surveillance was announced on May 18, 1977. Providing controls for electronic surveillance operations undertaken in the United States for foreign intelligence purposes, the bill had been drafted by an interagency committee headed by Attorney General Griffin Bell, with significant assistance from Vice-President Mondale.[29] It was publicly praised by many members of Congress (who had been consulted throughout the drafting process).[30] It provided essentially two things: a procedure that superimposed a requirement for a judicial warrant on the executive approval process, and a standard to be applied by the courts in granting warrants which approached, but did not reach in all respects, the standard used in domestic law enforcement cases.

The administration saw this initiative as a confidence-restoring measure, helping to build public trust in the intelligence agencies by requiring them to expose their operational rationales to judicial scrutiny.[31] The proposal was advertised, and praised, as an improvement over a Ford Administration bill that had died at the end of the previous session of Congress.[32] The improvement was said to be three-fold. First, unlike the

Ford Administration bill, the Carter initiative made no explicit reservation of (or reference to) inherent presidential power. Secondly, the warrant procedure was to be applied to certain activities of the National Security Agency that had been excepted from the Ford proposal. And finally, if "United States persons" (generally, American citizens and resident aliens) were to be subjects of surveillance, the bill required that high-level executive officials certify that the information was needed for national defense or for the conduct of foreign policy, and that judges be permitted to review and evaluate that certification.

The normal executive approval procedure worked as follows. Written proposals and supporting justifications were reviewed by an interagency panel chaired by the director of Central Intelligence. Proposals which were approved (some were not) were forwarded to the president's national security advisor who, if he approved, sent them to the attorney general for final review and authorization.[33] If the attorney general approved, the operation could be initiated. Approvals were for periods of ninety days, renewable upon reapplication and rejustification. The Carter Administration's proposal sought to add to this process the scrutiny of designated federal district courts. If the federal judges approved use of electronic surveillance operations, they were to be empowered to issue two kinds of "warrants": a "special" warrant with a one-year limit if officials of foreign powers were targeted, and a ninety-day warrant where U.S. persons were involved. In exercising that review authority the judges were to make four findings for each warrant granted:

(1) That the target of the surveillance was a foreign power or agent thereof. No U.S. person was to be targeted unless the judge found (a) probable cause to believe that the person was engaged in clandestine intelligence, sabotage, or terrorist activity for or on behalf of a foreign power in violation of law; or (b) that, pursuant to the direction of a foreign intelligence service, that person was collecting or transmitting in a clandestine manner information or material likely to harm U.S. security. This latter proviso was the so-called "non-criminal" standard which we shall shortly note generated much controversy.

(2) That the facilities or place targeted was being used or was about to be used by a foreign power or agent thereof.

(3) That the acquisition, retention, and dissemination of resulting information would be "minimized" – strictly limited to the uses contemplated by the operational proposal and the warrant.

(4) That the assistant to the president for national security affairs or a similar official had certified that the information sought was needed for defense of the nation or for the conduct of its foreign policy.[34] If a U.S. person was the target of the operation, the judge was empowered to review that certification.

The Carter bill was introduced in the House and the Senate within a few weeks. Hearings began in the Senate in July 1977 before the Subcommittee on Intelligence and the Rights of Americans of the Select Committee on Intelligence. Preliminary remarks by members of the subcommittee reflected their eagerness to delve into the issues opened by the proposal, as well as their high hopes for follow-on legislation to establish charters for the intelligence agencies. Senator Walter D. Huddleston, in particular, who was chairman of the subcommittee then engaged in drafting the larger charter, indicated that he hoped soon to introduce a draft that would capitalize on the momentum established by the Carter initiative. Senators also voiced much appreciation for the Carter Administration's more modest postures on the extent of the president's inherent authority to act unilaterally in the interest of national security.[35] But there were important reservations, too, because the proposal would not regulate surveillance activities conducted abroad. There presidential authority remained untrammeled, if controversial. Congress must act, many said, in that arena, too.

Other misgivings were evident, as well. There was specific concern about the lack of an across-the-board criminal standard for initiating these operations. Hard bargaining between the administration and the Intelligence Committee had considerably narrowed the deviation from that standard.[36] But there was strong feeling that even that narrow variance rendered the proposal unconstitutional. Senator Joseph Biden outlined that perspective by pointing out that the Fourth Amendment has two components protecting citizens' privacy, a procedural protection (judicial scrutiny and issuance of a warrant), and a substantive protection ("the judge must have probable cause to believe the search will seize particular evidence of criminal activity").[37] While the administration did propose to submit to a process of judicial review, the bill did not establish the necessary substantive standard for all cases, and so it must fail the ultimate test of constitutionality.

Attorney General Bell, Admiral Turner, and other officials of the intelligence community argued for the proposal in both House and Senate hearings. The attorney general noted the obvious advantages of the president's decision to submit to legislative regulation and judicial review in this arena: it would help restore public confidence and clarify important issues of legality. He also defended the special standard for authorizing surveillance activities as not only constitutional but sensible in view of the plain realities of national security.[38] If the world would permit America to constrain her international tools by the same standards as were used to assure domestic law and order, then there would be no objection to imposing "law enforcement" rules on these foreign intelligence activities. But the distinctive imperatives of international life, and compelling national security needs, dictated acceptance of this narrowly drawn exception.[39]

An array of critics challenged the bill in both the House and the Senate hearings. The special standards and procedures of the "pseudo-warrant" system were attacked as an attempt to circumvent the clear mandate of the Fourth Amendment. In the House hearings, moreover, a note of skepticism was introduced concerning the efficacy of the judicial review procedure, aside from the debate about the substantive standard to be applied.[40] Judges, it was argued, tend naturally to respect (and defer to) the rationales associated with national security operations, and so they would be unlikely to operate as a substantial check on what the executive wanted to do. Further, as Attorney General Levi had pointed out in the Ford years, no amount of outside review could erase the fundamental reality that at some point we must simply trust the executive to perform his duty to the nation faithfully.

With some modifications the Carter proposal was ultimately signed into law as the Foreign Intelligence Surveillance Act of 1978.[41] The outlines of the original concept had survived the legislative process: the attorney general was to approve government applications, accompanied by justifications and certifications, destined for a "FISA" (Foreign Intelligence Surveillance Act) court. The court could then issue warrants permitting initiation of those electronic surveillance activities meeting the requisite standards.

Although critics regretted the limitation of this legislation to activities conducted in the United States,[42] it was nevertheless, as informed observers had noted earlier, a major, historic executive concession. Not only did the executive submit to congressional rulemaking power in a field long held to be within his protected sanctuary of prerogative,[43] but he also submitted to a system of judicial review of specific operational proposals. President Carter, in his public statement at the signing of the bill into law, noted that the statute was, indeed, unprecedented, but he avoided speaking of the power he had bargained away. He observed, instead, that the new law would introduce clarity where before there was contention, and that it provided assurance to intelligence and counterintelligence personnel that the authorized electronic surveillance activities they undertook would henceforth be lawful.[44]

Indications are that the court created by the act has functioned substantially as originally intended − or, in the view of some, as originally feared. In its first seven and a half months it issued 207 warrants; in 1980 and 1981 it granted 322 and 433, respectively. In no case was a government request turned aside. For some observers this has reinforced suspicion that the court was intended as, and is functioning as, a device to legitimize, pro forma, government activities which had been vigorously challenged in the public debate. But the response on behalf of the new procedure is that it made operational planners more careful in selecting cases for which electronic surveillance was proposed.[45] It amounts, then, to a real control mechanism, though it operates subtly and, for outsiders, invisibly.

Executive Order 12036

Immediately after taking office the Carter Administration began to revise EO 11905. Ultimately a replacement directive was issued, EO 12036, but it took a full year to develop, a year of intensive internal debate and of detailed negotiating with members of Congress working simultaneously on a draft legislative charter. Disputes within the intelligence community proved especially difficult to resolve, forcing several postponements of forecasted completion dates.[46]

In the interim, the administration announced management and organizational reforms via executive orders of more limited scope, and also reorganized national-level administrative functions within the intelligence community. In May and June of 1977, two brief directives aligned certain structural provisions of EO 11905 with the new administration's reorganization of the National Security Council.[47] Under President Carter and his national security advisor, Zbigniew Brzezinski, two new NSC committees, the Policy Review Committee (PRC) and the Special Coordination Committee (SCC), had been created. Each was given intelligence responsibilities, and these new executive orders formalized that arrangement. The duties formerly assigned to the Committee on Foreign Intelligence in the Ford Administration were given to the PRC, and those formerly assigned to the Operations Advisory Group were given to the SCC.

When the PRC met to discharge the EO 11905 functions of the CFI (dealing chiefly with resource allocation, budgetary matters, and collection priorities), it was to be chaired by the director of Central Intelligence and to include the deputy secretary of defense, the deputy assistant to the president for national security affairs, and "a senior representative of the Department of State." Inclusion of this last official was a departure from the original EO 11905 design, in which the Department of State had had no formal CFI role at all.

The SCC, chaired by the national security advisor and composed of the secretaries of defense and state, the DCI, and the chairman of the Joint Chiefs of Staff (with the attorney general and the chief of the Office of Management and Budget as observers), took over responsibility for reviewing and recommending to the president on covert action proposals, for approving sensitive collection operations, and for conducting periodic reviews of programs previously considered and approved.

Beyond these organizational arrangements, on August 4, 1977, the president announced a substantial realignment of the major functions and responsibilities of national intelligence management, a move which was interpreted in many quarters as significantly strengthening the roles and institutional stature of the director of Central Intelligence.[48] The purpose of the realignment, according to the White House, was to centralize the most critical national management functions under the director, and to insure "strong direction" of the overall effort by the president and the National Security Council, while retaining the basic structure and distribution of operational responsibilities then prevailing within the community. The president and his advisors indicated that these decisions would later be incorporated in an "umbrella" executive order then in the drafting process, which later became EO 12036. They also indicated, reflecting the cooperative and collaborative tenor of the times, that this order would itself be an interim measure, to be effective "until appropriate charter legislation can be introduced and enacted by Congress."[49]

This realignment left intact the DCI's authority over collection "tasking," resources, and analytical production. It also left unchanged the existing division and assignment of operational and support activities, as most executive officials agreed that these were functioning adequately. It did, however, seek to rationalize collection management functions – to make the collection-production-dissemination process conform more closely to the "intelligence cycle" paradigm explained in chapter two, above. Major features of this effort were as follows:

(1) Users of intelligence were charged with formal responsibility for announcing their own special information requirements. This would emphasize that it is the real needs of policymakers which energize the intelligence agencies, not some parochial desire to exercise operational capabilities simply because they exist, or simply to reinforce or expand claims to spheres of operational authority. Only those imperatives derived from policy needs would generate intelligence collection activities.

(2) The DCI was given three specific responsibilities: (a) supervision of a new National Intelligence Tasking Center, which would establish peacetime intelligence tasks for all collection organizations, based on users' announced needs; (b) budget management authority for all national intelligence activity (except "tactical intelligence") – put most simply, the DCI was given the responsibility to review and approve the National Foreign Intelligence Program budget before it was submitted to the president; and (c) supervisory responsibilities for preparation of all national intelligence analytical products.

(3) The National Security Council system was reinforced as the framework for administering, managing, and controlling the intelligence community. The roles of the SCC and the PRC were of course continued, but the PRC was made a truly cabinet-level organ. Still chaired by the DCI for

intelligence subjects, it was to include the secretaries of defense, state, and treasury, the national security advisor, and others as the DCI deemed appropriate.

Although realignment of these responsibilities was explained as an attempt to improve "management," it clearly supported the president's effort to convince attentive observers that the intelligence agencies were operating within a well-defined framework of control. "Management" of resources and declaration of priorities and needs seem in some respects less controversial and less significant efforts than the definition of boundaries within which those resources can be used. But for a society that still sought reassurance about controls placed on governmental power, any strengthening of management capability was a matter of prime interest. Even as these new directives and decisions were being implemented, "revelations" of intelligence agency activities were still being prominently publicized in the media and were still generating criticism and debate.[50]

Executive Order 12036 was finally issued on January 24, 1978. In public remarks at the signing ceremony, the president emphasized its clear delineation of responsibilities and limitations, especially its protection of civil liberties. He also noted that it would be the basis of a legislated charter to follow from Congress. Similarly, the remarks of Vice-President Mondale emphasized the order's enhancement of operational control and its preservation of important national security capabilities.[51] Their observations reflected the hope that the executive order and its obvious emphasis on controls would reassure the nation about the intelligence agencies.

Executive Order 12036 designated the National Security Council as the highest executive-branch entity directing intelligence activities,[52] and also incorporated the earlier division of labor between the Special Coordination Committee and the Policy Review Committee. The PRC was to be the resource allocator, the budget overseer, the deviser of collection priorities, and the quality controller. The Special Coordination Committee was to participate with the president in review of covert action proposals and had approval authority for sensitive collection operations. The SCC was also assigned a new responsibility, the development of national counterintelligence policy. Additionally, the SCC was required to conduct annual reviews of ongoing covert action and sensitive collection operations – to recheck, in essence, on what had already been approved.

To enhance national-level management, a National Foreign Intelligence Board, chaired by the director of Central Intelligence and including representatives of all agencies within the intelligence community, was established to assist the director in preparing the intelligence budget, in supervising and evaluating community-wide coordination, and in disseminating intelligence products. The National Intelligence Tasking Center, created the previous year, was also formally incorporated into the management superstructure.

The new executive order, like EO 11905 before it, outlined how the high-level review of operational proposals and ongoing activities would be accomplished. Again approval authority for sensitive operations was elevated to levels of supervision outside the intelligence community. Though intelligence professionals had resisted this in the Ford Administration and fought it again when President Carter and his advisors considered the matter anew, these most visible control and accountability mechanisms survived all charges that they were unnecessary, unwise, cumbersome, and even disabling.

More recently, looking back on his years as director of Central Intelligence, Admiral Turner has argued that these formalized external review procedures proved in fact to be quite useful. They helped him resolve the conflict inherent in his dual role as head of an intelligence bureaucracy and an important functionary in the administration of intelligence controls.[53] In the first role he needed to encourage subordinates' initiative, but in the second he was expected to enforce rules about limits vigorously. He found that the external review process at National Security Council level helped him shoulder both burdens more easily. He also found that the process worked to broaden government perspectives on proposed operations by exposing them to review by officials cognizant of their possible impact on U.S. foreign policy at large.

Turner has also indicated that the Carter NSC scrutinized not only individual proposals for certain collection operations, but also the criteria by which he decided which operations were sensitive enough to require NSC review. Ever since issuance of EO 11905, collection proposals thought sensitive had been reviewed at NSC level, but it was the DCI and his advisors who determined whether or not particular operations should be placed in that process. Under the new regime, however, the NSC also evaluated how well such decisions had been made, and could direct any adjustments it thought necessary. As Turner noted, "This is part of an important system of small checks insuring that as operations become more significant, approval and supervisory authority automatically move upward."[54]

Both structure and process, then, as installed in the Carter Administration, worked to regularize self-examination within the community and to assist the director of Central Intelligence in accomplishing his twin, yet in important senses competing, responsibilities as leader and as regulator.

In the significantly upgraded roles assigned to the attorney general, the Carter directive provided additional control mechanisms outside the intelligence community chain of command and therefore divorced from the pressures of leading the regulated. Earlier, President Ford had been careful to introduce the attorney general into the regulatory scheme established by EO 11905. But the Carter order took that initiative even further, which pleased many who thought that a stronger voice for the legal perspective would make intelligence controls more trustworthy.[55]

In the operational approval process, the attorney general's status under EO 12036 was that of a full participating member of the Special Coordination Committee.[56] Under the earlier provisions of EO 11905, by contrast, the attorney general had attended Operations Advisory Group meetings as an "observer." Clearly he could make his views heard in either case, but in the Carter design they had stature equivalent to those of all others.

The attorney general's oversight role was subtly but significantly enhanced, too. In addition to his responsibility to review IOB reports about illegalities, he was also to receive reports from the heads of the intelligence agencies concerning possible unlawful activity by their subordinates. He, in turn, was to report those activities to the president.[57] Under the prior executive order he was required to report periodically about those activities, but not necessarily upon discovery of possible irregularities.

He also had a much more prominent role in reviewing and evaluating specific methods of operation.[58] EO 11905 had assigned him certain functions in that area, particularly with regard to electronic surveillance, and he was also responsible for writing the FBI's operational guidelines. But under EO 12036 he became nearly ubiquitous as a reviewer and approver of guidelines developed for "intrusive" techniques (especially electronic surveillance, television or other mechanical electronic monitoring techniques, physical searches, mail surveillances, penetration of domestic organizations, and collection of information not publicly available on United States persons).[59] This, according to Admiral Turner, eventually produced operating strictures which were more confining than necessary, mainly because the attorney general had no institutional incentive to preserve aggressive intelligence operations.[60] He had no responsibility for contributing to foreign policy formulation, no formal function in helping the nation cope with challenges in the world at large. He understood well only half the intelligence "problem" – the need to protect American citizens' privacy rights, and to insure strict compliance with law. The other half of the problem – helping the nation understand and deal with international environment – was not part of his ordinary responsibility or expertise. His perspectives on operational rules must, according to Turner, inevitably be dangerously unbalanced, favoring internal societal values and pressing toward operational strictures which, in view of external needs, were badly misshapen.

Whether that assessment of the attorney general's natural inclinations is correct or not, it is true that any attorney general, even one sensitive to the problems of survival in an insecure world, would have taken instruction from President Carter's guidance stated in the executive order itself. The directive expressly told him to evaluate operational procedures in the light of their potential effect on citizens' rights, not in terms of other standards.[61] Further, he was told to insure that operational guidelines incorporated the rule that the least intrusive methods were to be techniques of first resort. This "degrees of intrusiveness" rule was a significant, formalized refinement of decisionmaking criteria. Operational effectiveness or national security need would no longer dictate the choice of methods. Potential impact on Americans was now, by presidential directive, the prime consideration.

The order also expanded the responsibility of the intelligence agencies to limit the effects of their operations on Americans. The uses and storage of information resulting from their activities were to be limited to those needed for lawful governmental purposes. In a sense this was by now a familiar principle, but in EO 12036 President Carter elevated it to the level of presidential directive and made the attorney general his deputy in enforcing it.

The "elevation" of counterintelligence was another important innovation in EO 12036. For many years, specialists in covert action and collection operations had regarded the counterintelligence effort as secondary in importance to their own disciplines. It was a necessary endeavor, to be sure, but it was a small activity on the periphery of the main operational concerns of the intelligence community — to understand the world and to help the nation shape its destiny in international affairs. Partially as a result of this attitude, CI had no institutional home of its own. Some of it belonged to the FBI as an adjunct to law-and-order duties, and some belonged to the various intelligence agencies. Since it was oriented mainly on protecting individual departments and specific operations against foreign agents, its management and control were viewed as properly decentralized to the agencies conducting mainstream collection and covert action.

Executive Order 12036 instituted a major change, raising counterintelligence to a matter of NSC concern. It charged the Special Coordination Committee with developing national CI policy, including promulgation of standards and doctrine.[62] The SCC was also required to approve proposals for certain operations and, more broadly, to evaluate the effectiveness of CI programs.

There were two very different reasons for this raising of consciousness about CI. First, there was explicit sensitivity to the threat to United States interests from intelligence and security services of foreign powers and from terrorist activities.[63] In fact, the SCC was directed to prepare a yearly report to the president about that threat. As concern about hostile activities increased at high levels, so did concern for rationalizing the nation's capability to respond.

Secondly, the overarching concern in all quarters about controlling the intelligence agencies demanded that attention be devoted to CI operations. No framework of operational controls would be credible if it did not address them. By this time the attentive public and knowledgeable members of Congress had become far too sophisticated in their grasp of the intelligence control problem to settle for less. EO 11905 had been inadequate in that regard, and the drafters of EO 12036 attempted explicitly to remedy that deficiency.

EO 12036 was also notable for its recognition of the intelligence-related interests of non-executive authorities. President Ford's order had done this only fleetingly and obliquely in the appointment of the DCI to be the community's chief spokesman to Congress. President Carter's order, by contrast, expanded the DCI's role as communicator to embrace contacts with Congress, the news media, and the public.[64] He was also directed to facilitate the use of intelligence products by Congress in a secure manner, an instruction that recognized the legislature's right to use the best available information to discharge its foreign affairs duties. The proper bounds of those duties could of course still be debated, but the executive order recognized the need for collaboration on the mechanics of making them work.

There were also repeated admonitions in the directive to report illegalities and improprieties to the intelligence committees of Congress as well as to executive authorities (the Intelligence Oversight Board and the attorney general).[65] The order thus served congressional oversight interests, too, and by offering up reports, not just on illegalities but on improprieties, it acknowledged that extralegal principles were relevant to that outside oversight function.

The executive order further instructed the DCI and the heads of the intelligence agencies to keep the two intelligence committees "fully and currently" informed, not only about their ongoing activities but also about "any significant anticipated activities."[66] In its insistence on prior notification to Congress wherever possible, the order made room for the legislature to influence operations while they were being planned, not simply while they were being carried out. This was a role that had been urged on Congress by its most aggressive and hopeful supporters for some time. The directive also provided, however, that this requirement to keep Congress informed was not to be construed as a condition precedent to implementation of activities which the executive had decided to conduct. President Carter was willing to inform concerned and responsible members of Congress about how the executive was using the nation's instruments of power, and even about how the executive planned to use those instruments. But no executive authority to decide or to act had been bargained away. Only the veil of secrecy had been lifted, so that the spotlight of external scrutiny might fall on plans, activities, and rationales at an earlier time.

Section 2 of the order stated a number of "Restrictions on Intelligence Activities," and certain elements of the Ford administration's philosophy reappeared here, notably the principle that the law was to be the central determinant of specific prohibitions announced by the executive. It was, furthermore, "established concepts" of law that were to be applied, not ideas about what the law should be. While standards of propriety were recognized (as noted earlier) as appropriate for after-the-fact reviews about operations, legality was the standard around which prohibitions were fashioned. Abrupt departures in the status of the law were for other branches to initiate.

Several of the order's most prominent limitations prohibited activity which was already against the law.[67] This approach had not satisfied a number of critics of the Ford executive order, who believed that the permissions for intelligence operations then embodied in the law were too expansive. But the Carter approach tried to address these concerns also by specifying that the president himself would be involved in approval procedures for the most controversial operational techniques: electronic surveillance, the use of television cameras and other surreptitious monitoring devices, physical searches, and mail surveillance. In this way, operations which were not subjected to judicial scrutiny were required to be conducted pursuant to specific authority granted by the president himself, and only after approval of each operation by the attorney general.[68] Though the courts had not been given the roles hoped for by some who were distrustful of executive judgment, constraints – in the form of approval procedures installed at the highest executive levels – had in fact been created in an effort to accommodate pressures for reform.

For certain collection techniques particularly susceptible to abuse, moreover, the Carter Administration did impose the "least intrusive means" rule discussed earlier. This required operators to choose techniques in an order of precedence shaped by concern for possible impact on citizens' rights. National security imperatives were to be balanced against the need to protect all citizens against intrusive governmental powers. And some of that balancing was accomplished by the order itself, with the result that techniques that threatened important internal societal values were relegated to instruments of last resort. Operators and their mid-level superiors still had to make decisions about which techniques to use in particular operations. They were human and could make errors of judgment, even when the standards for exercising judgment were directed in some detail from above. But little could prevent that in any case. In simply stating those standards, EO 12036 identified the major counterpoised values implicated by "intru-

sive" instruments — national security and protection of citizens' rights —
and arrayed those tools of national power in accordance with a value synthesis favoring the latter.

President Carter also went farther than EO 11905 in regulating domestic informant operations, or "undisclosed participation in domestic organizations." The Ford directive had allowed infiltration of a domestic organization within the United States in order to report on or to influence its
activities if the organization was composed "primarily" of non-United
States persons and was "reasonably believed to be acting on behalf of a
foreign power."[69] The Carter approach imposed significantly more formal
regulation and review by giving the attorney general explicit approval roles
for the general procedures to be used in such operations, by requiring
disclosure of the government agent's affiliation unless the chief of his agency
(or a subordinate official approved by the attorney general) "finds that non-
disclosure is essential to achieving lawful purposes," and by making that
finding of essentiality subject to review by the attorney general.[70] The order
limited these activities to three kinds of cases: those in which the participation is undertaken on behalf of the FBI in the course of a lawful investigation; those in which the organization infiltrated is composed primarily of
non-U.S. persons and is reasonably believed to be acting on behalf of a
foreign power (this was the Ford administration's formula); and those in
which the participation is limited in nature, scope, and duration to that
needed to serve lawful purposes related to foreign intelligence, and is a type
of activity that the attorney general has approved. Significantly, "no such
participation may be undertaken for the purpose of influencing the activity
of the organization or its members." Covert action at home, in other words,
was specifically prohibited.

Even so, the reasons ("lawful" — i.e., not illegal — purposes) for which
such operations could be generated were still more permissive than some
observers preferred. Further, all this regulation and review was to be
accomplished within the executive branch. Other institutions of government were not to be involved in authorizations or approvals, even in the
sense of granting general operating authority.

The order also announced special restrictions on collection, dissemination, and storage of non-publicly-available information about United States
persons, limitations that were more detailed and confining than those in
Executive Order 11905. For these activities, as for others thought particularly intrusive, the attorney general was to approve general operational
procedures. But even more, the scope of the restrictive provisions had been
expanded. For example, whereas the limitations of EO 11905 had applied to
collection of information about the domestic activities of United States
persons, the more numerous and more specific limitations announced by
President Carter applied to protection of all activities of those persons,

regardless of their location.[71] There was still language which carefully preserved the distinction between law enforcement rules and foreign intelligence rules. But the unmistakable intention of these restrictions was to establish clearer protections for Americans by forcing internal review and approval, by legal authorities, of methods of operation; by announcing which kinds of activity were permitted; and by accomplishing all that on the open record.

Indeed, it is fair to say that protecting Americans from abuse of power by their government, and restoration of public confidence that such protections were in place and effective, were the main preoccupations of this part of the Carter Administration's executive order. The directive did, however, also impose limits on American power vis-a-vis the world outside United States borders in restrictions for the covert action function. President Carter retained the Ford Administration's prohibition of assassination, but broadened it (at least arguably) by eliminating the adjective "political" as a qualifier of the kind of assassination proscribed.[72] On covert action operations more generally, administration officials were openly skeptical about their utility, and there was real reluctance to engage in them.[73] But the administration was also unwilling to abandon the capability altogether.[74] It had a place in the nation's arsenal, but not a prominent one.

Overall, then, President Carter's directive continued the Ford Administration's concern for placing significant operational constraints before the public — "constraints" in terms of authorization and approval mechanisms and delineation of operational boundaries. In addition to closer and higher-level scrutiny of operational proposals and of individual ongoing activities, the review process external to the intelligence community now involved examination of the methods by which it operated. These review procedures succeeded in confining intelligence activity within bounds acceptable to legal authorities, if not intelligence professionals, within the executive. Indeed, it was later suggested (and argued by others at the time)[75] that the resulting operational limitations were too confining, that the Carter approach had swung the policy pendulum too far against the interests of the nation in maintaining potent intelligence capabilities. These criticisms objected in particular to curtailment of counterintelligence techniques. But there was concern, additionally, that the less-visible rules, standards, and attitudes applied to the covert action function would be equally harmful. President Reagan's director of Central Intelligence has indicated that the Carter Administration did in fact set the covert action tool aside for its first two years in office (one year each under EO 11905 and EO 12036). In the last two years of the Carter watch, increasing numbers of operations were undertaken, but the effects of previous neglect were not completely overcome.[76] At the time EO 12036 was issued, Admiral Turner argued that no such dismantling was intended, but evidently operational atrophy set in much more quickly or more pervasively than the administration had expected.

The Congressional Charter

With the issuance of EO 12036 the focus of attention shifted to the effort in Congress, led by the Senate Select Committee on Intelligence, to draft a charter for the intelligence community.[77] The executive order itself had been warmly received by members of Congress, including those who were working on the charter. But they were also looking beyond that directive, which they saw as an interim measure.[78] They hoped that their own work would bear fruit in a comprehensive statute that would replace the 1947 National Security Act and remedy its most glaring flaws. By late 1977, in fact, some critics had become impatient with what they perceived as unwarranted delay in the charter-writing effort. Senator Walter Huddleston, who headed the subcommittee writing it, felt compelled at that point to defend his work against charges of "dawdling." He explained that a painstaking – and necessary – process of coordination had been undertaken with presidential advisors working simultaneously on the executive order, and that the senate committee had agreed to let the president issue EO 12036 first, before the charter proposal was introduced in Congress.[79]

In early February 1978 Senator Huddleston finally introduced his charter: S. 2525, the National Intelligence Reorganization and Reform Act of 1978.[80] It was a massive compendium of details about organization, control, accountability, and oversight. Hearings on it began in April and continued intermittently for five months.[81] This draft and successive alternative proposals for a comprehensive legislative charter ultimately died in Congress, overcome by "counterreform" initiatives. Certain of its major features are worthy of some discussion, however, because they indicate the extent to which informed viewpoints in Congress wished at that point to go even beyond what presidents had done in rectifying control problems.

The charter stated its purposes as follows:

(1) to authorize the intelligence activities necessary for the conduct of the foreign relations and the protection of the national security of the United States;

(2) to replace the provisions of the National Security Act of 1947 governing intelligence activities;

(3) to insure that the national intelligence activities of the United States are properly and effectively directed, regulated, coordinated, and administered;

(4) to insure that the Executive and legislative branches are provided, in the most efficient manner, with such accurate, relevant, and timely information and analysis as those branches need to make sound and informed decisions regarding the security and vital interests of the United States and to protect the United States

against foreign intelligence activities, international terrorist activities, and other forms of hostile action directed against the United States;

(5) to provide for the appointment of a Director of National Intelligence, to delineate the responsibilities of such Director, and to confer on such Director the authority necessary to fulfill those responsibilities; and

(6) to insure that the Director of National Intelligence and the entities of the intelligence community are accountable to the President, the Congress, and the people of the United States and that the intelligence activities of the United States are conducted in a manner consistent with the Constitution and laws of the United States and so as not to abridge any right protected by the Constitution or laws of the United States.

Two points warrant special notice here. First, this act by its own terms would replace the 1947 National Security Act as the fundamental statutory authority for the intelligence community and its activities. This was a step that nearly all participants in the public debate had supported for some time. Practitioners felt that the vague provisions of the 1947 act ought to be made more elaborate and more specific, so that the lines of responsibility would be clearly drawn for all to see, and so that the limits of authority would be established with some degree of certainty. They were not anxious, of course, for tighter restrictions, but they did seek clearer guidance as to what the restrictions were. Critics of intelligence operations, on the other hand, hoped that executive controls would be substantially strengthened and lines of accountability clearly specified. In some respects the charter responded to both interests. But the bill was intended to do much more than that. It was meant also to give Congress better access to intelligence products and stronger roles in control and oversight. In this respect it dealt with the problem of sharing and distributing power within the federal government, in addition to its concern with controlling that power in the aggregate.

To some extent the charter proposal incorporated concepts and lan- guage taken from the president's postures in the executive order. This was the result, and arguably the advantage, of letting the president "go first" with announcement of his directive. But the bill's central and distinctive themes were those dealing with the roles of Congress and the courts, rearrangement of direction and control mechanisms within the executive, and announcement of operational standards and limits.

We have just seen that the bill's statement of purpose reflected a commitment by Congress to insure that the legislative branch had access, on the same basis as the executive, to information needed for national security decisions. The bill, accordingly, would have renamed the director of Central Intelligence, giving him the broader title of director of National Intelligence.[82] As the nation's (not just the president's) principal foreign intelligence officer, he would also have been told to serve Congress, as well as the executive, in providing information supportive of the foreign and national security policymaking process. Such a provision would not have given Congress the ability to direct and manage the business of collecting that information – few argued for such a role in any event. But it would have solidified in statute the coequal rights of Congress to use the intelligence product.

The bill adopted the Hughes-Ryan reporting requirement for covert action – the president himself was required to make certain findings (to be discussed shortly) and to report, via the director of National Intelligence, any approved proposals to the intelligence committees of Congress. The bill also adopted the procedure established in EO 12036 for NSC review of sensitive clandestine collection operations, and extended to them the director's responsibility to notify Congress.[83] A similar reponsibility was imposed on the attorney general with regard to CI and counterterrorist activities approved by the president or reviewed by the NSC. (The bill permitted the president to decide which operations ought to have presidential or NSC approval, but required him to tell Congress what those rules were.[84])

Congress's role in oversight was to be reinforced by adopting the procedures of EO 12036 regarding the Intelligence Oversight Board and associated reporting channels, and further by including the intelligence committees as recipients of the resulting reports. The attorney general was required to tell Congress about the activities that he believed raised questions of legality. And the heads of the intelligence agencies were similarly required to report activities that raised questions of propriety in the eyes of their inspectors general or general counsel. The attorney general was further required to report annually to Congress, in writing, on activities discovered by executive branch oversight procedures which he believed violated provisions of the Constitution, statutes, executive orders, or other presidential directives. For those who were concerned as to whether Congress might treat the information given it in a responsible manner, the proposal also outlined procedures for protecting the interests of secrecy within its chambers.[85]

The charter proposal included several provisions which would regulate the use of electronic surveillance within the United States. These were later enacted separately (with some modifications) as the Foreign Intelligence Surveillance Act of 1978. As in that act, the provisions of the draft charter established a procedure by which a special court would review proposals for electronic surveillance, granting authority to use that technique where the judge was satisfied that specified requirements had been met. The charter also went further than the FISA, however, by seeking to impose the warrant procedure on proposals to use electronic surveillance outside the U.S.

as well as on operations within American borders. In doing so, it made certain concessions to arguments that this impinged too much on national security interests, allowing the targeting of persons in certain cases not permitted under domestic rules. But the fundamental point remained: even activities abroad would be scrutinized by the special judicial institutions created to protect privacy rights. Furthermore, the charter sought to apply that procedure to operational techniques other than electronic surveillance, including unconsented physical searches and mail openings.[86]

To the dismay of some critics of intelligence operations, however, the charter preserved elements of the "noncriminal" standard for approving those techniques. Intelligence operators were not required to demonstrate in all cases that there was probable cause to believe a crime was being or was about to be committed in order to gain approval for intrusive methods of operation.

As might be expected, the legislators were also anxious to establish a statutory framework of control structures and procedures within the executive. The bill would have assigned roles and functions in the operational approval process, basically adopting procedures established under EO 12036: presidential approval of covert action operations after NSC (or a subcommittee thereof) had reviewed and approved the proposals, NSC approval of sensitive clandestine collection operations, and NSC or presidential review of such CI and counterterrorist operations as executive procedures would thereafter require.[87]

The charter also followed the lead of EO 12036 in elevating management and policy guidance for counterintelligence and counterterrorism to the level of the National Security Council. The NSC was assigned responsibility for formulating broad policies applicable to those programs. And it was also to be responsible for ensuring their "unified direction" within the boundaries of applicable law.[88]

Where the NSC or a subordinate organ met to consider proposals for covert action or collection operations, the charter required the secretaries of state and defense, the director of National Intelligence, and the attorney general (or their delegates) to be present. Where it met to consider CI and counterterrorist activities, attendees were to include the DNI, the director of the FBI, an official of the CIA, and again the attorney general. As these provisions indicate, the bill assigned substantial duties to the attorney general. Indeed, a separate section of the charter was to be entitled the "Intelligence Activities and Constitutional Rights Act of 1978," intended in part "to delineate the role of the Attorney General in ensuring that intelligence activities of the United States are conducted in conformity with the Constitution and laws of the United States."[89]

Oversight procedures envisioned in the bill were essentially those mechanisms, established by EO 12036, designed to facilitate discovery and investigation of problems of legality and/or propriety. The attorney general again was given prominent roles in that system, both as recipient and transmitter of reports about possible violations of law, and as an investigator of them.[90]

It was in the area of operational authorizations and restrictions that the charter illuminated most clearly the divergence between Congress and the executive. As one might expect of legislation intended to replace a statute now criticized as inarticulate, the charter would have specifically authorized all three kinds of intelligence operations: covert action, collection, and counterintelligence. But that authority was carefully confined, especially with respect to covert action and CI. For covert action a number of specific prohibitions were stated. Assassination of foreign officials in peacetime (defined as periods other than during a war declared by Congress or situations encompassed by the 1973 War Powers Resolution) was prohibited. Additionally, the Senate committee wanted to prevent the United States from engaging in activities which had as their objective or as a likely result any of the following: support of international terrorist activities; mass destruction of property; creation of food or water shortages or floods; creation of epidemics of diseases; use of chemical, biological, or other weapons in violation of treaties or other international agreements to which the United States is a party; violent overthrow of the democratic government of any country; torture of individuals; or support of any action which violates human rights, conducted by the police, foreign intelligence, or internal security services of any foreign country.[91] As operational restrictions stated on the public record, all these would have been new, representing the Senate Intelligence Committee's judgment that the United States ought not to engage in these kinds of international activities, and that the rules excluding them from our repertoire ought to be made part of the statutory foundation for the intelligence community.

The impetus to state clear constraints did not stop there, however. For both covert action and collection operations the bill would have further stated rules about categories of people who could not be used as intelligence operatives. There was strong feeling that certain occupations and institutions must be kept separate from and untainted by the official pursuits of government, and their independence was deemed so important as to warrant specific guarantees and protections in the law. The prohibitions applied to journalists, persons pursuing full-time religious vocations, and persons traveling abroad under United States government programs promoting education, the arts, the humanities, or cultural affairs. The Senate committee also wanted to prohibit the use of those occupations as operational "covers" – notional identities assumed by U.S. agents to disguise their intelligence affiliation and activities.[92]

According to later revelations by intelligence officials, some of these restrictions, at least those concerning the types of persons or cover that may be used, had already been put in place by the Carter Administration in internal, unpublished directives.[93] But there were strong reservations within the administration about stating flat prohibitions in statutory form, for fear of binding the hands of the executive too tightly. And future administration postures on proposed legislation would repeat those admonitions.[94]

The charter proposal attempted to accommodate this interest in flexibility by permitting the president to waive certain of the limitations in three specified circumstances of emergency: during any period in which the United States was engaged in a war declared by Congress, in situations where action abroad was undertaken pursuant to the War Powers Resolution, and in "any period when the President determines that there is a grave and immediate threat to the national security of the United States" and when "it is vital to the security of the United States for one or more entities of the intelligence community to engage in the activities."[95] In the latter case, the president was required to notify the intelligence committees seventy-two hours before executing the waiver, or forty-eight hours afterward if prior notification was not possible. Presidential waivers could be applied to the prohibition on using persons in the religious vocation and officially sponsored travelers, but the prohibition as to journalists was nonwaiverable. In all cases the limitations on cover identities could be lifted. And the president was further empowered to waive the restrictions on support of international terrorist activity, mass destruction of property, creation of food and water shortages or floods, and the violent overthrow of democratic foreign governments. It is worth repeating here that the circumstances in which the president was "empowered" to liberate intelligence agencies from the specified restrictions were limited to cases in which Congress had authorized a larger national commitment in the same direction (by declaring war or approving the dispatch of troops under the War Powers Resolution), or in which Congress was informed of the executive decision to engage in the activity.

As if these restrictions were not enough, the proposed charter would also have told the president and the National Security Council how to make decisions about operations. It outlined the decisionmaking criteria as follows:

(c) Whenever the National Security Council or the President reviews any special activity or clandestine collection activity, careful and systematic consideration shall be given to all appropriate factors, including, but not limited to –

(1) the justification for such proposed activity;

(2) the nature, scope, probable duration, estimated costs, foreseeable risks, likely consequences of disclosure, and actions necessary in the event of the termination of such activity;

(3) the relationship between the proposed activity and any previously approved activity;

(4) the likelihood that the objectives of such activity would be achieved by overt or less sensitive alternatives; and

(5) the legal implications of the proposed activity.

(d) No special activity may be initiated unless the activity has been approved by the President and the President has made a written finding that, in the President's opinion —

(1) such activity is essential to the national defense or the conduct of the foreign policy of the United States;

(2) the anticipated benefits of such activity justify the foreseeable risks and likely consequences of its disclosure to a foreign power;

(3) overt or less sensitive alternatives would not be likely to achieve the intended objectives; and

(4) the circumstances require the use of extraordinary means.

(e) No clandestine collection activity requiring the President's personal approval, under standards and procedures established by the President . . . may be initiated unless the President has made a written finding that —

(1) the information to be obtained by such project is essential to the national defense or the conduct of the foreign policy of the United States;

(2) the importance of the information justifies the foreseeable risk or the likely consequences of disclosure to a foreign power; and

(3) overt or less sensitive alternatives would not be likely to accomplish the intended objectives.[96]

In these provisions we see several important perspectives emerging. In the first place, the standard for approving covert action and sensitive collection operations was stated in terms of essentiality to United States interests. The drafters of the charter knew full well that this would raise the operational threshold from the Hughes-Ryan Amendment's focus on importance to national security. They knew also that the administration would have reservations about that. But the bill reflected their conscious choice to make such operations truly instruments of emergency and last resort. Secondly, the impetus behind the movement for greater accountability resulted here in a proposed requirement to have the president himself make written findings on each operation that he approves. Thirdly, the legislators wanted to declare operational priorities in statutory form, favoring overt methods and operations of lesser sensitivity and risk. Decisionmaking discretion previously left to mid-level managers would be in effect preempted by this congressional declaration of preference. Finally, we see that in addition to all the other mechanisms facilitating the interposition of legal judgment in the operational approval process, the proposed statute would have directed the National Security Council to consider the lawyers' view. Other provisions said the attorney general must be present when operations are reviewed for approval. The rule just quoted would have told other authorities to listen to him.

Counterintelligence and counterterrorism operations had their own approval criteria, shaped importantly by safeguards for constitutional rights. They had their own operational limitations, too, stated in almost excruciating detail. And, as with the covert action and collection provisions, the bill stated priorities – in a "least intrusive means" rule – which decided, as a matter of national policy, certain matters previously left to operators' discretion.[97] If it was poor operational judgment which was in part to blame for the abuses of the past, then the sensible remedy seemed to be to limit the areas in which that judgment could be exercised.

S. 2525 never became law, as we shall see in the next chapter. But as the legislative counterproposal to EO 12036, it embodied congressional perspectives as of 1978 in great detail, focused on several areas. The first of these was authorizing specific categories of operations to be carried out by the intelligence agencies. This in effect would make public the functions they were to perform in service of the national interest. Secondly, Congress was interested in prohibiting certain kinds of operations in explicit terms, and applying restrictions to those activities thought permissible. The constraints on operations were meant to protect citizens' right to be free from unnecessary governmental interference and surveillance, and also reflected distinctive ideas about how America ought to behave in the international arena. Congress also specified the factors which were to govern decisions about which operations to undertake and about which techniques to use in approved projects. Finally, the bill sought to make congressional participation in regulation and oversight a matter of statutory requirement.

S. 2525 met opposition from knowledgeable observers on all sides of the intelligence debate. The American Civil Liberties Union regarded it in general as a modest improvement on EO 12036, but objected to many of its most important features. Particularly objectionable, in the ACLU's view, was the breadth of CI and counterterrorist activity the bill would have authorized. This resulted from the lack of a criminal standard for initiation of intrusive investigative techniques, and from insufficient procedural safeguards against abuse. The ACLU also urged Congress to prohibit covert action abroad. They argued, among other reasons, that the costs associated with it outweighed the asserted benefits, that it threatened precepts of shared and balanced power within the federal government, that it would tempt presidents to use secret activity abroad to avoid troublesome intra-governmental debate about American behavior and commitments, that it had been used too often to undermine fundamental freedoms in foreign societies, and that it inevitably colored the perceptions of foreigners about the United States, in ways not compatible with America's professed ideals.

The ACLU also argued that the intelligence community's charter ought to prohibit espionage in peacetime.[98]

Morton Halperin and the Center for National Security Studies had reservations about the charter, too, fearing that it would legitimize controversial activity without imposing sufficient controls. Halperin objected more specifically that the charter "implicitly assumed that the intelligence agencies and presidents and attorneys general will operate in good faith with an effort to comply with both the letter and the spirit of the legislation." In view of the recent past, said Halperin, this assumed too much. He also believed that covert action operations were useless, counterproductive, difficult to control, and ought to be abolished — or, as a less preferable alternative, limited to "most extraordinary" emergency circumstances in which a "large proportion" of Congress or the public would support use of that capability. Finally, he argued that the charter lacked an across-the-board warrant procedure and criminal standard for authorizing the use of intrusive operational methods.[99]

The views of intelligence professionals who were free to speak were equally critical, but of course for different reasons. Richard Helms, for instance, objected strenuously to the loss of "flexibility" which imposition of an elaborate framework of statutory controls and reporting requirements entailed. Such flexibility, he argued, was needed in order to permit the intelligence agencies and their activities "to shift quickly in the face of new conditions."[100] A statement by retired U.S. Army General Richard Stilwell, speaking as president of the Association of Former Intelligence Officers, elaborated on this point and made clear the major perceptions and values at its center:

The indispensable condition precedent for U.S. and/or Allied actions to checkmate the Soviet Union is advance knowledge of the substance and timing of specific actions to further its expansionist policy. Our intelligence capabilities must coalesce to meet this requirement. Like the strategic nuclear TRIAD, our various intelligence capabilities — conspicuously including human intelligence — are interdependent and mutually reinforcing. Yet S. 2525, in its present form, imposes troublesome — approaching prohibitive — operational restraints on the conduct of clandestine collection, i.e., old-fashioned espionage.

. . . Never before has the security and well being of the United States been more susceptible to disturbance by events abroad. . . . Thus situations continue to arise in which we will find it necessary to try to influence the course of events in furtherance of our legitimate national interests. Sometimes these situations may be most prudently dealt with through some means short of direct U.S. involvement. But again, S. 2525 imposes significant obstacles, inhibiting the flexibility which is essential to the success of such operations.

. . . Without effective counterintelligence, neither intelligence operations nor covert actions can be pursued with confidence. The examples of audacious and aggressive KGB operations in the United States and abroad, including the "bug-ging" of our embassy in Moscow, which have recently surfaced, are but the tip of the iceberg. . . . Moreover, that threat is growing. Identification of the specifics of that threat and the countering of penetrations of our security necessitates a major effort, sophisticated means and a high degree of operational resourcefulness. Some of the provisions of S. 2525 are not in consonance with the magnitude of that task.[101]

In the months ahead, this perspective would gain in visibility and power in official circles. It held the seeds, indeed, of a significant counter-reform movement which in the end would defeat the effort to legislate a new charter. It would also shape executive approaches to the intelligence control problem, even in the time remaining to the Carter Administration.

Looking back over the Carter Administration's own pre-1979 reform effort, several major features and themes are apparent. In the area of the most critical civil liberties concern, the Carter Administration had sup-ported the Foreign Intelligence Surveillance Act of 1978, instituting judi-cial review of proposals for electronic surveillance within the United States. But while it submitted to that procedure, as a result of extended bargaining with Congress, the administration also contended − successfully − that the substantive standard for authorizing these foreign intelligence opera-tions could not be so confining as the classic standard of "probable cause" in criminal investigations. In order to soften that posture, for the benefit of those who had hoped his administration would be even more forthcoming on the substantive standard, President Carter gave his chief legal officer prominent responsibilities in the devising of operational rules, in the approval of individual operations, and in the administration of oversight procedures. Additionally, the president decreed that regardless of perceived operational need in particular cases, operators and their supervisors were to select the least intrusive operational technique available. He also made counterintelligence policy a matter of concern and official responsibility for the National Security Council itself, raising CI to equal status with other operational disciplines, and also, not incidentally, raising the visibility of CI controls in the executive regulatory scheme.

President Carter's policies were also importantly reform-minded in their public focus on value-based principles as sources of guidance for controls and oversight. Though his rules for particular operations were fashioned around the precepts then embodied in law, this was in recognition of his position as executive, or implementer of the law. References to "fair play" ideals and to traditional standards of justice and decency were equally prominent in the president's public utterances about the kinds of actions America should undertake and the kinds of policies it should adopt. Evidence now available, furthermore, indicates that the administration did set aside the covert action instrument in its first two years in office, declining to engage in techniques of manipulation, at least on the scale of previous practice. In its bargaining with Congress on the comprehensive charter proposal, moreover, the administration acceded to certain limits on types of operations and on operational techniques (categories of persons and/ or covers to be used, for instance), though it would have preferred not to state those limits in a statute, leaving them to more flexible internal executive regulations. These positions encouraged many critics and con- tributed significantly to the growth and sustenance of a major reform movement in Congress and elsewhere.

The early Carter years also saw the institutionalization of regularized scrutiny of intelligence affairs by Congress and, as just noted, in some instances by the courts. Oversight by the intelligence committees of the House and Senate was routinized, with members of both committees satisfied that the procedures devised for them to influence, to participate in the control of, and to benefit from the products of intelligence activities were sufficient to satisfy all reasonable interests. The administration ac- ceded to congressional assertion of its regulatory authority by means of a comprehensive charter and by means of the FISA, which in fact intruded on spheres of executive rulemaking authority that had been defended vig- orously for years. This, too, was regarded by reformers as a giant step forward. But the story was not yet ended.

6

The Carter Endgame and the Reagan Administration

Even as S. 2525 was being scrutinized and criticized during the remainder of 1978 and 1979, there were perceptible indications that the momentum was beginning to shift in favor of those who were concerned as much about the effects of regulatory reform as about the need for it. The earlier emphasis (some would have said near-fixation) on constraining intelligence operations now began to be tempered by growing doubts, more frequently expressed officially and in public, about the ability of the intelligence agencies to serve the national interest under the strict regulatory regimes many still advocated. Increasingly, members of Congress as well as spokesmen for the administration and the intelligence community found opportunities to go public with their concern for the effectiveness of the intelligence effort if it was burdened by rules meant mainly to restrain power rather than to rationalize it, to focus it, and to place it in perspective in the nation's behavioral repertoire.

This trend was visible particularly in early 1979, when the Subcommittee on Legislation of the House Committee on Intelligence began a series of hearings which explored the growing difficulties caused for the intelligence agencies by restrictive rules and procedures. Though ostensibly focused on narrow issues, these hearings provided repeated opportunities for the agencies to explain and to criticize the larger efforts of the regulatory reform movement. Headed by Congressman Morgan Murphy, the House subcommittee proved a most sympathetic forum for these views. Since it was the counterpart of Walter Huddleston's charter-writing group in the Senate, the Murphy committee's evident reservations about the effects of reform had important implications for the prospects of the ongoing charter effort.[1] The dissatisfaction it expressed would ultimately grow into a widely supported movement which would defeat the charter proposals and pursue legislative relief for some of the most burdensome effects of the 1970s restraints. But in the end, as we shall see, it would be the course of international events that would provide this movement a rationale persuasive to large segments of the public, and a distinctive and lasting impetus of its own.

In January 1979 Congressman Murphy's subcommittee began a series of hearings on the nation's espionage laws, generated by concern about the vulnerability of our intelligence agencies and information to foreign spying.[2] From the start, however, members of the subcommittee made no attempt to hide their anxiety about the effects of information "leaks", revelations, and disclosures not related to hostile espionage. The activities of investigative journalists and exposé writers, especially, were singled out for explicit and even scornful criticism.[3] Deeply implicated in the inquiry, then, were principles of "open government and robust debate," as well as more specific First Amendment freedoms of speech and press which promote those central societal values.[4] For all participants and observers the tension was clear between those values and the nation's security interest in protecting legitimate government secrets. And equally clear was this House subcommittee's concern that on this issue the proper balance had not yet been found in reform measures – which of course included the ongoing work in the Senate on a legislative charter.

Administration witnesses testifying at these hearings were mainly lawyers, general counsels of several intelligence agencies, who described the impact of information leaks on their agencies and evaluated various ways to cope with that problem. But views on wider issues were evident, as well. Anthony A. Lapham, the CIA's general counsel, for instance, told the subcommittee that in recent years it seemed that the "legitimate and strong national interest" in protecting intelligence secrets had been "crowded out by others and . . . is not being served very well." Existing law, Lapham felt, was not adequate to prevent, deter, or punish leakers and others who participate in the unauthorized disclosure of national security information.[5] Testimony by Daniel Silver, general counsel of the National Security Agency, agreed, pointing even more starkly to the tension between national security interests and disclosure activities which had been cloaked in the protective mantle of the First Amendment. The problem, moreover, as seen by the intelligence community, was not limited to leaks from executive branch sources. Mishandling of sensitive information by Congress was a major concern.[6]

These arguments supported proposals for modifications in the law and in the practice of sharing information with Congress. The proposals themselves need not detain us here. What is important is the fact that the hearings on this issue gave vent to perceptible antireform sentiment within the Carter Administration and in Congress. There was a shared belief among members of intelligence agencies and a number of congressmen charged with oversight responsibilities that certain rules and practices associated with the era of regulatory reform had had untoward effects on important national security interests, and that more sensible regimes had to be devised to ameliorate those effects.

Those views were controversial, however, and there was extensive opposition testimony by persons concerned about interference with media and publishing activities and with the public's "right to know." The American Civil Liberties Union was a prominent critic.[7] Senator Joseph Biden (a member of the Senate's intelligence committee) appeared in the House hearings to counsel caution, too. He feared that legislative remedies for "leaks" might intrude on the legitimate interest of the public in being informed about the activities of their government.[8] Several legal experts agreed: some disclosures are helpful, not harmful, they argued, and ought to be protected, not proscribed. They were especially concerned about the impact of proposed remedies on journalists, academics, and other concerned citizens. Publication of national security information that has come, somehow, into the public domain serves everyone's interest in promoting public discussion, and it also enhances citizen participation in the affairs of government. These are values which, in the American scheme of things, ought to be preferred over others.[9] The value of this kind of public discussion was regarded as simply too great to justify curtailing it in the name of national security.

Several months later, in April 1979, the Murphy subcommittee held another set of hearings on a related issue: the impact on intelligence operations of information disclosures required under the provisions of two related statutes: the Freedom of Information Act and the Privacy Act of 1974.[10] The Freedom of Information Act (FOIA) had been passed by Congress in 1966 and amended substantially in 1974. In the late 1970s the Carter Administration regarded it as an important way to make government responsive to the needs of an open society. It required government agencies to make available to the public, on request, information held in their files if the requestors followed designated procedures and if one or more of nine specified exemptions was not claimed by the agency or agencies concerned.[11]

The Privacy Act, enacted in December 1974, stated similar disclosure requirements specifically intended to enable citizens to discover, on their request, what information about them was held in government files. Exceptions were again provided for national security and foreign policy secrets. In the case of both acts, exemptions claimed by the government could be (and often were) challenged in federal courts.

In the years since enactment of those laws, requests for information and files had burgeoned, imposing significant financial and manpower costs on all intelligence agencies. These were explained at some length in the April 1979 hearings. But the agencies' worries went far beyond those administrative burdens. They were concerned more specifically about the threat, or simply the perceived threat, of forced disclosures that would compromise sensitive sources and methods of operation.

Deputy Director of Central Intelligence Carlucci was the first witness to appear before the subcommittee. He began his testimony by making it clear that "Admiral Turner and I support the general concept of openness in government." Indeed, he observed that the DCI had been criticized by some for bringing too much openness to the Central Intelligence Agency. Media representatives and academics in particular had benefited from this new orientation, and the administration by no means intended to back away from it. But, Carlucci argued, the intelligence agencies had been seriously harmed by the government's failure to protect them sufficiently from the FOIA and Privacy Act disclosure requirements applied to all other agencies. To be sure, open government is an important principle to uphold in a free society and the administration intended to respect it fully. But certain instruments of the state, including the intelligence agencies, cannot be subjected to accountability procedures which assume that the public at large can sensibly oversee their activities without vitiating their effectiveness.

The administration recognized that in our scheme of things the people's knowledge is the people's power. But in this area of government capability and activity, Carlucci asserted, dispersion of knowledge must inevitably erode the society's aggregate power by informing potential enemies about strengths, resources, and weaknesses. The best course, accordingly, seemed to be to trust Congress, the people's elected representatives, to discharge oversight responsibilities in a way that serves all interests. This was an arena, the administration argued, in which public scrutiny could do, and was doing, much more harm than good.

The particular harm, as Carlucci described it, was this: foreign and domestic sources alike increasingly feared that their association with American intelligence would be revealed through the FOIA and Privacy Act – if not with the intelligence agencies' concurrence, then pursuant to the directives of a court after review of contending arguments about exemptions. The CIA, for instance, might itself feel confident that it could protect information which might later facilitate identification of its source. But no amount of persuasion could reassure those potential and existing agents who did not wish to subject themselves to that extra risk, over and above the normal risks of intelligence activity. This "chilling effect," Carlucci argued, had seriously hampered the nation's intelligence effort in ways he could not elaborate upon in open session. More certain guarantees of protection were needed, or else the value of the human collection effort to the nation's security interests would be severely undercut. In fact, he said, the American intelligence effort might be rendered second best when compared with its competitors on the international scene.[12]

Members of the subcommittee were most receptive to the administration's views. One, in fact, stated flatly that the time had come to try to strengthen the intelligence agencies and that some better balancing of "open government" interests with the need for secrecy was clearly an important part of that effort. [13]

Testimony by the National Security Agency then expanded the focus of concern from protection of human sources to protection of the highly sensitive technical sources and methods used by that collection agency. And, concluding the administration's testimony, representatives of the FBI described the impact of the FOIA and Privacy Act on counterintelligence operations, referring especially to documented instances in which potential agents had refused to cooperate with the bureau because of fear of exposure under these acts. [14]

A few months later, in August and September 1979, the subcommittee held a third set of hearings meant to shed light on the threats to security interests posed by procedures and practices required of the intelligence community in our free society. This time the problem addressed was the "graymail" phenomenon, in which a defendant in a criminal case argues that he must have and use classified information in his defense. [15] The administration had proposed new procedures which, it contended, would better serve the government's interest in secrecy and the defendant's (and society's) interest in a fair trial. They amounted, in the administration's view, to "modest" changes altering the timing of rulings on relevance and admissibility of evidence. Civil liberties activists were not so sure, however, and urged careful scrutiny of the proposal. But even more significantly, they were disappointed that this issue had been detached from the charter proposal and movement. [16] They feared that any fragmentation of the regulatory effort would dissipate reform momentum by diverting the attention of reformers, dividing their resources, and providing multiple opportunities for pressures toward more permissive rules to prevail.

While the hearings in the House were providing an outlet for warnings that our intelligence agencies could not serve national security properly when bound too tightly by "free society" strictures, events in the Middle East and Persian Gulf provided spectacular evidence of the vulnerability of many of America's far-flung interests in the world. In Iran, which for a quarter-century had stood as a bastion of American presence and influence in the Middle East, the shah's regime tottered under the long-suppressed pressures of internal dissent and revolt, and finally fell. In the midst of convulsive revolutionary turmoil there, the American embassy in Tehran was seized by militants on November 4, 1979, along with fifty-two American hostages imprisoned in the embassy compound. (Several others were trapped in diplomatic legations elsewhere in Tehran.) The Iranian revolution spawned anti-American unrest in Saudi Arabia and Pakistan, too, including an attack on the U.S. embassy in Islamabad a few weeks later.

President Carter and his closest advisors saw these events as "grave threats to world peace."[17] It became known soon thereafter that the president was most displeased with the intelligence agencies because they had failed to detect and monitor these revolutionary impulses in their early stages.[18] That "intelligence failure" left America woefully unprepared for the outburst of anti-shah and anti-American fervor when it did finally occur. Before the year was out, the Soviet Union's invasion of Afghanistan on December 27 redoubled the president's concern for threatened U.S. interests and international stability. The invasion, he observed, constituted "gross interference" by the Soviets in the internal affairs of Afghanistan, in violation of "accepted international rules of behavior" and raising "the most fundamental questions" about world order.[19]

In both cases the administration immediately began to evaluate courses of action available to cope with these developments. Insofar as intelligence operations are concerned, the full extent to which capabilities were activated is of course hardly a matter of public record. But President Carter himself has provided some insight into the kinds of things the intelligence agencies were given permission to do in this time of perceived need. In the case of Iran, American secret agents were early infiltrated into Tehran under various covers to help with rescue plans for American diplomats who had taken refuge in the Canadian embassy.[20] Also, in preparation for the ill-fated military mission to rescue the hostages held in the U.S. embassy compound, the president has now indicated that American agents had "moved freely in and out of Tehran under the guise of business or media missions."[21] His revelations about the use of journalistic cover in this operation immediately caught the eye of watchful observers in the press, who pointed out that the president in this case must have waived his own previously-issued rule against such use.[22]

In the case of Afghanistan, President Carter has indicated that he and his advisors at least considered providing weapons and other aid, through covert channels, to the Afghan freedom fighters conducting guerrilla operations against Soviet occupying forces.[23] The president's account suggests, furthermore, that such a plan may have been thought feasible and actually executed. It would certainly have raised the cost of Soviet activity within Afghanistan, and Mr. Carter was most concerned to insure that the USSR paid a high price for its adventurism.[24] It has been reported elsewhere that the CIA did in fact engage in an operation to aid the Afghan forces and deepen Soviet difficulties in that country.[25]

What was known at the time, of course, was hardly this specific. The president was clearly concerned about the effects of these untoward events on U.S. interests in a most volatile region, and all knew that his attention turned immediately to mobilizing the instruments of foreign policy to cope with these external challenges. It was also clear from the start that he understood their impact in global terms, not simply in terms of regional strategic implications. His annual State of the Union message to Congress, delivered in writing to the legislators on January 21, 1980, repeated that assessment and argued that America now faced some of the most fundamental foreign policy challenges in its history. We must deal, he said, with "a world in which democracy and freedom are still challenged, a world in which peace must be re-won every day."[26]

To equip the nation to respond, the president set a number of legislative priorities, including enactment of a charter for the intelligence agencies. He noted that the lengthy process of consultation with Congress on the previous charter proposal had resulted in a new draft which the administration hoped to introduce for legislative action shortly. He still spoke of the need to define roles and missions as one reason to work for such a charter. But he also noted that "events of the past year" indicated a further need for strengthened intelligence agencies.[27]

Two days later, in his State of the Union address to Congress and the nation, the president observed that "it has never been more clear that the state of our Union depends on the state of the world," and that recent events had served to remind us that the world is a most dangerous place.[28] The prospects – and the goals and hopes and expectations – of America as a society were linked inextricably with developments in the larger world. To see America's internal goals as separated from events in the international arena was an intellectual artifice blind to plain reality. To preserve and protect the "state of the Union" desired by Americans, the nation required (among other steps not relevant here), "quick passage of a new charter to define the legal authority and accountability of our intelligence agencies. We will guarantee that abuses do not recur, but we must tighten our controls on sensitive intelligence information, and we need to remove unwarranted restraints on America's ability to collect intelligence."[29]

This latter declaration – that the intelligence agencies should be liberated from certain operational restraints in the name of national security – had now been raised from the level of "expert" testimony by intelligence officials before Congress to the level of firm and public presidential conviction. Mr. Carter expanded upon that position in a news conference a week later, arguing before the press and the public that the regulatory reform movement had imposed too many burdens and restraints on the intelligence agencies: too many reports to too many committees in Congress, and too many disclosures of sensitive information not protected from the Freedom of Information Act and Privacy Act. He also remarked, significantly, that "there's been an excessive restraint on what the CIA and other intelligence groups could do."[30]

The irony of the president's highly visible posture in favor of stronger and freer intelligence agencies was not lost on some observers who had watched the reform movement closely in recent years, and they were anxious to understand exactly where the president – once a prominent reformer – now stood.[31] Hearings convened (again) by the Subcommittee on Legislation of the House Permanent Select Committee on Intelligence, within a week after the president's remarks, provided a forum for the new perspectives to emerge.

The lead witness was the majority leader of the House, Representative James Wright of Texas, who underlined the importance of passing legislation to revitalize the intelligence agencies, as the president now desired. Though he hoped to do this in the charter effort, his most immediate concern (and the focus of the hearings) was to provide better protection for the agencies from the activities of exposé writers who disclosed the names of intelligence operatives. This, he said, was a priority item on the legislative agenda, and "we in the leadership will certainly be responsive to the requests of those handling the bill on behalf of this subcommittee for early scheduling."[32] Among the further measures then contemplated by members of the subcommittee and others in Congress were reduction in the number of committees to which the intelligence agencies were required to report (then numbering eight and involving perhaps 200 individuals – members of Congress and their staffs) and greater protection for the agencies from the disclosure requirements of the FOIA and the Privacy Act.[33]

The Deputy Director of Central Intelligence also appeared before the subcommittee to argue for remedial legislation on the relatively narrow identities disclosure issue. But he noted, more generally, that in light of "recent events" the president was determined to increase protections for intelligence operations and methods beyond the safeguarding of agents' identities.[34] In his statements, as in the president's own postures, the challenges the world presented for American foreign policy were clearly now a major preoccupation and a major factor shaping regulatory perspectives at top levels in the administration.

In the debate to this point, much of the national security argument in favor of strong and vigorous intelligence agencies had been mainly abstraction, focused upon "threats" about which reasonable men could (and did) differ. Now concrete events made the import and urgency of that argument plain. Even the Department of Justice believed that, although espionage laws already in place were sufficient to cover the exposé activities of concern here, passage of a statute focused specifically on those activities was advisable in order to clarify prohibitions and facilitate enforcement.[35]

Not surprisingly, observers concerned primarily about protecting civil rights and liberties differed sharply with the administration insofar as it appeared to be departing from earlier positions. Their fears stemmed in large part from their sensing that the policy tide was turning against them at the more general level of the charter effort itself.[36] An exchange between Jerry Berman of the American Civil Liberties Union and Representative Edward Boland (chairman of the House intelligence committee) illustrates their concern. Berman began:

We think it would really be in the wrong direction to use or respond to the current crisis and react in a way which removes accountability and removes the public sense that matters are discussable and debatable in this country.

MR. BOLAND.   You would prefer to leave this whole thing hang until we get to the charter legislation because these issues are more narrowly drawn and defined.

MR. BERMAN.   Well, the agencies have been complaining about this problem for a very long time, and they have not moved very fast with this charter, and I don't think anything in Iran or Afghanistan, serious as those matters are, have changed the situation with respect to the names of the agents, the Freedom of Information Act, or Hughes-Ryan. Those are continuing problems.

If they wanted to come up in March of 1978, after you introduced the comprehensive charter, and put a counterproposal on the table, we would have a charter now, or perhaps we would be close to having a charter, but suddenly, the crisis and names of agents have been linked together. Now the agencies believe it is an appropriate time to come forward, get the authorizations and standards that they want, and perhaps leave the charter in the train station. I am afraid that if the kind of package that Senator Moynihan proposed last week, which is what the agencies say they need, and maybe on the merits they need, is passed, I don't think that they are going to come back next year and support the charter restrictions to protect the rights of Americans. That will have gone by the wayside.[37]

The discussion about charter prospects and contending views on the advisability of charters were repeated throughout the hearings, even though their declared focus was much more limited.[38]

As if all this had not made the views of the House intelligence committee plain, as well as those of many other members of Congress and the administration, a week later (on February 6, 1980), its Subcommittee on Oversight began another set of hearings to expose Soviet covert action operations against the United States.[39] Such activities were seen and presented, of course, as part of the "threat" environment surrounding American society. In the subcommittee's view, however, they had not received the public attention they deserved.

In preliminary remarks, one member exhorted administration witnesses to "tell us a little bit about what goes on out there in the real world, about an adversary that is not constrained by congressional oversight or even the same kind of Western morality that most of us advocate."[40] The witnesses, drawn mostly from the CIA, readily obliged, pointing at length and with documentary evidence to Soviet use of propaganda and covert action as a major arm of foreign policy. Soviet capabilities went far beyond political manipulation, it was explained, to embrace terrorist and radical organizations used in furtherance of Soviet purposes abroad.[41]

At this point, too, a renewed charter proposal was introduced, and it was brought quickly to center stage in legislative efforts. As the hearings on narrower issues showed, however, the climate of opinion in Congress had changed importantly. National security interests and rationales, which only a few months earlier had been viewed as suspect, now had regained their prominent place in the search for regulatory principles, alongside concern for civil liberties, for conformance to American ideals, and for adherence to our constitutional design of shared and balanced governmental power.

Renewed Charter Debate

In February 1980 the Senate Select Committee on Intelligence began hearings on S. 2284, the National Intelligence Act of 1980, which was introduced as the successor to the 1978 charter proposal. The earlier debate on S. 2525 had been arduous and prolonged because of profound disagreements about what kinds of structures and complaints to legislate. Now, however, in the 1980 debate, the question of whether or not to legislate at all was far more prominent. There was considerable opinion that a statutory charter might not be an appropriate – or feasible – regulatory device, in view of all the untoward effects said to be associated with it.[42] And even those who still wanted to legislate (a significant number, to be sure) were not convinced that an omnibus, "comprehensive" statute was the correct course to pursue. Alternative, "smaller" charters were proposed, as well as more specific initiatives addressing problems explored in the recent House hearings.

Administration witnesses still went on record in favor of comprehensive charter legislation, especially since the prevailing view in Congress seemed clearly to favor strengthening the agencies. But at the same time they supported more specific proposals to eliminate administrative burdens and rules now viewed as unwise. Although there was nothing inherently contradictory in this bifurcated posture, it was by now clear that the dynamic of legislating small, remedial statutes was working distinctly against the dynamic of legislating a large statute. Energy spent on the smaller problems dissipated resources available for the larger one.

In a real sense, however, the commitments of the administration were dual in nature. It had an obligation to protect the intelligence agencies on behalf of a society needing their capabilities. To that extent it had to argue for elimination of unnecessary constraints. But the administration also had an obligation to control those agencies, and a long-term and public investment in an omnibus charter as the proper means to do that. It had, after all, helped develop both major drafts of that charter (S. 2525 and S. 2284). These positions had been on the public record far too long to abandon so suddenly.

Work on an administration-initiated statutory charter had in fact been in progress since mid-1978. There had been much internal debate about how far to go in constraining the intelligence community, especially for operations conducted within the United States. Vice-President Mondale worked strenuously for tight constraints, as did Attorney General Bell and the State Department. But there were insistent pressures from the intelligence agencies for a freer hand. And, according to some reports, top-level officials of the Defense Department were among the most persistent advocates of more permissive rules.[43]

The competition within the executive branch between these two perspectives was so intense that it emerged in confrontations at the National Security Council. And even in that forum the difficulties were hard to resolve.[44] The ultimate effect was delay in development of a consolidated administration position and proposal, as well as uncertainty about the bonds cementing the alliance which would have to speak for it. By the middle of January 1980 the bargaining within the administration and with Congress had produced agreement on many issues, or at least on enough to warrant bringing the draft and the final negotiating about it into the legislative arena. Hence the introduction of S. 2284.

Senator Huddleston, who again headed the Senate's participation in the drafting of the bill, acknowledged publicly that, while it would codify many existing operational constraints, it would relax some, too.[45] Most notable among these "loosened" regulations and practices were limitation of the impact of the Freedom of Information Act and the Privacy Act on the CIA and other agencies, and modification of the Hughes-Ryan reporting requirements to reduce the number of congressional committees involved (from eight to two). The senator also acknowledged that, in contrast to the mood of the mid-1970s, there was now appreciable sentiment in Congress and among the public for giving the intelligence agencies more operational latitude – in large part because of the crises in Iran and Afghanistan and resulting fears about a hobbled America in an unfriendly world. Indeed, he observed, in the House of Representatives there were many who favored rolling back all of the constraints imposed in the last few years. And there was serious doubt about whether any "comprehensive" statutory charter could be passed in that body. Some attentive critics outside the government, hoping to the end for an ambitious charter, lamented the decline of its prospects.[46] But even for the writer of the comprehensive charter proposal there was no denying these legislative – and political – realities.

In his formal description of the new proposal at the beginning of the

Senate's hearings, Huddleston deemphasized the charter's role as a constraining device and focused attention instead on its enhancement of control and accountability, management functions exercised from atop the administrative hierarchy. [47] There was, as well, a faint note of discouragement and loss of confidence about the bill's prospects because of concurrent efforts to solve specific problems in smaller statutes.

In testimony and resulting exchanges it was evident immediately that the extended executive-congressional bargaining had not resolved all differences. Admiral Turner, the administration's lead witness, disagreed with the bill's approach in several important respects. [48] One was its requirement to report significant anticipated operations to Congress. A statutory requirement for prior notice, Turner argued, was unnecessary and unwise and would also be an unconstitutional interference with the president's powers. The administration preferred that the charter simply codify existing practices by which Congress was informed of sensitive activities in a timely fashion (but not necessarily beforehand). Also, the DCI hoped that the proposal would be amended to give the president authority to waive any of its provisions in wartime or in a War Powers Resolution situation. S. 2284, like the earlier charter proposal, permitted such waivers only for certain specified operations; for others, statutory constraints bound the president irrevocably. The Carter Administration now had to attack it in public as too confining.

The executive also wanted changes in the bill's provisions concerning congressional oversight, and it argued against prohibitions on the use of the media, clerics, or academics as agents or as cover identities. Turner also wanted better protection of all intelligence agencies from the FOIA and the Privacy Act, and explicit proscription of unauthorized disclosure of the identities of intelligence officers, agents, and sources. And finally, he argued for adjustments in the Foreign Intelligence Surveillance Act that would facilitate the targeting of additional categories of people (foreigners within the United States).

Testimony by Attorney General Griffin Bell, FBI Director William Webster, and the director of the National Security Agency, Admiral Bobby Inman, also welcomed the charter proposal, if adjusted in line with the DCI's recommendations. Not surprisingly, given earlier postures in intra-executive negotiations, the Department of Defense was much less enthusiastic about the bill and much more detailed in its description of the untoward effects of unwise legislation. [49]

Hearings in the House had, of course, aired many of these administration positions already. Many in the House had sympathized with them. But in the Senate proceedings, even after months of negotiating, the lines of battle in the charter debate were still defined by unreconciled, and seemingly irreconcilable, views. Those watching the debate could hardly have been blamed for wondering whether the comprehensive charter effort was indeed too ambitious a project, given the irreducible opposition of professionals, as well as many congressmen, to central reformist precepts. All that was, of course, quite separate from the question — which was hotly debated — of whether the charter itself was any longer necessary, in light of executive self-regulation.

Predictably, the views of informed "outside" observers called to testify were sharply split. Some, such as former Director of Central Intelligence James Schlesinger, flatly opposed even the idea of a new, omnibus statute. Others, such as former DCI William Colby, supported it and believed furthermore that this bill would return intelligence regulation "to a sensible middle position" which avoided the exaggeration, sensationalism, and overreaction of previous iterations.[50] But many who hoped for a comprehensive statute were deeply dissatisfied with this version. Any adjustment in the applicability of FOIA provisions, for instance, was adamantly opposed as a retreat from "open government" principles. The American Civil Liberties Union criticized the bill on two major grounds: its preparation in secret bargaining sessions between Congress and the executive, and its abandonment of "nearly every significant principle of reform" that the Church Committee had recommended, that S. 2525 had earlier adopted, and that civil liberties activists held to be central to meaningful regulation. In particular, the lack of a "criminal standard" for initiation of intrusive investigative actions was still the classic civil libertarian barometer for measuring the acceptability of any code of constraints, and the bill failed that test.[51]

The hearings also provided a forum for those who argued against this charter proposal because it did not regulate international activities sufficiently, wholly aside from any domestic applications. From their perspective it did not show enough concern for protecting foreigners under principles of international law dealing with prohibition of aggression and protection of human rights.[52]

Several other aspects of the renewed debate in 1980 indicated that the charter effort itself was in deep trouble, even beyond criticism of its latest offering (S. 2284). First, even after years of consultation and negotiation between the executive and Congress, there still remained sharp disagreement about the role of Congress in monitoring intelligence operations. Debate about the "prior notice" requirement for sensitive operations, which the administration steadfastly resisted, and concern for limiting the number of committees involved in oversight matters, illustrated this. But even more significant was the fact that many members of Congress now clearly and publicly supported the administration, arguing against the most expansive roles for Congress that had been advocated or put in place by reformist pressures. This indicated to many observers that the reform effort had gone about as far as it could on such matters and that the policy pendulum was indeed beginning to swing back the other way.[53]

The same was true for the role of the public in intelligence regulation and oversight. Accountability of intelligence officials to the public, and opening of intelligence files so that the public could discover what those officials and their agents had actually done, had been a major reform goal, supported by arguments about "open government," the public's "right to know," and the need for popular vigilance against abuses of power. Skepticism of governmental power was still evident, to be sure. But it was no longer the dominant sentiment behind congressional pressures for reform. The prevailing view within Congress, as within the executive, seemed clearly to be that a framework for oversight could not be informed by "open government" values alone. The result would simply be too unwieldy, unworkable, and unwise.

It was not that the more sweeping arguments for reform had disappeared. They were resurrected from time to time, but adherents were fewer and more deeply ideological in their rhetoric. They had lost much of their audience in Congress, the policymaking forum in which they had pressed their claims most vigorously, the one in which they had made the most progress, and the one whose institutional interests (in asserting its own power) had aligned generally with their arguments. The diminution of congressional support was, then, a costly loss indeed, sapping the reform movement of substantive weight and vitality and in effect closing down a most lucrative arena in which to showcase evidence and arguments.

All this made quite plain the erosion of support for a comprehensive statute replacing the 1947 National Security Act. And this, many knew, presaged far more important difficulties. The reform movement's substantive goals – imposition of constraints and accountability procedures – had long been linked by reformers themselves to a comprehensive, permanent charter as the only appropriate means to achieve them. All knew therefore that widening disputes about the tools of reform indicated widening reservations also about the goals.

At the conclusion of the Senate hearings (in April 1980) the charter movement was in great disarray: its underpinnings were fractured and its impetus was rapidly dissolving into smaller contests in which many sought to redress agency grievances about burdensome procedures and unwise constraints. The Senate Intelligence Committee, long in the vanguard of the comprehensive charter effort, immediately went to work on shortening and simplifying the proposal.[54] Even with those adjustments, however, it appeared to many observers that the prospects for an omnibus statute were dim in a legislative year foreshortened by political conventions and a presidential election.

In May 1980, in fact, the Senate committee decided it would be impossible to bring a comprehensive charter to the floor of that body before the next congressional session, so it agreed on two courses of action for the remainder of the year: it would report out a much smaller bill intended essentially to revise the Hughes-Ryan reporting requirements, and it would continue active consideration of other issues raised in the debate about the comprehensive charter bill. [55]

The first action was accomplished on May 8, when the committee approved a 750-word bill entitled the "Intelligence Oversight Act of 1980." This was all that then remained of the original charter. It proposed to give the Senate and House intelligence committees the sole authority to oversee the intelligence community, in effect revising the 1974 Hughes-Ryan Amendment by reducing the number of committees receiving notifications about covert action operations. It demanded prior notice of those operations, too, although it left room for the president's authority to take action first and then inform Congress in emergency circumstances. The bill also required the president to keep the intelligence committees "fully and currently informed" of all intelligence activities, and also directed Congress to devise reliable procedures for protecting information given to it. Soon approved in the House, [56] the bill became law in October 1980 as part of that year's Intelligence Authorization Act.

The second commitment made by the Senate intelligence committee in May had been to keep alive other major issues raised by the broader, but abandoned, charter bill. It tried to do that, too, but, significantly, it chose to focus on an issue that had been placed in the forefront of the emerging counterreform movement, largely through the efforts of the House intelligence committee in its recently completed hearings: protection of the identities of intelligence officials, agents, and sources. Senate hearings on that subject began in June and essentially rehearsed old perspectives previously outlined before the House. [57] The committee's favorable report on the bill was most supportive of the intelligence agencies. [58] And this exhausted the committee's energy until the next session of Congress, when it began hearings on another emerging concern: limiting the applicability to intelligence agencies of disclosure requirements ultimately derived from "open government" principles. [59]

The comprehensive charter had died, then, and had left in its place far more modest legislation which essentially ratified existing oversight practices but narrowed them to include a smaller number of persons outside the intelligence community. No operational constraints were enacted in statutory form (beyond the earlier provisions of the Foreign Intelligence Surveillance Act). And the focus of concern even in the Senate — the last fortress of reform fervor — had shifted to grievances about the excesses of reformist zeal. The 96th Congress and President Carter had together brought the work of clandestine intelligence at least partly under the surveillance of a legislative body and had established that general oversight regime by statute. This new statutory framework was a compromise unsatisfying to many who had hoped for broader legislation with more rigorous constraints.[60] But as 1980 ended and President-elect Reagan prepared to assume office, it seemed clear that the reform movement had already had its heyday. Another era was opening.

The Reagan Administration

The new Administration's interest in the intelligence community was evident very soon after Ronald Reagan's election victory. For the first time in the memory of informed observers, a "transition team" was appointed specifically to review and evaluate the activities of the CIA and the other intelligence agencies and to make recommendations about changes. That team quickly gave the president-elect a report which recommended, inter alia, that our national intelligence capabilities be improved and used more aggressively. It envisioned, in particular, an expanded role for covert action and greater emphasis on counterintelligence tools to combat Soviet espionage and international terrorism.[61] Prominent students of national security affairs outside the government publicly urged Mr. Reagan to restore the vitality of intelligence capabilities that had been undermined in "the recent orgy of revelations and restraints."[62] As such themes began to emerge in public, counterpoised viewpoints were energized and a new watchfulness for Reagan Administration postures developed.[63]

The first firm indicators of official views came in the confirmation hearings of William J. Casey, who had been nominated for the position of Director of Central Intelligence. Casey, who had served in the OSS in World War II and who had also been a member of the President's Foreign Intelligence Advisory Board in the Ford Administration, gave early notice that the emphasis would henceforth be on enhancing intelligence capabilities in order to prepare America for the international crises that were likely to arise in the months ahead. In part, this required significant reorientation of public attitudes about intelligence in order to make clear the agencies' important contributions that had been obscured – and, indeed, greatly jeopardized – in the era of reform. Casey indicated that he was going to review the existing set of rules to evaluate their impact on the agencies' effectiveness and to see how restrictions that impair performance might be minimized. He promised to keep the Senate Intelligence Committee informed on those matters and to consider any "input" the committee might offer.[64]

By January 1981 it was already clear, of course, that this input would be importantly influenced by a desire to strengthen the intelligence agencies. There was clear agreement among all members of the Senate committee that the three main operational missions of the agencies – collection of foreign intelligence, covert action, and counterintelligence – must remain intact and be energetically exercised, in the light of international exigencies. As Senator Malcolm Wallop remarked, a "mature nation" needed good intelligence simply to continue to exist with reasonable assurance of security and to compete viably in the world.[65] In itself, of course, this assertion added nothing to the traditional national security rationale supporting active collection operations. But its prominence in congressional perspectives is important, especially in comparison with the views which had prevailed in Congress two years earlier, when recitation of security-oriented formulas was regarded with much skepticism and suspicion. Now in 1981, furthermore, Senators were not afraid to extend those supportive formulas beyond the arena of intelligence collection to embrace also the more controversial covert action and counterintelligence functions, and to do that on the public record.[66]

Further, there were no more attempts to tighten the oversight mechanisms instituted by the new, shortened statutory charter. The statute's brevity was not a matter of concern, nor was its reliance on executive good faith (e.g., on the president's diligence in keeping oversight committees "fully informed"). Legislative attention had clearly moved beyond questions of control to questions of performance: how to insure that the intelligence community can and does in fact help the nation cope with foreign challenges. A particular concern was improvement of the quality of intelligence analysis – an important challenge, to be sure, but a far cry from the committee's earlier preoccupation with intelligence controls and with legislating detailed operational and oversight guidelines.[67]

There was, additionally, action in both houses of Congress on two outstanding proposals to help the agencies: protecting the identities of intelligence personnel and providing some relief from FOIA disclosure requirements. Hearings on the "Intelligence Identities Protection Act" began in the House (the second series of House hearings on this issue) in April.[68] At the end of the 96th Congress, House Majority Leader James Wright had appeared before the intelligence committee to testify strongly in favor of the proposal, as we have already seen. He repeated that performance in the new round of hearings, and in addition Minority Leader Robert Michel also went on record in support of the bill. As before, the hearings provided a forum for restatement of classic pro and con positions, administration witnesses and members of the committee (and other members of Congress) clearly favoring legislated remedies, and groups concerned about restraints on First Amendment freedoms arguing for limitation or rejection of the proposed legislation.

In July the Senate Select Committee began hearings on a bill which would amend the Freedom of Information Act to give intelligence agencies more protection from its disclosure requirements.[69] These hearings, too, aired now-familiar arguments, with the senators themselves indicating much support for the executive contention that such remedial legislation was needed.

The legislation to protect intelligence identities was ultimately enacted, over dwindling objections.[70] But the FOIA relief remained beyond the reach of the counterreformers, to the Reagan Administration's continuing dismay.[71] What was especially important in 1981, however, was the clear commitment, on the part of the congressional oversight committees, to reexamine and if necessary overturn specific accountability and control measures installed in the era of reform. They would do this, moreover, in the face of cautionary arguments about abuse of domestic political values reflected in the Bill of Rights. Thus, the instincts which generated and informed the Reagan Administration's review of intelligence policy were reinforced by similar perspectives in Congress, specifically in the committees charged with responsibility to supervise the intelligence community. The rhetorical climate in 1981 was, then, far different from that which prevailed when the Carter Administration began to write its executive order and charter proposal. Perspectives in the Reagan camp and among its philosophical allies in Congress now made national security the dominant concern, the most frequently heard formula for expressing the major values thought to be at stake, or at risk.

The changed climate of opinion did not mean, however, that proposals to reinvigorate the intelligence agencies had clear sailing thereafter. Within the administration a draft revision of EO 12036 was circulated for study and preliminary comment early in 1981. It had been written by an interagency group that included all agencies responsible for collecting and producing intelligence, but it had not acquired widespread support at policy levels. When it was leaked to the press,[72] there was startled and dismayed reaction at its obvious departures from the Carter executive order.[73] Reports disclosed, for instance, that the draft recommended the following:

(1) In order to reflect a new attitude about intelligence generally, major sections of the order would be renamed. "Restrictions on Intelligence Activities" would become "Conduct of Intelligence Activities." Similarly, "Restrictions on Certain Collection Techniques" would become "Use of Certain Techniques."

(2) The role of the attorney general, which had been enhanced by the Carter directive, would be downgraded, specifically curtailing his power to review and evaluate operations.

(3) The requirement to collect information by the least intrusive means available would be eliminated.

(4) Restrictions on infiltration of domestic organizations for intelligence purposes would be relaxed.

(5) The definition of "United States person" — the category of individual protected by the order — would be narrowed.

(6) Restrictions on certain intrusive techniques would be loosened, and the president's role in approving them would disappear.[74]

(7) The CIA would be permitted in certain circumstances to engage in electronic surveillance within the United States, reversing a Carter Administration prohibition.[75]

The proposal dealt with other matters, too, but even those provisions which were "leaked" convinced many that genuinely radical departures from Carter Administration postures were being planned. Immediately the Reagan leadership attempted to assuage resurrected fears about the direction in which policy was moving. Admiral Bobby Inman, the new deputy director of Central Intelligence, acknowledged that there was indeed much opinion within the administration in favor of removing some operational constraints, particularly in the light of an increased international terrorist threat.[76] But he also made it clear that he personally opposed the sweeping relaxation of current restrictions that some conservative forces in the executive and Congress were seeking. He was as much concerned as anyone about protecting libertarian principles, and the public could be assured that there were others like him watching over the process of developing the new executive order.[77]

Within a few days the White House itself was drawn into the public controversy.[78] Presidential Counsellor Edwin Meese indicated that the final version of the executive order, which the White House hoped to issue in April, would not substantially change CIA roles and functions, nor would it liberate the intelligence agencies from the existing framework of constraints. He did, however, restate an important aim of the policy review then in progress: to improve the nation's ability to cope with terrorism. That, he indicated, could produce some change from the Carter rules, but it would be done for good reason if that proved to be the case. His remarks gave little comfort to some critics, however, who feared that "a new talisman, 'terrorism,' may come to center stage in Washington" to sanctify the reinstatement of dangerous investigative powers in the government.[79]

A revised draft of the order was prepared in May and was again circulated within the administration for review and comment. It, too, was subjected to criticism from "liberals" and "conservatives" alike within the executive, the former arguing that its safeguards against abuse were inadequate and the latter arguing that it did not provide enough operational flexibility. Some officials also argued that the revision had failed to address major deficiencies they saw in the Carter order and was therefore inadequate in that respect. Details of this version appeared in press accounts of the renewed executive debate, and animated criticism arose once again.[80]

Another draft began to circulate for executive branch review in September and October. At about that time the administration, in order to inform the public about the need for vigorous intelligence agencies, also began to publicize information about specific Soviet intelligence activities inimical to U.S. interests and the interests of international peace.[81] Administration officials briefed Congress about the draft in closed hearings, specifically declining to do so in public hearings.[82] But that was to no avail; critics in both the Senate and the House objected to the proposal as too permissive.[83] Particular concern was raised by provisions that would give the attorney general authority to approve use of intrusive techniques, such as mail opening, without obtaining a judicial warrant. The order also contemplated removing prohibitions on CIA covert action and infiltration of domestic organizations within the United States as long as such operations were not intended to influence official policies or politics. That brought objections from those who believed CIA operations must be kept outside the borders of the United States in order to preserve the agency's role as a foreign intelligence arm.

As review of the draft progressed in Congress, it became apparent that the administration would face bipartisan opposition on the Hill if it did not try to accomodate these reservations. By early November, strongly worded senatorial warnings were being communicated privately but directly to the White House.[84] Shortly thereafter the administration abandoned some of the proposals that had been singled out as most objectionable, including the authority for domestic infiltration activity by the CIA. Still there were critics inside and outside of Congress who were not satisfied.[85] When they evaluated the draft order in the light of other initiatives, such as the attempt to limit use of the Freedom of Information Act and to criminalize disclosure of intelligence agents' identities, they saw "a systematic assault on the concept of Government accountability and deterrence of illegal Government conduct."[86] They awaited issuance of the new executive order with no little sense of trepidation.

The New Rules

On December 4, 1981, President Reagan issued two executive orders, one to govern the activities of the nation's intelligence agencies (EO 12333) and a separate one to reconstitute the Intelligence Oversight Board (EO 12334). Together, he said, the orders were designed to provide clearer and more positive guidance for the intelligence community and "to remove the aura of suspicion and mistrust that can hobble our nation's intelligence efforts." The orders also reflected his belief that the misperceptions and regulatory overreactions of the past must be set aside in devising and implementing rules for the 1980s. With these orders he fully intended to chart a new course to enhance the strength and efficiency of the agencies, despite the objections still raised in some corners of the debate. This was required in order to improve the president's ability to defend the nation against pressing external threats.[87]

The administration was by this time on record, of course, with a multitude of descriptions of these perceived threats and of the behavioral imperatives derived from them. Most importantly, as Secretary of State Alexander Haig had recently observed, there would be no relief from Soviet antagonism, belligerence, and interventionism worldwide.[88] Dealing with the Soviets would require renewed American strength and the will to use it in defense of American ideals. And one part of the program of enhancing and using strength, as the president had indicated, was the reenergizing of intelligence.

President Reagan knew that this would be controversial, despite the growing number of sympathetic voices in Congress and elsewhere. But he urged critics who remembered past abuses to free themselves and their thinking about operational constraints from those memories. They were not indicative of how this president or this administration would behave. If existing laws and rules were not sufficient in themselves to inspire public trust and confidence in the intelligence agencies, then faith in the character and good intentions of the man directing them might suffice.

But in an important sense these public utterances were mainly atmospherics. When the public had a chance to examine the directive in detail, they found the "new direction" clearly stated on every page. The order's most significant themes were the following:

(1) Enhancement of operational capabilities as the overriding purpose. Part Two of the new directive was the direct descendant of the 1978 list of operational restrictions in EO 12036. It was, however, retitled, as it had been in the earlier drafts, as "Conduct of Intelligence Activities," in lieu of "Restrictions on Intelligence Activities." It began, moreover, with a statement of the need for vigorous intelligence operations and a frank description of the purpose of the order: "This Order is intended to enhance human and technical collection techniques, especially those undertaken abroad, and the acquisition of foreign intelligence, as well as the detection and countering of international terrorist activities and espionage conducted by foreign powers."[89]

Though this part of the order does specify which activities are permitted and which are not, the word "restriction," so prominent in the Carter order, never appears. Provisions are phrased in terms of "authorizations" (except for a flat prohibition of assassination), and constraints are then stated as exceptions to authorized activity. As a result, the language of the new directive is much more positive than either previous executive order. This reflected the more affirmative attitude now dominant in the administration, but more than rhetorical nuance was involved. The authorizations stated in the order, and the exceptions to them, were given special meaning by the context of purpose in which they were announced. It was clear from that context that the rules had been shaped mainly by considerations based on a sense of external threat. The Carter Administration had known about that threat, too, but its order had also deliberately served other values, at clearly recognized cost to efficiency and security, in the rules it announced. In this respect alone the new directive evidenced a new, more aggressive operational ethos now ruling the business of intelligence.

(2) Raised expectations for intelligence operations, and the role of law and constitutional rights. President Carter's executive order had demanded "adherence to law" and had required that the measures used to acquire information necessary for national security decisionmaking "should be *responsive* to legitimate governmental needs and must be conducted in a manner that *preserves* and respects established concepts of privacy and civil liberties."[90] The intelligence agencies were thus directed to stay within the clear confines of law and to hold inviolate the well-recognized spheres of individual rights implicated by particular operations. The message to operators and their managers was clear: find authority in law for what you want to undertake; wherever the boundaries of individual rights are now drawn, they delimit a true sanctuary forbidden to governmental intrusion. It was not a message calculated to excite operational enthusiasm or initiative.

Similarly, the Carter order (and the order issued in 1976 by President Ford) had instructed operators to respond to governmental needs, but this is not quite the same as levying on the agencies a mission to satisfy those needs. Intelligence operations should, indeed, attempt to satisfy them; the Carter order was not a codification of excuses for failure. But operational success was not an explicit expectation. It was a hope that might not be fulfilled for any number of reasons, including the intervention of other values indicating that collection capabilities must be confined.

The Reagan order was very different in all respects. In the first place its introductory phrases assigned the intelligence agencies the responsibility, indeed, the mission, to satisfy – not just react to – governmental information needs. The directive further instructed the agencies that "all means consistent with applicable United States law and this Order, and with full consideration of the rights of United States persons, shall be used to develop information for the President and the National Security Council."[91] And in the text's preamble the agencies were told that "all reasonable and lawful means must be used to ensure that the United States will receive the best intelligence available." The mere fact that these exhortations were included as part of the foundation document for the intelligence community was in itself of no small significance. But even more important was the substance of these admonitions when compared to principles expressed and perspectives evident in the Carter order. Intelligence operations were now to be "consistent with" law, which meant essentially that if an activity was not prohibited by law, then the intelligence agencies could be directed to do it. The law, in this view, exists as a body of prohibitory rules with which operations must surely comply, but in areas where no such rules exist, there is no impediment to intelligence activity unless the operational approval process states one as a matter of policy or practicality. And that operational approval process was to be informed in large part by the overarching statement of mission: to inform the president and his advisors. The new executive charter was no timid, self-denying document. It assigned missions and told the agencies to get on with them.

Similarly, the weight now accorded to the constitutional rights of the individual was different from that of 1978. In choosing among the methods available to them to satisfy the government's informational needs, the agencies were told to give "full consideration" to spheres of individual rights that might be affected, but there was no instruction to preserve those spheres inviolate. There was room for those domestic political values to lose in the balancing process that arrayed them against perceived operational imperatives.

This point must be made clear here: the Reagan Administration did not condone or encourage lawless or unconstitutional behavior in its executive order. Quite the contrary — it recognized the major competing interests and attempted to reconcile them. It did not, however, as a matter of national policy, adopt a presumption in favor of individual rights over satisfaction of governmental information needs. The Carter Administration had done exactly that, preempting the process of balancing that might otherwise have been conducted in the review of individual operational proposals, and specifying the primacy of "established" constitutional principles confining governmental power. The Reagan Administration reintroduced the balancing approach and trusted the operational approval process to do it well in specific cases.

(3) Disappearance of "propriety" as a standard for evaluating activities. In the Carter Administration, the executive oversight mechanisms supervised and administered by the Intelligence Oversight Board were designed and instructed to discover evidence of improprieties as well as illegalities. President Reagan's oversight institutions had no such instruction. His executive order reconstituting the Intelligence Oversight Board, issued the same day but separately from EO 12333,[92] said only that the IOB had been created "to enhance the security of the United States by assuring the legality of activities of the intelligence community," and it directed the board to report to the president activities which any member believed might violate

law or executive directives. Beyond the proscriptions of law, however, the new order discarded the notion of propriety as an additional criterion against which to measure operations.

(4) Treatment of counterintelligence as a tool of foreign policy as well as national security. President Carter's executive order had shown heightened concern for counterintelligence by identifying specific national-level responsibilities and functions with respect to that discipline. The Reagan directive went even further, declaring early in its general instructions that "Special emphasis should be given to detecting and countering espionage and other threats and activities directed by foreign intelligence services against the United States Government, or United States corporations, establishments or persons."[93] Although information about external events was clearly necessary for decisionmaking, that was not the only intelligence capability which needed to be reenergized in the light of perceived international imperatives. There was also a pressing need to be able to defend vigorously against security threats.

It is also significant here that the Reagan Administration had explicitly adopted a rather broad concept of the kind of security interests which might be vulnerable to foreign spying or disruption and which must therefore be protected. A governmental interest was asserted, for instance, in protecting private corporations or "establishments."[94] This widened scope of counterintelligence interest reflected a broader policy, then just emerging on the public record, to close down Soviet access to American technology in hopes of maximizing U.S. advantages in the superpower competition. It was not just government secrets and the official decisionmaking process that needed protection; it was the entire product of our national technical energies, which could be stolen and turned against us, directly or indirectly, by our military competitors, notably the Soviet Union.[95] Vigorous counterintelligence capabilities would clearly have much to contribute to protection of those resources, and EO 12333 laid the groundwork for exactly that contribution.

(5) Disappearance of the inclination to move responsibility upward. As the era of reform had gathered momentum, the tendency had been for operational approval authority, and responsibility for reviews of ongoing activities, to move upward. The order issued by President Reagan reversed that process and also substantially decreased the personal involvement of the president in the control framework. He was, of course, still responsible in a general sense for the activities of his executive branch. And he was still responsible for approving covert action operations, after review of proposals by the NSC – this procedure was required by statute. But in other respects his role receded. In the case of sensitive collection operations, where the Carter directive had required the president to state standards for the NSC review and approval process, no such presidential involvement was con-

templated in the Reagan order.[96] Further, the 1978 directive had indicated that the president would establish standards and criteria for determining which counterintelligence operations must be elevated to the NSC for approval. No such presidential guidance was promised by the Reagan order.[97]

Treatment of duties assigned to the NSC was also different. In the Carter administration, authority assigned to the NSC was to be exercised, whether in the Policy Review Committee or in the Special Coordination Committee, by a body whose membership included the secretaries of defense and state. And in the case of the SCC, when it performed its operational review and approval functions, there was no provision for those persons to designate others to act for them. In the new directive, however, the NSC was permitted to create subordinate committees to discharge its functions, including principally the preparing of recommendations on covert action proposals and the reviewing of proposals for sensitive collection operations.[98] In January 1982 Mr. Reagan announced that such a subcommittee had in fact been formed: a "Senior Interagency Group – Intelligence," consisting of the director of Central Intelligence (acting as chairman), the assistant to the president for national security affairs, the deputy secretaries of state and defense, and the chairman of the Joint Chiefs of Staff.[99] One of the duties specifically assigned to this committee was to review collection and counterintelligence proposals submitted by the DCI for approval. Cabinet-level officials were no longer required to be involved in the review and approval process, however, at least for those kinds of operations, and the chairmanship of the reviewing body was entrusted to the nation's chief intelligence officer. (The Carter Administration had vested that responsibility in the national security advisor.) In both respects the Reagan order provided evidence that the impetus to move responsibility upward and away from intelligence officials had begun to dissipate. Informed observers noted this immediately, and some, including President Carter's director of Central Intelligence, Admiral Turner, regretted it, fearing that the Reagan Administration had too hastily decided that a rigorous process of clearance would diminish the quality of intelligence.[100]

The Reagan order, additionally, discarded the previous directive's requirement[101] that any dissents from the NSC's covert action recommendations must be given to the president along with the majority assessment. It is of course true that a dissenter in the Reagan Administration might well obtain a presidential hearing on his views, whether the order said so or not. But that entitlement was not made plain in the executive order, a clear departure from the Carter approach, which had gone to great lengths to publicize the image of an enlightened national leadership making clear choices among values and upholding central ones against baser instincts.

The order issued by President Carter had further provided for presidential authorization of types of intrusive techniques that could thereafter be used by the intelligence agencies upon the attorney general's approval.[102] This reflected the Carter Administration's sensitivity to criticism of the "non-criminal" standard governing decisions about intelligence operations. It did not retreat from that special standard, but it made application of it a Cabinet-level matter, with some involvement on the part of the president. The Reagan order addressed that issue, too, but again eliminated the requirement that the president be involved even in approving general categories of activities, assigning that authority to the attorney general.[103]

(6) Overall diminution of the attorney general's role and influence. It would be a mistake to conclude, on the basis of the approval authority which devolved upon the attorney general from the president, that his role and influence had therefore been expanded. In fact and on balance, the opposite was the case. Under EO 12036 the attorney general had been firmly installed in the NSC's operational review and approval process. He was expected to evaluate and approve operational practices, and he also performed important oversight functions. Under EO 12333, he retained several prominent and significant functions, particularly in relation to oversight. But in other areas his role was reduced. For instance, whereas the Carter order had required his attendance as a full participant at NSC meetings on operational approvals, the Reagan order did not.[104] Additionally, he was empowered, as before, to approve procedures for using operational techniques, but now if he disapproved of any of those procedures written by agencies other than the FBI, he had to provide a statement of reasons for the disapproval.[105] If the reasons were other than constitutional or legal, the NSC – the nation's political leadership – would then provide guidance about resolving any continuing disagreement. The attorney general's sphere of special competence was, in essence, limited to legal advice, or to the boundaries of his official duties. Outside those boundaries his advice was worth no more than that of others, including the intelligence professionals, at least on the face of EO 12333.[106]

(7) Revised definitions that expand the sphere of permissible activity. Two definitions were notable here. The first was the treatment of "United States person," the category of individual whose privacy rights were protected by the order against governmental abuse. The Carter order had defined the types of people and organizations within that category and had conferred protected status on them regardless of whether their qualification for that protection was known to the intelligence agencies, and, in the case of corporations, regardless of whether they might be extensions of a foreign government. The Reagan order modified the definition so that protected status was not so automatically conferred, and so that the agencies were not so automatically disarmed.[107]

A second definitional change worthy of note pertained to "special activities." The new order appeared to permit certain unspecified aspects of covert action operations to be carried out in the United States as long as they were "not intended to influence United States political processes, public opinion, policies, or media."[108] This provision, too, quickly caught the eye of knowledgeable observers sensitive to any increase in CIA authority to operate at home.[109] Fears were raised also by the order's explicit language permitting CIA collection and CI operations in the United States upon coordination with the FBI.

(8) More discretion at lower levels to choose operational techniques based on considerations of effectiveness. President Carter's order had required that the procedures for using operational techniques must set aside "more intrusive" techniques if operational success might arguably be achieved by "less intrusive" means.[110] This formula in essence immobilized much of the nation's collection capability whenever that capability confronted a person protected by the order. The amount of capability immobilized depended, to be sure, upon one's perspective on degrees of intrusiveness. But once the rights of a United States person were implicated, some kinds of activities were precluded at the outset. The Reagan approach, by contrast, permitted operators and their managers to select techniques based on their own appraisal of "feasibility" – the prospects for success.[111] Even though the rights of a protected person or organization might be affected, the Reagan formula allowed a very intrusive technique to be selected at the outset, based on an expert evaluation of operational necessities. After all, the overarching thrust of the executive order, as we have seen, was to improve the agencies' performance. In that respect it is not surprising that it made more room in the decisionmaking process for the professionals' views about what must be done.

Provision-by-provision dissection of the rules announced in the Reagan order would identify many additional differences from the Carter approach.[112] But that analysis would only cumulate evidence about what should already be eminently clear: that the Reagan executive order was firmly focused on its appointed task—enhancement of operational performance by elimination of burdensome procedures and restraints now thought unwise. The pattern of emerging purposes was now plainly laid out on the public record – renewal and reinvigoration was the goal. And once the executive order was announced, quality of performance, not liberation from rules, would become the main concern.

The Reagan Administration had stood solidly in support of the contentious distinction between law enforcement and counterintelligence, the touchstone of civil liberties concern. Indeed, EO 12333 made administrative control procedures for CI somewhat less burdensome than before by eliminating the requirement for presidential participation in the authorizing process. And even in writing definitions of the categories of persons whose rights were protected, the Reagan Administration revised prior formulas in ways that permitted more operational latitude, not less.

Similarly, on a second touchstone of the public debate, the role of extralegal policy considerations in shaping constraints, the Reagan perspective disappointed the advocates of "ideals" or "values" as independent sources of rules. Illustrative was the executive order's circumscribing of the sphere in which the attorney general's evaluation of operational procedures was to be taken as authoritative.

Even more generally, the administration argued repeatedly that there was no inherent, irreconcilable conflict of values between intelligence capabilities and the protections for citizens recognized in the law. Both serve the same ends: preservation of an orderly and secure American society. As a result, no argument based on "values" could be used to deprive the nation of self-preservation tools exercised by competitor states and therefore mandated by the realities of international politics. Obviously, one could take that argument too far, and the Reagan Administration knew this. But at the level of general perspective, President Reagan declared that there was no special sanctity about "restraint" arguments that were couched in terms of conformance to traditional American ideals. Equally cogent value-based arguments supported the maintenance of sufficient strength to insure the international viability and vitality of American society. And the Reagan administration intended to make sure that the latter perspectives were not eclipsed by the former.

With regard to participation of other, extra-executive institutions in the operational control framework, Reagan postures maintained the status quo inherited from the Carter years. The "shrunken" legislative charter had already reduced the number of congressional committees to which the intelligence community had to report, and there was of course no inclination in the administration to widen that practice. Defenses were also maintained against further expansion of the roles of the judiciary in the intelligence arena. The administration did show concern about, and tried repeatedly to limit, public access to intelligence information and public surveillance of intelligence affairs. This was most visible in attempts to limit the application of the Freedom of Information Act to the intelligence agencies. So to the extent that the Reagan forces showed any movement on the third barometer of official policy, they again disappointed observers who had been pleased about the "open government" and "accountability" achievements of the era of reform.

The extent to which operational performance was in fact improved or even affected by all this is of course not a matter of public record. And in any event final judgment on that point must await the passage of time. Nevertheless, from time to time there have been indicators that the Reagan

Administration has attempted to put into practice the more aggressive themes preached in the executive order in the interests of operational efficiency and effectiveness. In one report published shortly after the order was issued, senior officials described new "cover" practices that had been instituted at the DCI's initiative.[113] These were intended to provide more security for collection operations abroad, and they involved increased use of private commercial identities rather than diplomatic. As William Casey then noted in a public interview, it was unlikely that the nation's intelligence-gathering capability would be quickly restored to the position of strength the administration felt was needed in the 1980s, but the intelligence community had been given "a general go-ahead to carry out that buildup."[114] Deputy Director of Central Intelligence Inman further noted that, although the intelligence community was then only "marginally capable" of meeting future requirements, the administration knew what the major deficiences were and was attending to them. Notable among these deficiences, he said, was overemphasis on technical means of collection at the expense of classic human espionage.[115]

Covert action, too, was an area of operational capability in which the administration was concerned to maintain strength, and it did not shrink from saying so in public.[116] This was a subject of some controversy; a number of observers were still not convinced that this was a business in which America ought to be engaged.[117] Others, of course, *were* so persuaded. In the Senate, once a paramount reform forum, ninety-nine senators coauthored a resolution asking the administration to increase covert aid to the Afghan guerrillas resisting Soviet occupation troops.[118] But independently of that admonition the renewal of covert action begun in the latter part of the Carter Administration was carried forward under President Reagan. Early disclosures about operations in Central America, notably to finance, train, and arm exile groups opposing the Sandinist regime in Nicaragua, were later confirmed.[119] It was also reported in the national press that as many as ten other such operations were being conducted, including the one in Afghanistan, which had been reported earlier but never officially acknowledged.[120]

Intelligence activities which might affect the constitutional rights of individual Americas but which were intended to defend the society at large against foreign threats were a major concern of the Reagan Administration, as evidenced in public statements and in the new executive order itself. This was an area in which operational rules continued to be tested and redefined in public forums, notably in the courts, where major issues were still working their way through the litigation process.[121] Continuing public sensitivity about the matter was shown graphically in the immediate alarmed reaction to the resignation of Admiral Inman, effective July 1, 1982. The departure of Inman, a noted believer in much of the civil libertarian perspective on intelligence operations, was seen by many as a product of the overwhelming momentum behind an "unleash the intelligence agencies" movement — a movement many understood to be led by presidential advisors in the White House.[122] In this view, Inman, grown tired of the ceaseless struggle for a losing cause, simply retired from the battlefield. The administration and Inman himself denied this, but these sensitivities and suspicions still hung palpably in the air as the Reagan program moved onward.[123]

7

The Critique and the Debate: An Overview

In John LeCarre's popular novel about British intelligence *Tinker, Tailor, Soldier, Spy,* one of the major characters, looking back over his many years in the business of espionage, muses aloud that a nation's intelligence service is the only real measure of its political health, the one true expression of its collective subconscious. Perhaps as no other national institution, it embodies the societal psyche, reflecting interwoven images of national "self" and alien "other." As we in America look back over the last decade's intelligence debate, it is plain that a good many of us in that time came to share that view. From that perspective, the long and painful inquiry into intelligence control issues now appears as nothing less than a public probing of the nation's soul, a probing which uncovered sometimes disquieting perceptions of men, of the nation's needs, and of the nature of the world at large.

The debate at times seemed directionless, even dizzying, as it thrashed through a profusion of complicated problems and grappled with contending perspectives on how to resolve them. At first, perhaps understandably, the nation's policymaking institutions responded to those issues which had received the most public attention and for which pressures for action had become the most compelling. Later, in the era of "counterreform," concern focused on ameliorating the most objectionable side-effects of measures taken earlier to enhance control and accountability. In retrospect, however, it is clear that in neither case did the rulemaking effort explore the length and breadth of issues raised or implicit in the public critique. Important problems were left unaddressed in the interstices of a regulatory agenda forged, ad hoc, in the heat of controversy.

Nor was the explicit debate often able to illuminate the underlying tension of grand values at its center – the conflict of world views and national self-images which defined the most basic decisionmaking dilemmas and explained their persistence. There was, to be sure, a kind of peripheral awareness of the dimensions of this hidden, unarticulated agenda. Some participants sensed this more clearly than others. For them, the result of the inquiry – a series of executive orders and associated coordination routines – seemed little more than a patchwork of rules and procedures thrown over larger problems of setting national directions and defining national purposes in a self-conscious and open manner. But for the most part the regulators themselves were not anxious to tarry over the extended public probing that would require. For them – or for those of them examined here – it was as if they were struggling through a dismal regulatory swamp as they prepared their own policy postures. Once having waded to solid ground they were anxious to push onward, away from the marshes, rules tucked safely under their arms as charms against the night. None wanted to peer back through the reeds to see what demons had been roused by their hurried passage.

It is not, of course, that the haphazardly composed explicit agenda and the record of official response were insignificant. As we pause here to take stock of what we have seen in this study, a sense of impressive – if uneven – effort and accomplishment emerges. Yet it seems singularly unsatisfying, too, for we know that there are lingering questions unanswered. Or, to return to the earlier metaphor, we know that the demons now lie awake in the darkened marshes, waiting for the next set of regulators to come through.

The Explicit Issues and Arguments

This book has traced the gradual development of a critique of intelligence that began with the work of scholars in the 1950s and early 1960s. Working from the detached vantage point of the universities, and in several cases using insights drawn from their own or others' service in government, they early identified many of the issues relating to control of intelligence operations which were to become, in the 1970s, the object of so much concern, even consternation, and remedial action. The prospect of unacceptable intrusion on individual liberties in the name of national security was outlined, even though there was as yet no publicized pattern of arguable abuses to drive the point home for an American public caught up in the Cold War's confrontational ethos. Also outlined was the equally perplexing problem of making American behavior abroad reflect, to one degree or another, the traditional liberal and humanitarian ideals at the center of the nation's collective self-image. And the work of these early observers explored as well the challenge of fitting intelligence activity into the Constitution's design of shared, balanced, and accountable governmental power. All these themes reemerged in the public debate of the 1970s, given special urgency by the revelations and allegations which flew about, substantiated and unsubstantiated, beneath the pyrotechnics of widespread public alarm and surprise. To make matters worse, even by that time the American public had acquired no enduring, explicit understanding of intelligence functions, purposes, and rationales. The critique of the 1970s, in a context of national self-questioning about the uses and ends of power, struck quite literally at the very foundations of an intelligence community whose place in the governmental and societal fabric was not well understood.

Criticism converged, in the final analysis, on several major questions or problems which thereafter served, for many observers, as touchstones in the debate and as barometers of official reaction to pressures for reform. The first of these reflected the tension between advocates and defenders of civil liberties, on the one hand, and proponents of vigorous national security instruments, on the other. It centered on the special distinction, well-recognized in policy and in law, between activities undertaken for the purposes of preserving domestic law and order and activities undertaken for purposes of foreign intelligence or counterintelligence. The instruments of government which served domestic law enforcement needs had tradi-tionally been confined and controlled by one set of rules, procedures, and constraints, while the instruments having significant external missions or supported by national security rationales were governed by another, more permissive set. The special status of foreign intelligence and counterin-telligence had to do essentially with the thresholds at which operations could begin to monitor American citizens, and with the institutions and officials required to participate in authorizing such activity. In the case of national security operations, the monitoring could begin earlier than in criminal investigations, in which the procedural and substantive provisions of the Fourth Amendment were rigorously applied, and decisions about those operations were left mainly in executive hands.

Civil libertarian pressures against those more permissive rules were exerted in Congress, in the courts, in executive councils, and in various corners of the public debate for a decade. Their argument amounted in essence to the proposition that all instruments of government which threat-en the civil rights of citizens must be ruled by the same principles, procedures, and regulations, whether they are directed at antisocial forces at home in the name of law and order or at anti-American forces anywhere in the name of national security. Tools of foreign policy which may also be asked to cope with threats within our borders must be confined by the same constraints as internal tools when they implicate the privacy rights of Americans. Advocates of this perspective urged the writers of intelligence controls to jettison the "non-criminal," or "national security," standard for initiating intrusive investigative activities against Americans, and to re-quire that all such operations be authorized by a judicial warrant issued after a showing of probable cause to believe a crime has been or may be committed.

The countervailing argument insisted that those procedural and substantive strictures were too confining, given the nature of the security threat involved and the magnitude of the potential costs attending failure to cope with that threat. For the most part, domestic law enforcement institutions must combat and counter singular instances of illegal activity, or perhaps certain patterns of activity generated by habitual miscreants whose purpose is only to serve their own personal interests but not to destroy the society as a whole. Indeed, it could be argued that criminals depend on the continued existence of the society whose energies they pirate and whose openness they exploit. In stark contrast, the operational techniques of the intelligence community must combat the concerted, persistent activities of hostile forces whose unchanging design is to destroy or appreciably weaken the American nation in its competition with other nations. This enduring security threat is of such importance as to justify more permissive rules for the policy tools which must counter it. The interests of American society in the aggregate are not arrayed here against the interests of individual privacy and liberty at home. They stand against the interests of other societies whose purposes, vis-a-vis the United States, are at least competitive and often combative. From this standpoint, it was argued, there are more numerous and more serious factors involved in the "balancing" process than the civil libertarian perspective will admit, and these make, or should make, a difference in the kinds of controls devised for intelligence capabilities.

The second touchstone in the public debate dealt with the argument that America must confine its international activity within boundaries of permissibility that have been shaped by "fair-play" ideals, or by humanitarian values, or — somewhat less frequently — by principles said to be derived from international law. Values which are at the center of American political culture, including belief in democratic principles and practices and respect for human dignity, must govern the nation's official behavior abroad. This is so, and must be so, even though other nations devoted to different and even antithetical values may behave quite differently. America is not the kind of nation that conspires to kill foreign leaders or that secretly manipulates the politics of other societies in order to create a more compatible world. America stands for more than that. Certainly there are risks involved in abstaining from practices that others have apparently adopted as part and parcel of their behavioral repertoire. But choices about instruments of policy are also choices about the purposes and values which policy must serve. They express and define and ultimately help to shape the society which uses them. Ideals at the center of the American essence are, if not truly distinctive, then at least different from those animating hostile competitors. And that difference is precisely what the international competition is all about, what in the final analysis must be defended and preserved at all costs. The struggle for survival in the world at large must not press

American behavior toward that of less restrained, less principled enemies, or else the struggle will have been lost in the only way that really counts.

This perspective argued for specific prohibitions, in published rules, of specific actions thought to be incompatible with American ideals, such as assassinations or the influencing of foreign electoral (particularly democratic) processes. Its proponents wanted prohibitions not only regarding the kinds of operations America might undertake, but also regarding the kinds of mechanisms (types of agents, covers, and so forth) that might be used in those activities declared permissible.

The contrary argument came from those who were not persuaded that traditional American principles worked against the maintenance and exercise of important self-defense capabilities, or against the strength and activities needed to help the nation navigate through an uncertain future. No one argued that America must kill foreign leaders in order to survive, or that the tools of policy must work secretly and incessantly everywhere to engineer a compatible world. But many believed that the national government had an obligation to the society which it served to maintain effective intelligence-gathering tools and also to install in its apparatus some capability to influence foreign events. This perspective naturally resisted attempts to eliminate or to confine such capabilities, and it saw the more radical or strident arguments for restraint as unrealistic and dangerous.

The third focus of the critique, and the major arena of contention, was largely about institutions: what roles should Congress and the courts (and, in some formulations, the public) play in creating and administering rules and controls? The central problem lay in supervising executive branch power and making it accountable. Contentious issues were raised about either invading or asserting authorities said to be assigned to one branch or another in our Constitution's design. Those concerned about codifying control procedures and constraints were not satisfied with oversight mechanisms devised and operated solely within the executive branch. They believed that the constitutional mandate of checks and balances, or of shared governmental power, required more surveillance of the executive's intelligence activities by coordinate branches of government. There was a wide array of expectations in this regard. Many hoped for assertion of the legislature's regulatory authority in a new, comprehensive statutory charter that would explicitly authorize all intelligence activities. They also wanted to state clear operational prohibitions and establish responsibilities and procedures for enforcing them. Others wanted even more: to insert the relevant committees of Congress into the process of reviewing and essentially approving operational proposals before the intelligence community implemented them. There were parallel arguments for close and continuous congressional review of ongoing and completed operations. Some critics also wanted to involve the judiciary in scrutinizing operational proposals that entailed significant intrusion into the private lives of American citizens.

At the center of this critique were serious reservations about the extent to which we as a nation could and should trust executive officials to discharge their duties faithfully — that is, within the letter and spirit of the law and in conformance with traditional American values. This viewpoint argued that we must, in the end, place our collective trust not in men but in institutionalized rules and procedures that make plain the limits of permissibility and that facilitate the patrolling of those boundaries and the discovery of mistakes and venality. In this imperfect world, and in light of the kind of society that America tries to be, rulemaking should move in the direction of supervising the executive, not in the direction of liberating him from restraint.

The opposing perspective recognized that external (in the sense of extra-executive) review mechanisms had an important constitutional role to play, but it was more optimistic, or more charitable, in its expectations about executive performance. It was receptive to some collaborative interaction, but it also drew a firm line at recommended procedures which seemed to interfere with the president's responsibility — and therefore his right vis-a-vis the other branches of governement — to take action that he felt was required by the foreign affairs and national security interests of the society he had been elected to serve, represent, and defend. Advocates of this viewpoint did not object to legislative renewal of the intelligence community's foundation statute. But they had deep reservations about formalized, publicized lists of operational inventories, which is the way they tended to see detailed descriptions of authorizations and prohibitions. They also hesitated at suggestions that other branches should participate in the planning, proposing, and approving of collection and covert action operations, though many were prepared to recognize a somewhat larger sphere for collaboration in counterintelligence in view of the important civil liberties values implicated. And this perspective was always concerned about the chilling effects of open scrutiny of any operational capabilities. It tended to prefer after-the-fact reviews of executive actions, conducted by only a few responsible outsiders, who would keep their judgments and recommendations within specific, and nonpublic, channels.

Governmental Performance

The Ford Administration's response to the intelligence critique disappointed many who were convinced that serious reform was needed. Its specially-appointed commission to investigate the CIA's domestic activities proposed nothing truly innovative. The president's executive order frustrated civil libertarians by ratifying the contested distinction between law enforcement and counterintelligence. And though the order required a good deal more awareness among operators of rules and boundaries for operations, its restrictions did not significantly constrict the arena of CI authority. It prohibited mainly what was already against the law, and it provided some internal mechanisms (such as elevated approval authority) which rationalized and facilitated executive self-control.

More disruptive within the intelligence community were the disclosure requirements of the Freedom of Information and Privacy Acts, which imposed distracting administrative burdens and frightened away potential sources and agents. Also important was the "chilling" effect of lawsuits for money damages, as operators and their managers faced the prospect of civil liability if after-the-fact disclosures revealed challengeable activities. This tended to deaden initiative and enterprise in a profession reliant on intellectual creativity and operational vitality. There was also a growing morale problem among human intelligence and CI operators, who felt deeply the criticisms that argued that their work was outside the boundaries of law and morals.

President Ford's focus on the law – or as some said his inclination to take refuge in expansive interpretations of what the law allowed – also affected his postures on incorporation of extralegal policy considerations (or "ideals") as operational constraints. He was willing to recognize and live by ideals which had been made visible in American law, but beyond a prohibition of assassination he did not reach out for other "value-based" restrictions.

The Ford Administration cooperated with congressional inquisitors during the long Senate and House investigations, and agreed to important collaborative procedures with Congress thereafter. It also indicated willingness for the courts to play a limited – but new – role in reviewing some operational proposals having important implications for citizens' rights of privacy. But it surrendered no executive power, nor any arguments about executive power, to manage the business of intelligence. It was determined, in fact, to defend that authority, and the executive order and associated positions in Congress and in the courts reflected that conviction.

In important respects Carter Administration policies underwent two phases of development. In the early phase arguments for constraints had ascendancy. The FISA was enacted with administration support, the administration's own charter detailing restrictions was issued, collaboration with Congress was initiated on a comprehensive statutory charter, and regularized scrutiny of intelligence affairs by the legislature became commonplace.

In its later phase the administration's concern shifted to improvement of the intelligence agencies' ability to perform all their operational missions. Now there was concern that the earlier reforms – rules imposed by the executive and by Congress – had so burdened the agencies that they could not take action to cope with security threats. A succession of international crises reinforced that view and seemed to highlight American disabilities. It was also widely believed that earlier moves toward multiple outside oversight mechanisms and many knowledgeable external supervisors had been overdone, and that much more limited participation to the same ends should be instituted. The impetus behind the effort in Congress to legislate a comprehensive charter declined, and the emphasis there too turned to exercising and reenergizing the intelligence agencies.

There was little solace for critics of the agencies in any of the Reagan Administration's policies. From the outset, and in all available forums, the administration worked consciously and conspicuously to strengthen intelligence operations, a clarion call which by this time meant reexamination of the reforms of the 1970s and elimination of those which appeared in the 1980s to be too confining or cumbersome. The administration's own charter for intelligence, EO 12333, reflected that spirit. Its spokesmen took on the most visible "open government" issues of the time – the Freedom of Information Act and the "leaking" of secrets (including intelligence identities) – before Congress and the public. And these assertive, more aggressive inclinations were matched by more activist operational approaches, which the administration was not at all shy about defending.[1] Close collaboration with the intelligence committees in Congress was continued. But as a rule the members of those committees shared administration perspectives on intelligence: the focus was on enhancing effectiveness, not on circumscribing capabilities and activities.

In chapter one I noted three fundamental questions that have animated this inquiry: What did the process of decision about intelligence controls look like? What were the main concerns of those who participated? What were the choices made and what do they say about our nation and its larger purposes? The chapters that followed showed that even in this most sensitive, most protected policy arena, the process of decision entailed bargaining, negotiation, and compromise among many official and nonofficial actors over a long period of time. It is, in fact, an unfinished process. An array of players, both within and outside of the government, has sought actively to influence the way policymakers define the problem and, ultimately, the way they resolve it. Presidential advisors of all sorts, intelligence professionals (past and present), scholars, former officials of the national security and foreign policy establishment, civil liberties activists and their organizations, journalists, judges, senators and congressmen, and others among an increasingly knowledgeable and watchful public pursued their individual or institutional purposes in a multitude of forums: in Congress, in the courts, in executive policy councils, and in the wider arena of public inquiry and debate. Once the critique of intelligence operations had gained momentum and credibility, reform pressures pushed tirelessly forward on all fronts.

The lines of argument did not reflect constant, uniform positions maintained by officialdom versus the public, nor by the executive versus Congress, nor by intelligence professionals versus policy-level controllers. Presidents differed in their preferences and decisions, though all were custodians of the contested power and authority. Views in Congress – those of individual members, the responsible committees, and the legislature as a whole – also shifted over time as the contending arguments developed, clashed, and pressed on. The investigative zeal of the Church and Pike committees was passed on to their successors, the standing committees on intelligence in the Senate and the House. The Senate committee in particular led the effort to insert the legislature and the judiciary into the regulatory and oversight arena and to devise a comprehensive statutory charter. But within two years its companion committee in the House was working to strengthen the agencies, and ultimately the policy momentum in Congress as a whole shifted markedly away from the remedial goals originally set by reformers. A smaller statute, and oversight practices worked out largely informally with the executive, set the policies ultimately accepted by Congress as satisfactory. Dissenters there were, of course, and they remained active before the legislature and in the courts. But by 1980 the center of the reform coalition had moved away from them, converging with defenders of the intelligence agencies on compromise proposals.

The players' main concerns were evident quickly, and I have already surveyed them at length. Four major perspectives were evident. The first sought above all to equip the national government to deal with security challenges. A second focused on protecting individuals from potentially abusive powers of government. It granted that tools of national security are necessary, but it gave the societal interest in protection from foreign threats no greater standing than the interest in insuring that power cannot be abused at home. The tools of government must be controlled and confined deliberately with the purpose of preserving inviolate certain spheres of personal privacy and liberty.[2] Also at the center of this second perspective was a sense of confidence in the ability of American society to survive in the competitive world sketched out by the national security advocates, even if operational capabilities retained by other nations were set aside in America. Even in the world as you describe it, the civil libertarians told the national security advocates, America can cope with external challenges without abandoning the internal political principles and practices it values.

A similar point was made by those who argued the third position: that certain core democratic and humanitarian ideals must govern American behavior abroad. American actions must not descend to the level of instinctual responses to perceived provocations or to presumed threats. They must be guided by a rational, conscious striving to transcend baser instincts, to maintain civilized values, and to set an example for others to follow.

A fourth set of arguments focused on arranging controls and constraints in such a way as to serve the interests of constitutional government: to divide the national government's power among its component branches. While the civil libertarians and the advocates of humane, principled external behavior pressed for delimitation of boundaries on government power, those whose primary concerns were institutional wanted to apportion power within those boundaries to insure adequate supervision of the executive. This, they argued, was a societal purpose of such magnitude that no security-oriented protestations about unwieldy or unwise burdens could overturn it. The mechanics of collaboration could be adjusted to reasonable security needs without unilaterally disarming the nation's intelligence community, and so mechanics there must finally be. That was the inevitable price – if indeed it was a price – for living in this society as opposed to living in others less devoted to formalized checks and balances.

Which of these perspectives "won"? In a real sense they all did, for all were heard and at various times all had their day. To be sure, security concerns were constant, even in the Carter Administration's first and more reformist phase. All three administrations maintained, against great pressure, a more permissive regulatory framework for counterintelligence tools than for domestic law and order tools. All three administrations, additionally, resisted the disestablishment of intelligence capabilities attacked by some as inconsistent with American ideals. The Carter Administration went the farthest toward reform prescriptions in this regard, but only in its first phase. And all three presidents retained unilateral executive authority and flexibility they thought sufficient to deal with the world as they understood it. In these senses, particularly if themes of policy are seen over the long term, the security imperative was a powerful factor leading to decisions which sought to fortify the government for the demands of international life.

But when analysis descends beneath the level of long-term trends and main policy themes, we find smaller, significantly restrained postures where "security" arguments have been frustrated. We see the Carter Administration, in its first years, essentially abandoning covert action operations and devising significant administrative controls for intrusive counterintelligence techniques. We see Congress imposing statutory rules and procedures, and participating vigorously in collaboration and oversight routines. We also see that certain of the 1970s reforms have survived the most insistent counterreform pressures to overturn them. These have included, most prominently, the disclosure requirements of the Freedom of Information Act, which into 1984 continued to apply to intelligence agencies in ways understood by the national security perspective as most unwise and unrealistic.

Where do such policies come from, and how do we account for them and understand their import? Samuel Huntington's analysis, in its emphasis on the values imbedded in American society and their influence upon external tools and behavior, offers an explanation.[3] Decisions which impose control-related burdens on intelligence operations, or which set aside certain capabilities or techniques, even though other nations may use them for combative, self-aggrandizing ends, reflect conscious, deliberate choices in America to respect and conform to central societal ideals and political principles. A collective American self-image is itself a powerful force in the policy process, independent of, but in the end intertwined with, an image of what the world is and requires. In particular cases, indeed, this self-image may be more important in that process than any argument pointing to the imperatives of international life or describing the venal designs of particular competitors. But in all cases it will play an important role, attempting to channel actions in directions that uphold the ideals. If it did not play such a role, especially in the intelligence arena, at the intersection of self-image and international imperative, then the American essence would have been changed beyond recognition, if not beyond imagination. Perspectives which do not embrace these factors cannot fully understand America or the domestic and international society toward which American values strain.

Lessons for Policy

Two related lessons for policymakers – specifically, for the writers of intelligence rules – might be drawn from this study of the explicit debate. The first argues that they must prepare for a large and diverse array of credible, yet divergent, pressures from increasingly knowledgeable, watchful, and concerned interest groups. The issues involved are momentous. They touch the essence of America as a "founded society." They have been widely publicized and politicized, and they will not go away. Rulemakers need not accede to such pressures, of course. Arguments are free to win or to lose in our system. But if policy moulders do not accede to them they must know how to defeat them or to deflect them, and how to respond to them in terms of the values they espouse. Moreover, the makers of intelligence policies cannot presume that opposing perspectives will fall forever silent upon losing any particular policy contest. Critics now know what is at stake, and their attention and efforts will not dissolve or swerve in their commitment to their own visions of what America must be. This is true even though on intelligence issues one might expect most Americans to be inclined to respect executive preferences, simply because of secrecy and security interests that many understand and would otherwise wish to accommodate. Where critics believe that decisions about intelligence capabilities have subverted central values, or that such values have been placed too low in the policy calculus, they will work energetically and unceasingly to put them back where they think they belong.

The second lesson has to do with the need to justify intelligence capabilities, to explain the rationales which support them, in order to build enduring foundations in public legitimacy. The intelligence community's reliance upon widespread acceptance of the Cold War's conceptual framework was perhaps defensible in the 1950s, but in the 1980s it can no longer suffice. At the level of underlying world views and of visions of what America must do or be able to do, there is now significant divergence.

For that reason the intelligence debate is unfinished. We still have not found a way in the public domain to explain, rationalize, and thereby openly legitimize the intelligence capabilities the nation's leaders have chosen to retain. Despite years of policymaking agony, we have not been able to say what capabilities are needed and why, or to make operational rules which can be defended as an explicit synthesis of national goals and values.

The efforts to legislate a comprehensive intelligence charter confronted that problem squarely, but in time it lost momentum and dissolved into smaller contests about initiatives meant to strengthen or reenergize the intelligence agencies.

The main regulatory burden has thus fallen on the executive branch. The clipped, often cryptic, language of successive executive orders has been the only attempt as a matter of public policy to rationalize American intelligence capabilities and controls for a most attentive citizenry. Unfortunately, it has been in the nature of these executive orders only to describe the activities and responsibilities of the intelligence agencies, not to explain them. As a result, in the public domain there is still no clear, unified vision of intelligence purposes to broaden and integrate thinking about these issues, no comprehensive set of principles outlining how intelligence operations serve central national values.

This stands in marked contrast to the careful, public thought given other major instruments of policy. In the arena of strategic warfare and deterrence, for instance, analysts, decisionmakers, and operators stand literally knee-deep in strategies and military doctrines thought out at length both within and outside of government. Weapons of strategic warfare have been examined and reexamined from every possible angle; contingencies and capabilities have been elaborately explored; and doctrines for various uses of those weapons abound. Whether or not all Americans are comfortable with the existence of these weapons and with the possibility that they might actually be used, many have come to understand the place of such armaments in the nation's life and purposes.

But because no such body of thought has developed or been made explicit for the intelligence agencies, they have no solid underpinning of legitimacy, no operational rationale and *raison d'être* accepted as a matter of broad public policy. Largely for that reason they are often treated roughly in recurrent debates about familiar, unresolved issues and challenges. Attempts to use the capabilities sensibly, and to make rules about them, are cast adrift without map or compass on essentially uncharted seas. Resulting operations and rules, moreover, in effect lift themselves into the air by their own bootstraps, supported, if at all, by rationales conceived within the same professional services charged with conducting the regulated operations.

To be sure, the need for operational secrecy and the reluctance of government officials to enter a potentially inflamed public debate help to account for the nation's failure to develop an overarching manifesto for intelligence activities. But neither of these constraints is unique to the intelligence problem. In other highly sensitive areas they have not impeded open discussion and explanation of official postures. The huge and useful "civilian" literature on strategic warfare, for just one example, was developed despite obvious secrecy needs concerning weapons characteristics and capabilities and concerning specific operational or contingency plans. One need not disclose the full details of actual capabilities and intentions in order to describe general purposes and to prescribe operational parameters.

No one can argue that explication of rationales will forever preempt debate about the capabilities they support. But it is axiomatic in the development and administration of public policy that those who make decisions should first identify and articulate the purposes which their choices must serve. Without clear connection to some concept of goals, decisions may seem to wander aimlessly and resulting actions can have no legitimizing foundation, no grounding in any underlying consensus, even a partial and temporary one. But to the extent that policymakers do attempt to make plain the central and enduring principles from which their choices spring, Americans may be made more comfortable with the operational capabilities – the security instruments – we have retained and which from time to time we have decided to use despite contrary pressures. Within executive councils what may be required, in the end, is some small dose of humility, at least enough to understand the need to explain why certain tools of policy are valuable to America. There is, as Stanley Hoffman once said, the need for a rationale, and it seems well within the resources of American leaders to provide one.[4]

We should not leave the explicit debate, however, without also noting this judgment: that critics outside the government, especially those who attack the "national security" perspective, have much work to do to make their participation more useful in the future. Too many have sought to maximize their own preferred set of values and have obdurately insisted that decisions which also serve other interests cannot be legitimate. They fear the directions in which the national security perspective tends because what awaits us at the extremes is a state which behaves lawlessly abroad and sets itself above the law at home. But the patent undesirability of that remote extreme hardly justifies the radical preventive measures some still insist upon: the jettisoning of security tools needed and utilized in everyday life by even the most democratic societies abroad, or the weakening of those tools by exposing their inner workings to many layers of supervision and outside scrutiny. We need not flee from one specter into the clutches of another.

Too many "critics," furthermore, have approached the discussion from rigidly narrowed, and therefore unhelpful, perspectives. An example is the viewpoint which finds in our Constitution mainly a set of rationales for prohibitions and restrictions to protect citizens' rights. That is certainly an important purpose of the constitution, but as I argued earlier in this study, the framers also intended to establish a viable and competent national government and to equip it for life in the world at large. If we are to take bearings from the Constitution when we write intelligence rules, we must also remember that purpose. True, this makes the process of decision more difficult. But it makes the outcome of that process more likely to align with the framers' original design and with the totality of the values at the center of our national essence.

The Remaining Agenda

This study suggests that both policymakers and other participants in the debate about controls can do much to illuminate threshold questions left implicit in the 1970s discussion. In doing so they may open the way to the building of stronger public foundations for intelligence functions. No one can expect that true consensus about underlying perceptions – of America and the world – can be forged. At those levels dissonance is unavoidable,[5] but at least it can be made plain in all its aspects. And further, it may well be possible to begin to box in common ground, or to bring into greater relief the contours of an acceptable operational and regulatory rationale, by confronting certain prior questions not yet fully explored. Working largely invisibly, unspoken perspectives on these threshold matters set contending policy preferences at loggerheads from the beginning. They still compose, in a real sense, a "subliminal agenda" which we can begin to explore to our great profit.

At least four such agenda items suggest themselves: (1) the problem of what normative standards ought to apply to choices about intelligence operations; (2) the problem of persistent but unexamined beliefs about "national efficacy," about what America can achieve in the world and about what tools are useful to those ends; (3) the "fear of regulation" syndrome: the presumption of many observers that regulated and supervised intelligence is somehow less capable intelligence; and (4) the legalism/formalism syndrome: the presumption that "control" means mainly formalized rules and oversight routines imposed from outside the executive or at high levels within the executive.

For each of these items, the discussion which follows is intended to suggest how their exposure to close analysis may help to clarify the remaining policy challenge, and to point the way to solutions that many persons can support. And in significant respects it is also intended to suggest how the work of scholars may prepare the way for more enlightened and fruitful policy debates in the future.

At the center of regulatory controversies have been deep-seated beliefs and preferences about "moral" or "ethical" behavior.[6] All Americans want their government to behave in a moral way, though it is not easy to decide what that means in particular cases.[7] Two themes drawn from the writings of scholars who have devoted much of their work to the problem of morality and foreign policy may help to sharpen further discussion in this area.

First, it is illusory, as Kenneth Thompson has reminded us, to believe that insistence on "moral" behavior somehow injects more certitude into the policy calculation than might otherwise be the case. A commitment − in principle − to moral behavior does not obviate the need for choice among values. The hope, for those who wish to make explicit and binding the connection between morality and foreign policy, is to bring about a return to moral reasoning, not to fall headlong into the pursuit of any single moral value raised artificially and inflexibly to special status.[8] But what, then, is moral reasoning in the international context, and more specifically in our case?

A second principle can help to orient our thoughts here, especially in our approach to the challenge of reconciling the internal values of our own domestic society with the felt imperatives of life in the international system. It has to do with what the Catholic theologian John Courtney Murray once called "the gulf between individual and collective morality": "The private life is governed by the will of God as stated in the Scriptures. It is to bear the stamp of . . . patience, gentleness, sacrifice, forbearance, trust, compassion, humility, forgiveness of injuries and, supremely and inclusively, love. On the other hand, it is the plainest of historical facts that the public life of the nation-state is not governed by these values. Hardly less plain is the fact that it cannot be."[9]

In the American context, society and the state have a special character and mission structured by a framework of obligatory, value-oriented goals: to serve and promote the interests of justice, freedom, security, the general welfare, and civil unity or peace. This special set of obligations is quite separate from those that rest, at another level, upon the individual in domestic society. And the moral standards that apply at one level are not the same as those operative at the other.[10] For those empowered to act in the name of society and the state, the content of political and social morality derives from the nature of political and social reality they confront and from the posited goals they must serve. In that context, the centrality of national self-interest (including concern for security) does not itself raise moral issues as long as the ends of national action remain defined by all the public purposes entrusted to the American state.

Thus the moral situation of the public official is very different from that of a private person. He is the guardian of the national interest, which is composed of the collective societal purposes entrusted to the state. He cannot be generous or charitable to others outside the society at the expense of that trust. This does not, however, license the pursuit of unbridled, selfish, self-celebrating nationalist causes. That would be inconsistent with the overarching core values (such as justice and freedom) which set the standards for national behavior. The public official knows full well "that we must live in a brutal world and still remain civilized."[11] But it is a political and practical morality which he seeks. As Reinhold Neibuhr suggested, the special art of statecraft is to find the point of concurrence between the parochial and the general interest, between the national and the international common good.[12] A sense of justice for all, including those outside our borders, must prevent the national community's natural prudence from defining its interests too restrictively and from neglecting wider responsibilities and goals in the world at large. Yet those wider responsibilities must not be allowed to dissipate attention and resources needed for protecting the society. The regulator of that interest-defining calculation— political morality – must guard against dangerous, overgenerous sentimentality, on the one hand, and callous, self-serving cynicism, on the other.

Ernest Lefever has explored the implications of this line of reasoning in the intelligence arena, and specifically with respect to covert action operations.[13] He offers no prescriptions about particular constraints or controls, but with the help of classical "just war" doctrine he suggests three standards for determining what kinds of covert action undertakings may be morally acceptable. The standards are put in the form of questions the policymaker must be able to answer in the affirmative:

(1) Is the objective of the action just? Obviously there is difficulty in defining justice in particular cases. But the very naming of that goal-value

widens the criteria for decision beyond pure security formulas. Yet it does not ask the nation to disable itself, relative to others, in the name of ideals.

(2) Are the means employed both just and appropriate? Just ends may be corrupted by unjust and inappropriate means. Tools of force and coercion present the most difficult issues here, and by analogy instruments of manipulation raise similar questions. A "proportionality" rule is suggested to guide choices about using or not using such policy instruments. In certain contexts, both too much and too little force or coercion or manipulation may be wrong, in the sense of unjustified, since they betray the moral ends of policy and the societal trust reposed in the decisionmaker.

To answer this question with any assurance one must, of course, know a good deal about the effects of using the policy instruments in question. There must be some basis on which to judge their "appropriateness" to policy objectives. Whether we now have such knowledge in the case of intelligence tools (or any others for that matter) is of course questionable. But if we do not, we may find that research can redress this, over time, if scholarship can be activated to that end.

(3) Will the chances for justice be enhanced if the action succeeds? The ultimate practical *and* moral test of political behavior lies not in the nature of the ends sought or the means chosen, but in the consequences that flow directly from the action. Again, in order to apply this formula to an actual decisionmaking problem, public officials must know something about the likely effects of taking certain actions, or must have reliable means of forecasting their effects. Whether the requisite knowledge or forecasting methods are available at any time is once again problematical. This, too, suggests ways in which the work of scholars may be able to instruct the "moral reasoning" process in policymaking, and also to lead it meaningfully.

This framework of questions does no more than alert the policymaker to the considerations, and the kinds of empirical data, relevant to moral choice. It does not exclude any course of action *ab initio*. Nor does it make choices among available courses of action either evident or easy. Even assassination as a tool of policy is not ruled out. Those (especially intelligence operatives) who seek certainty and specificity in guidance, and those who hope to declare particular courses of action out of bounds as a matter of policy, are likely to be uncomfortable with this. But lack of specificity about prohibitions – the failure to compile a long list of "don'ts" – does not indicate moral ambiguity. The standards for judging behavior are stated. The decisionmaker's proper attitudinal orientation is made plain. The moral dimensions and consequences of his choices are recognized and ratified.

There are, of course, all sorts of reasons why assassination or any other activity might be declared impermissible as a matter of policy. Some might fear the proliferation of practices that must be treated as truly exceptional in any case. They might also fear for the safety of our own officials and society if assassinations or other manipulative activity were to be attributed (rightly or wrongly) to the United States. But these considerations bear upon the practical advisability of such activity. They do not make a case for morality or immorality in principle, though rhetoric often pushes them in one direction of argumentation or the other.

A framework for moral judgment, even as general as the one outlined here, might well provide the centerpiece of a regulatory structure around which significant public support could coalesce. It would give ethical coherence to the smaller, more specific rules appended as a matter of policy to the central framework. And it would make explicit at least the general moral grounds on which intelligence capabilities stand. If it were to be adopted, many Americans might then be able to come to terms with intelligence capabilities whose rationale, from the standpoint of public morality, is not well understood.

In another part of the normative realm, the public debate has not been well informed on the application of international law to intelligence operations, particularly to secret operations within the legal jurisdiction of other states. This is an issue which has been kept on the margins of the public inquiry, no doubt in part because there is a good deal of disagreement among scholars about whether such operations have legal sanction or not, and if they do, to what extent.[14] Moving that collision of expert opinion to center stage has seemed likely to shed as much darkness as light on the policy problem, and no one has been anxious to complicate things any further. United Nations Charter provisions and General Assembly resolutions forbidding intervention in the internal affairs of sovereign nations contend in the "real" world against de facto interpenetration of national societies, economies, and politics, as well as against proven or suspected manipulative practices repeated literally for centuries in the behavior of states. If experts cannot resolve those dichotomies and cannot say what the law (or the prevailing view of the law) permits, then the public debate can hardly be expected to venture usefully into that realm.

Yet those who wish to find legitimate grounding for intelligence functions and rules must do more with the legal perspective than has been done to date. Many intelligence professionals and others worry justifiably about imposing ponderous legal strictures on their work. But the law is not only a source of constraints. It takes full account of the practices of nations, and nothing in it requires that America abstain unilaterally or gratuitously from common international behavior. An explication of legal groundings in those terms would help to build citizens' confidence in the tools of power entrusted to the intelligence community, by explaining how those instruments can be exercised consistent with enduring principles sanctioned outside any particular administration.

Norms of international morality and law may suggest where the boundaries of permissible actions are, but we also need clearer ideas about "national efficacy," or about what is possible and feasible. The concern here shifts markedly toward assisting practical decisionmaking for intelligence, especially for covert action operations whose object is to produce favorable international outcomes for America. What many hope for is a more realistic appraisal of the limits of those operations, a clearer picture of what they can and cannot do.

Some analysts have attempted to draw attention to this problem for many years, questioning basic presumptions about America's ability to manipulate external events to her advantage.[15] They called for answers to such general questions as: What kinds of political or social events have proven manageable, which have proven intractable, and why? What tools have contributed to success or failure, and what have been the consequences of failure? Further scholarship pointed at these problems might clear much of the path toward intelligence rules that reflect not only proper values but good sense, as well.[16]

This is, of course, an area where intelligence collection and analytical capabilities also have much to contribute. As Adda Bozeman has observed, sound foreign policies and definitions of the national interest depend upon America's knowledge of herself and equally upon her knowledge of other societies – her sensitivity to the dynamics of political and social change.[17] This requires effective intelligence within the government, as well as reliable scholarship outside it.

No amount of data collection and careful assessment of the utilities of available tools can insure that wise choices will ultimately be made either about operational rules or about exercising capabilities. But nothing can guarantee wisdom. We can only be sure to choose leaders who ask the right questions and who then may choose wisely among various courses of action. In that regard there may be considerable benefit in widespread activation of research, within and outside of government, which might instruct both attentive publics and the nation's leadership about the foreign events which affect American interests, and about the tools of policy that may or may not be appropriate to those challenges.

Especially within the intelligence community, there is strong prejudice against extensive operational controls and comprehensive sets of rules.[18] Many believe that as control measures proliferate, performance must inevitably suffer. In large part this sentiment is a reaction to the era of reform, when there was great concern among professionals and others that the ability of the intelligence community to perform vital tasks had been undercut, perhaps irreparably. There was also a great deal of simple resentment about widely publicized allegations and grievances many saw as overblown and insensitive to important interests served by the challenged, and later constrained, activities. As a result, though in the American political context some sort of control and close supervision of executive power is imperative, many still reflexively resist such measures as inherently dangerous to the national interest. As some in the 1970s debate were (and still are) cynical and skeptical about intelligence operations, others are now cynical and skeptical about operational controls. They fear that any "reform" that works in the direction of closer management and oversight must inevitably compromise operational capability. On that point some minds seem, unfortunately, quite convinced and impatient with contrary views.

Future discussion of the issue might well profit from a more differentiated conceptualization of what "controls" are involved and in what relationships they are employed. Stansfield Turner has outlined four categories of control measures which drew attention in the 1970s: (1) those developed within the intelligence community and within the agencies themselves; (2) those established between the president (or national-level policymakers) and the intelligence community; (3) those developed between Congress (for completeness we must also add the courts) and the executive branch; and (4) those developed between the public at large and the institutions of government. [19] Even such a general categorization as this one begins to suggest how we might sketch out an allocation of control functions that serves all interests.

The most troublesome divisions of labor are those between the executive and the other institutions of the national government, and between all those institutions and the public at large. As between the president and the intelligence community, and within that community, authority and responsibilities for direction and supervision are well established and by comparison noncontroversial. Some may object to the substance of controls adopted in those relationships — as for instance in complaints that elevation of approval authority to very high levels is too burdensome, or that attorney general guidelines are too restrictive, or that approval criteria are unnecessarily confining. But there can be no question about the ultimate authority and indeed the responsibility to impose some such measures. It seems reasonable to expect, for instance, that rules and procedures will state governing principles, loci of authority, channels for approval and dissent, and processes for internal review and oversight. They should also state authorizations, allocate functions, and make clear what is forbidden. In general terms, these rules should be placed on the public record, as is now the case. What the rules actually say will of course be a product of the controlling perspectives an administration brings to executive leadership positions. They will also be affected by the views of others interested enough to try .to influence those perspectives. This is perfectly natural in our political system.

But the relationship between the executive and Congress (and the judiciary) is controversial on all counts. Thanks to the uncertain distribution of important foreign affairs powers, many intelligence control measures are contested not only on grounds of substance but also on grounds of authority. Inherent presidential power over tools of national security is the root problem. No one can be sure of its proper boundaries. Most recognize, however, that as a result of his national security responsibilities the president must be the primary controller and supervisor of intelligence. All acknowledge that Congress, too, has important rulemaking and oversight authority, and all know also that Congress has given the courts a role in the realm of electronic surveillance. But the president's managerial primacy makes practical sense, for all the reasons noted in the *Federalist's* recitation of his institutional advantages in foreign policy – unity, secrecy, dispatch, and so forth. The membership of Congress is simply too numerous, its procedures too unwieldy, open, and slow. Judges, too, have significant handicaps, aside from the obvious limitations of jurisdiction and expertise. To be sure, arguments for the president's day-to-day managerial primacy can be pushed too far. But to grant that they are compelling is not to argue for untrammeled executive primacy. Other branches have their own responsibilities in a system of shared power. The current state of their participation seems to have satisfied most mainstream concerns in that regard. But more ambitious proposals which move in the direction of intruding on routine executive functions (by, for instance, requiring congressional approval of all sensitive intelligence proposals before they are implemented) cut against both constitutional principle and good sense. The task for rulemaking is to recognize that control responsibilities outside the executive can be discharged effectively without straining toward such micromanagement of specific executive initiatives.

There are, however, equally persuasive arguments for congressional activity of two kinds: legislating a basic foundation statute for the intelligence community which articulates, independently, truly national preferences about missions, organization, and functions (and does this in more comprehensive fashion than does current legislation); and institution of oversight routines which keep relevant committees fully informed of executive activities, with a view toward assessing quality of performance and policing the boundaries of operational permissibility. The second task has, of course, been accomplished, and Congress has devised ways to surmount basic handicaps in order to perform this function responsibly. But it has not been well understood that the intent to exercise that supervisory authority in effect makes the first step – announcement of foundation organization and controls – imperative. Otherwise the collaborative, supervisory routines put in place essentially ratify executive preferences about such matters. Agreed routines take internal executive rules, organizational arrangements, and functions as given, and they monitor how well the executive manages them.

Current executive rules and procedures for collaboration do reflect congressional preferences to some degree, as a result of intense bargaining involved in preparing them. But still the public charter for intelligence is a self-imposed executive document. Moreover, supervisory interaction depends on executive diligence in living up to the informal bargains which defined relative roles and established the relevant action channels. With perhaps one prominent exception, the system has apparently worked satisfactorily to this point.[20] But whether we can be sure that this will be the case years hence, when times and personalities have changed, is problematical.

Beyond those practical considerations, there is much weight to the persisting argument that Congress should not recede from the challenge of "directing" the intelligence community in the most fundamental way: by enacting a foundation statute which makes expectations and operational guidelines explicit.[21] As this study has described in some detail, the nation's experience with the congressional charter effort in the 1970s was not a happy one. But that should have surprised no one who understood the challenge: to reconcile competing values when possible, and, when not possible, to choose among them and make the rationale for choice explicit. This challenge still remains, and we can be sure that our neglect of it only postpones the agony to another time.

The final relationship – between the public at large and the institutions of government involved in intelligence affairs – has also been troublesome, largely because some participants in the debate have expected it to accomplish too much. "Open government" measures, such as public access to intelligence files through the Freedom of Information Act and the Privacy Act, remain controversial as applied to the business of intelligence. The Reagan Administration and some members of Congress still seek to protect the agencies from these public monitoring devices. Others insist that such measures are mandated by our democratic values.

The "open government" arguments are surely important ones. Yet it is possible to take their concern for direct popular control of government much too far, at great cost to the nation's external interests. We are a democracy, but we are also a republic: the people's voice is expressed through elected institutions. On principle, then, as well as from the standpoint of practical administration of intelligence affairs, those who argue for extensive, direct public surveillance of intelligence activities simply address the wrong set of control relationships. The public is entitled, certainly, and indeed obligated, to be vigilant in assessing how governmental institutions perform their delegated functions, including the monitoring of intelligence. But should the public become dissatisfied with such performance, the remedy is not to bypass those institutions with direction and supervision by the general body politic. It is, instead, to make the system work by reconstituting the membership of those institutions, by insisting that they perform their proper direction and supervision roles diligently, by using the legislature and the courts to remedy deficiences and punish venalities, and by participating more generally in the actions which bring their views to bear in the policy process. That is, simply put, the American tradition and practice, and there is no reason to depart from it in the case of intelligence.

The last hidden agenda item deals with the view that enhanced control is synonymous with a formal structure of constraints and procedures. In the extremes, this view treats formalized, institutionalized regulatory frameworks and "high level" mechanisms as almost a panacea for all intelligence ills, and the more elaborate, detailed, and widely known the rules are, the better the controls will be.

Within the executive this argument's successes have pressed operational approval and supervisory authority upward, toward the president and his closest advisors, in hopes of achieving more rigorous control. They have also produced high-level panels for investigation of problems and for "detached" advice to the president as he exercises his leadership functions. This perspective has also pressed involvement in approvals and supervision outward, away from purely operational or intelligence channels, to include lawyers, inspectors general, and officials in other departments involved in the larger policy process. And all of these measures have been codified in a succession of executive orders and their subsidiary implementing directives.

Outside the executive branch, this perspective has sought a detailed, comprehensive charter in Congress that would specify exactly what kinds of activities are permitted and what are not, and that would describe in great detail all the approval criteria and procedures. It has also sought more formalized and wider congressional participation in approval and review of intelligence operations, as well as significant roles for the courts in reviewing proposals for "intrusive" activities.

It is incontestable that important benefits flow from our checks and balances system, from clear and systematic regulatory guidance and procedures announced at high levels, and from the discipline that results when responsibilities, functions, and expectations are made plain and unmistakable. But this perspective has all too often been undergirded by an unquestioning faith in the efficacy of formalized rules and procedures as constraints. Adherents of this view, reluctant to place trust in men, and suspicious of the natural tendencies of those in power, prefer to place their trust in law and in elegantly elaborate formalities prescribed by law. They tend to neglect much of the wisdom available in the literature of political science concerning the "capturing" or coopting of the regulators by the regulated,[22] and concerning the strength of subterranean bureaucratic preferences, patterns of behavior, and invisible bargains and judgments that are beyond the reach of formal rules and hierarchy.[23] Their presumption has been that establishment of routines for oversight, after articulation of detailed rules of law, will lead to aggressive, well-orchestrated, sustained, coordinated monitoring of intelligence activity. But history indicates that this is much too hopeful. As a rule, studies have shown that 'oversight' simply means talking with like-minded people in the bureaucracy on a routine basis to make sure that no major deviations are occurring in policies and programs that the members of the subgovernment have long since ratified."[24]

It would be well to remember that this generalization is an apt description of the nature and effect of congressional activity in the intelligence arena for many years. The 1970s debate stirred more intensive activity, but whether that burst of energy will have real endurance is a question about which a certain healthy skepticism seems in order. And it might also be recalled that much of the impetus to strengthen the intelligence agencies came from the relevant committees in Congress after concern had grown about untoward effects of the era of exposure and reform.

As a result of its faith in law, in regulations, and in formalities, this perspective tends to overregulate by proliferating detailed rules, requirements, and procedures that in the aggregate can impose significant, distracting burdens upon operators and their managers. At the same time, however, it risks undercontrol because it neglects the importance of the human element in improving the quality of governmental behavior.

In a real sense the fundamental problem in controlling intelligence operations is not simply the lack of rules, though where that is the case it is certainly an important deficiency. It is, additionally, the caliber of people involved and the nature of the views about America and the world that they hold. A prescription for remedial or preventive action, then, must attend to the recruitment into government – and at all levels of direction and supervision as well as at operational levels – of persons conscious of and committed to the full range of values and public purposes our government is constituted to serve and uphold. This is, of course, a perennial problem in American governance. But at times in the intelligence inquiry we seem to have lost sight of it, for all its obviousness, as we have rushed to grapple with one another in small contests about this or that particular rule or procedure.

In the final analysis, the enlightened prescripton calls not for placing our trust in law rather than in men. It calls, instead, for articulation of demanding, overarching standards and oversight procedures in our law, for strength of character in our officials, and for the placing of a well-supervised trust in both.

The challenge of controlling intelligence activity is not made simpler by that statement of the problem, to be sure. But as a beacon on the horizon of argument, it can provide us much-needed directional bearings. It has the virtue of reminding us that in order to promote the wise use of governmental power we must do more than fabricate elaborate frameworks of rules and intricate formalities of management. We must attend as well to the choosing of leaders and representatives who, in the interstices of written rules and behind the formalities of collaboration, will live the values which define the character of our nation.

Notes

Chapter 1

1. See, e.g., Harry Howe Ransom, *Central Intelligence and National Security* (Cambridge: Harvard Univ. Press, 1958), pp. vi-ix.

2. Roy Godson, ed., *Intelligence Requirements for the 1980's: Covert Action* (Washington, D.C.: National Strategy Information Center, 1981) p. 238. See also Harry Howe Ransom, "Being Intelligent about Secret Intelligence Agencies," *American Political Science Review* 74 (March 1980): 141; Roger Hilsman, "On Intelligence," *Armed Forces and Society* 8 (Fall 1981): 129.

3. See, e.g., John Prados, *The Soviet Estimate: U.S. Intelligence Analysis and Russian Military Strength* (New York: Dial Press, 1982); Richard K. Betts, "Surprise Despite Warning: Why Sudden Attacks Succeed," *Political Science Quarterly* 95 (Winter 1980-1981): 551; Robert F. Ellsworth and Kenneth L. Adelman, "Foolish Intelligence," *Foreign Policy* 36 (Fall 1979): 147; Raymond Cohen, "Threat Perception and International Crisis," *Political Science Quarterly* 93 (Spring 1978): 93. The work of Robert Jervis has also been influential: *Perception and Misperception in International Politics* (Princeton: Princeton Univ. Press, 1976).

4. See, e.g., Ray S. Cline, "Policy without Intelligence," *Foreign Policy* 17 (Winter 1974-1975): 121; Richard K. Betts, "Strategic Intelligence Estimates: Let's Make Them Useful," *Parameters* 10 (Dec. 1980): 20.

5. Prominent examples include Philip Agee, *Inside the Company: CIA Diary* (New York: Stonehill, 1975); John Stockwell, *In Search of Enemies: A CIA Story* (New York: Norton, 1978); and the selections in Robert L. Borosage and John Marks, eds., *The CIA File* (New York: Grossman, 1976).

6. Frank J. Donner, *The Age of Surveillance: The Aims and Methods of America's Political Intelligence System* (New York: Vintage Books, 1981), p. 7. See also Athan Theoharis, *Spying on Americans: Political Surveillance from Hoover to the Huston Plan* (Philadelphia: Temple Univ. Press, 1978), p. 230, arguing that the breakdown of the American constitutional system had produced an emergent "1984 Society." See also Noam Chomsky's introduction to Nelson Blackstock's *COINTELPRO: The FBI's Secret War on Political Freedom* (New York: Vintage Books, 1976).

7. Ray S. Cline, "Rebuilding American Intelligence," *New York Times,* Dec. 20, 1979, p. A 27.

8. See, for example, the caustic description of operational rationales derived in part from international factors in Donner, *Age of Surveillance,* pp. 3-29 (especially the treatment of "foreign influence," pp. 17-21.)

9. This analytical impediment is not, of course, a new phenomenon in America. Nearly two centuries ago President John Quincy Adams, hoping to strengthen America's defenses by upgrading her military forces, confronted intense opposition from persons fearing that those forces would be turned inward against political dissidents at home.

Adams's rejoinder held that this view erred in "confounding the principles of internal government with external relations." Those who espouse it, he said, dread too much "the force of executive power at home, and leave it therefore without any power to withstand force from abroad." Quoted in Paul A. Varg, *Foreign Policies of the Founding Fathers* (East Lansing: Michigan State Univ. Press, 1963), p. 135.

10. These include: Richard E. Morgan, *Domestic Intelligence: Monitoring Dissent in America* (Austin and London: Univ. of Texas Press, 1980); Stephen R. Weissman, "CIA Covert Action in Zaire and Angola: Patterns and Consequences," *Political Science Quarterly* 94 (Summer 1979): 263; Harry Howe Ransom, "Strategic Intelligence and Intermestic Politics," in Charles W. Kegley, Jr., and Eugene R. Wittkopf, eds., *Perspectives on American Foreign Policy* (New York: St. Martin's Press, 1983), p. 299; Emanuel Adler, "Executive Command and Control in Foreign Policy: The CIA's Covert Activities," *Orbis* 23 (Fall 1979): 671; Thomas Emerson, "Control of Government Intelligence Agencies – The American Experience," *Political Quarterly* 53 (July-Sept. 1982): 273; and a series of books edited by Roy Godson and published by the National Strategy Information Center (Washington, D.C.) under the general title *Intelligence Requirements for the 1980's*. Volumes are: *Elements of Intelligence* (1979); *Analysis and Estimates* (1980); *Counterintelligence* (1980); *Covert Action* (1981); and *Clandestine Collection* (1982). (All are hereafter cited by subtitle.)

11. Roger Hilsman, "The Foreign Policy Consensus: An Interim Report," *Journal of Conflict Resolution* 3, no. 4 (1959): 361; idem, *The Politics of Policymaking in Defense and Foreign Affairs* (New York: Harper and Row, 1971); idem, *To Move a Nation: The Politics of Foreign Policy in the Administration of John F. Kennedy* (Garden City, N.Y.: Doubleday, 1967). See also Richard C. Snyder, H. W. Bruck, and Burton Sapin, eds., *Foreign Policy Decisionmaking: An Approach to the Study of International Politics* (New York: Free Press, 1962), pp. 60-74.

12. Hilsman, *Politics of Policymaking*, pp. 136-38.

13. Hilsman, *To Move a Nation*, p. 4.

14. Ibid., p. 5.

15. Warner R. Schilling, Paul Y. Hammond, and Glenn H. Snyder, *Strategy, Politics, and Defense Budgets* (New York: Columbia Univ. Press, 1962), p. 23. Hilsman, *To Move a Nation*, p. 13.

16. Hans J. Morgenthau, *Politics among Nations*, 5th ed., rev. (New York: Knopf, 1978), pp. 4, 36. Idem, "Another Great Debate: The National Interest of the United States," *American Political Science Review* 66 (Dec. 1952): 961-98. Nicholas J. Spykman, *America's Strategy in World Politics* (New York: Harcourt Brace Jovanovich, 1942), p. 7.

17. See, e.g., Charles Burton Marshall, "The National Interest," in Robert A. Goldwin, ed., *Readings in American Foreign Policy* (New York: Oxford Univ. Press, 1959), p. 664 (reprinted from *Department of State Bulletin*, May 5, 1952).

18. Seyom Brown, for instance, argued that American foreign policy in the twenty years following World War II was driven by the need to maintain strength sufficient to protect and advance an "irreducible triumvirate of interest": survival, the perpetuation of the nontotalitarian condition of the nation, and economic well-being. Observable variances in policy were due not to changes in these fundamental purposes, but to changes in the premises of power, the means thought appropriate or necessary to serve those ends, given perceptions of the nation's attributes of strength and those of major competitors. Seyom Brown, *The Faces of Power: Constancy and Change in United States Foreign Policy from Truman to Johnson* (New York: Columbia Univ. Press, 1968). See also the earlier work by Robert Osgood, which discerned increased American attention to power imperatives as the nation matured in its outlook on international affairs: Robert Endicott Osgood, *Ideals and Self-Interest in America's Foreign Relations: The Great Transformation of the Twentieth Century* (Chicago: Univ. of Chicago Press, 1953), pp. 429-32.

19. See, e.g., Charles W. Kegley and Eugene R. Wittkopf, *American Foreign Policy: Pattern and Process* (New York: St. Martin's Press, 1979), pp. 29-50.

20. Paul Seabury, *Power, Freedom, and Diplomacy: The Foreign Policy of the United States of America* (New York: Vintage Books, 1967), pp. 84, 86-87.

21. Samuel P. Huntington, *The Common Defense: Strategic Programs in National Politics* (New York: Columbia Univ. Press, 1961), pp. 2-3.

22. Norman A. Graebner, *The Age of Global Power: The United States since 1939* (New York: John Wiley, 1979), pp. 302-6.

23. Arnold Wolfers, "The Pole of Power and the Pole of Indifference," *World Politics* 4 (Oct. 1951): 37, 48-52.

24. Ibid., pp. 54, 53.

25. Kenneth N. Waltz, *Theory of International Politics* (Reading, Mass.: Addison-Wesley, 1979), p. 105.

26. Ibid., p. 107.

27. Ibid.

28. Ibid., p. 125.

29. Ibid., p. 127.

30. Samuel P. Huntington, *American Politics: The Promise of Disharmony* (Cambridge: Harvard Univ. Press, 1981), pp. 1-12. See also Huntington, "American Ideals versus American Institutions," *Political Science Quarterly* 97 (Spring 1982): 1.

31. Huntington, *American Politics*, p. 237, 240.

32. Ibid., pp. 259-67.

33. Osgood, *Ideals and Self-Interest*, p. 437.

Chapter 2

1. Prominent alternative conceptions are noted in Hilsman, "On Intelligence," p. 129. See also, Ransom, "Being Intelligent about Secret Intelligence Agencies," p. 141.

2. U.S. President, Executive Order 12333, *United States Foreign Intelligence Activities*, sect. 2.1, *Federal Register* 46, no. 235 (Dec. 8, 1981): 59941, 59949. (Hereafter cited as EO 12333.)

3. See the survey of these factors in U.S. Congress, Senate, Select Committee to Study Governmental Operations with Respect to Intelligence Activities, *Final Report, Book I: Foreign and Military Intelligence*, S. Rept. 94-755, 94 Cong. 2 sess. (1976), pp. 257-62 (hereafter cited as *Foreign and Military Intelligence*). See also Ray S. Cline, *World Power Assessment: A Calculus of Strategic Drift* (Washington, D.C.: Georgetown Univ. Center for Strategic and International Studies, 1975); John M. Collins, *U.S. Defense Planning: A Critique* (Boulder: Westview Press, 1982), pp. 113-32.

4. *Foreign and Military Intelligence*, pp. 17-18.

5. Information needs generally fall into well-recognized categories: strategic warning; indications of crises or armed hostilities; foreign military deployments; foreign political and military capabilities and intentions; and economic, political, sociological, and tactical military information affecting American interests.

6. The names and purposes of the various intelligence "products" have varied, and it is not the intent of this study to describe them or to trace their evolution. An authoritative description of them is available in *Foreign and Military Intelligence*, pp. 259-62.

7. William J. Barnds, "Intelligence and Policymaking in an Institutional Context," in U.S. Commission on the Organization of Government for the Conduct of Foreign Policy (the "Murphy Commission"), *Report of the Commission, Appendix U: Intelligence Functions Analyses* (Washington, D.C.: GPO, 1975), pp. 21, 33. (Hereafter cited as *Murphy Commission Report*).

8. *Foreign and Military Intelligence*, pp. 83-92, describes continuing attempts to discipline and rationalize the intelligence production process. See also Robert E. Hunter's account of Carter Administration efforts in this regard: *Presidential Control of Foreign Policy:*

Management or Mishap, The Washington Papers no. 91 (New York: Praeger, 1982), pp. 37-38.

9. Taylor G. Belcher, "Clandestine Operations," in *Murphy Commission Report*, p. 67.

10. EO 12333, part 3, sec. 3.4(h).

11. Ibid. sec. 3.4(a).

12. Ibid., 3.4(f).

13. As Alexander Hamilton indicated in *Federalist 75*, they foresaw that "accurate and comprehensive knowledge of foreign politics" would be required in the management of our external relations. Similarly, John Jay, while addressing the treaty-making power of the national government in *Federalist 64*, recognized that management of the "business of intelligence" would be an important contribution to that process. And all understood the arena of international politics as one which mandated some capability to discern the shifting tides of events. See *The Federalist Papers*, with an introduction by Clinton Rossiter (New York: Mentor Books, 1961), pp. 452, 392-93.

14. Charles A. Beard, *The Idea of National Interest: An Analytical Study in Foreign Policy* (New York: Macmillan, 1934), pp. 33-49.

15. In *Federalist 4*, Jay surveys the world and finds much potential for conflict between America and the major European nations, especially because of commercial and navigational rivalries. In the natural order of things, America should expect to encounter conflict, competition, and the conscious striving of others for advantage. Inducements to war would abound, arising from the natural operation of the international system. Additionally, Jay knew that America would face adversaries who sought not simply advantage but preeminence, whose designs would include not only assertion of national interest but also diminution of their rivals' competitive capabilities. See *Federalist Papers*, pp. 46-47. Alexander Hamilton echoed that view in *Federalist 6*, finding power-maximizing motives and the urge to dominate inherent in the relations of nations; ibid., p. 54.

16. Ibid., pp. 42, 45-47.

17. "Additional Views of Senator Frank Church Concerning Covert Action," *Foreign and Military Intelligence*, p. 563. See also William E. Colby, "Intelligence Secrecy and Security in a Free Society," *International Security* 1 (Fall 1976): 3.

18. U.S. Department of the Army, Field Manual 100-5, *Operations*, July 1, 1976, pp. 7-2, 7-3.

19. Herbert Scoville, "Is Espionage Necessary for Our Security?" *Foreign Affairs* 54 (April 1976): 482, 484; Christopher Andrew, "Whitehall, Washington, and the Intelligence Services," *International Affairs* 53 (July 1977): 394.

20. E. Drexel Godfrey, Jr., "Ethics and Intelligence," *Foreign Affairs* 56 (April 1978): 624, 627.

21. Statement of President Reagan on issuance of Executive Order 12333, *United States Intelligence Activities, Weekly Compilation of Presidential Documents* 17, no. 49 (Dec. 7, 1981): 1335-36.

22. This categorization was offered in a July 18, 1982, presentation by Theodore Shackley (former CIA station chief in Saigon and former CIA associate deputy director for operations) to the Seminar on Intelligence for Teaching Faculty held by the National Strategy Information Center at Bowdoin College, Brunswick, Maine. Other professionals may use a slightly different categorization, especially with regard to the technical methods. See, e.g., Scoville, "Is Espionage Necessary," p. 484.

23. Testimony of William E. Colby before the House Permanent Select Committee on Intelligence, printed in U.S. Senate, Select Committee on Intelligence, *National Reorganization and Reform Act of 1978: Hearings Before the Senate Select Committee on Intelligence on S. 2525*, 95 Cong. 2 sess. (1978), p. 43 (hereinafter cited as *S. 2525 Hearings*).

24. Typical discussions of these points can be found in Ransom, *Central Intelligence and*

Naional Security, pp. 17-18; testimony of Thomas H. Karamessines, former CIA deputy director of plans, *S. 2525 Hearings,* p. 117; Barnds, "Intelligence and Policymaking," pp. 24-25, Samuel Halpern, "Clandestine Collection," in Godson, *Elements of Intelligence,* p. 37. Ray S. Cline, *Secrets, Spies, and Scholars: Blueprint of the Essential CIA* (Washington, DC: Acropolis Books, 1976), p. 10.

25. On ethical reservations, see Godfrey, "Ethics and Intelligence." On the relative importance of human intelligence see Kenneth L. Adelman, "A Clandestine Clan," *International Security* 5 (Summer 1980): 152-69; Scoville, "Is Espionage Necessary," p. 482; Richard K. Betts, "Surprise Despite Warnings," pp. 551, 556. One observer has suggested, more specifically, that human espionage provides only 5 percent of the volume of information collected by the intelligence community. Paul W. Blackstock, "Intelligence, Covert Operations, and Foreign Policy," in *Murphy Commission Report,* pp. 95, 101. Another, a former intelligence official, once suggested that its contributions are so minimal that it could be eliminated from the intelligence community's repertoire without appreciable damage to the nation. Testimony of E. Drexel Godfrey, *S. 2525 Hearings,* p. 106

26. See the Senate testimony of former CIA directors George Bush, William Colby, and Richard Helms in *S. 2525 Hearings,* pp. 59-60, 60-61, and 210, respectively.

27. William J. Barnds, "Intelligence Functions," in *Murphy Commission Report,* pp. 7, 15; Scoville, "Is Espionage Necessary," pp. 491-92.

28. Perhaps the best overview of collection techniques appears in Harry Rositzke, *The CIA's Secret Operations: Espionage, Counterespionage, and Covert Action* (New York: Reader's Digest Press, 1977), pp. 102-3. Statement of Frank C. Carlucci in U.S. Congress, House, Permanent Select Committee on Intelligence, *Impact of the Freedom of Information Act and the Privacy Act on Intelligence Activities: Hearings before a Subcommittee of the Permanent Select Committee on Intelligence,* 96 Cong. 1 sess. (1979), p. 4 (hereafter cited as *FOIA Hearings*). Testimony of E. Henry Knoche, former deputy director of Central Intelligence, *S. 2525 Hearings,* p. 61.

29. The categorizations used in this discussion are those provided in Colonel (USAF) George E. Daniels, "An Approach to Reconnaissance Doctrine," *Air University Review* 33 (Mar.-Apr. 1982): 62. See also Amrom Katz, "Technical Collection in the 1980's," in Godson, *Clandestine Collection,* p. 101.

30. Both optical and infrared techniques are limited by the time now required to retrieve and interpret the resulting imagery. For strategic crisis or for military applications in tactical situations, much research has been devoted to development of "real-time" collection and transmission techniques, including the use of television from satellites and aircraft. See Ford Rowan, *Techno Spies* (New York: G.P. Putnam's Sons, 1978), pp. 155-56; Scoville, "Is Espionage Necessary," p. 486.

31. Scoville, "Is Espionage Necessary," p. 486.

32. Information discussed in this section concerning signals intelligence is derived from: *Foreign and Military Intelligence,* pp. 354-55; statement of LTG (USAF) Lew Allen, Jr., director, National Security Agency, in U.S. Congress, House, Select Committee on Intelligence, *U.S. Intelligence Agencies and Activities: Intelligence Costs and Fiscal Procedures: Hearings before the House Select Committee on Intelligence,* 94 Cong. 1 sess. (1975) 1: 368-78; Daniels, "Approach to Reconnaissance Doctrine," pp. 65-66.

33. The controversy has involved mainly disputes about whether the definition of CI ought to treat it only as a set of activities, or whether it ought to be conceived as a category of information also. See Arthur A. Zuehlke, Jr., "What Is Counterintelligence?" in Godson, *Counterintelligence,* pp. 11, 13-16; Newton S. Miler, "Counterintelligence," in Godson, *Elements of Intellligence,* pp. 47, 49-50; *Foreign and Military Intelligence,* pp. 165-66. Some specialists might argue, as well, that operations against the terrorist threat are not the exclusive preserve of CI operatives.

34. Kenneth E. de Graffenreid, "Building for a New Counterintelligence Capability:

Recruitment and Training," in Godson, *Counterintelligence*, pp. 259, 263-64.

35. Arnold Beichman, "Can Counterintelligence Come In from the Cold?" *Policy Review* 15 (Winter 1981): 93, 98.

36. Statement of William H. Webster in U.S. Congress, House, Permanent Select Committee on Intelligence, *H.R. 6588, the National Intelligence Act of 1980: Hearings before a Subcommittee of the House Permanent Select Committee on Intelligence*, 96 Cong. 2 sess. (1980), pp. 50-51 (hereafter cited as *H.R. 6588 Hearings*).

37. Beichman, "Can Counterintelligence Come In," p. 93.

38. Arnold Beichman and Roy Godson, "Legal Constraints and Incentives," in Godson, *Counterintelligence*, pp. 279, 284-85.

39. See the testimony of FBI Director Clarence D. Kelly in U.S. Congress, House, Committee on the Judiciary, *Surveillance: Hearings before a Subcommittee of the Committee on the Judiciary on the Matter of Wiretapping, Electronic Eavesdropping, and other Surveillance*, Part 1, 94 Cong. 1 sess. (1975): 461, 462-63 (hereafter cited as *Surveillance*).

40. See, for example, the Supreme Court's support for the distinction between law enforcement and "security" surveillance rules in *United States* v. *United States District Court*, 407 U.S. 297, at 322 (1972).

41. *Federalist Papers*, pp. 148-52, 412.

42. Miler, "Counterintelligence," p. 51. See also statement of John McMahon, U.S., Congress, House, Permanent Select Committee on Intelligence, *Soviet Covert Action (The Forgery Offensive: Hearings before the Subcommittee on Oversight of the Permanent Select Committee on Intelligence*, 96 Cong. 2 sess. (1980), pp. 2-3 (hereafter cited as *Soviet Covert Action Hearings*). See also, Herbert Romerstein, "Soviet Intelligence in the United States," in Godson, *Counterintelligence*, pp. 161-62. It is common for counterintellience specialists to buttress arguments about the magnitude of the Soviet challenge with statistics showing the number of Soviet diplomatic and other personnel working in or visiting the United States. All are viewed as potential spies or spymasters. See Miler, "Counterintelligence," p. 51; *Foreign and Military Intelligence*, pp. 557-62.

43. U.S. Department of State, Bureau of Public Affairs, *Soviet "Active Measures": Forgery, Disinformation, Political Operations*, Special Report No. 88, Oct. 1981, p. 1.

44. Ibid., pp. 2-4.

45. U.S., Congress, Senate, Select Committee on Intelligence, *Activities of "Friendly" Foreign Intelligence Services in the United States: A Case Study*, Committee Print, 95 Cong., 2 sess. (June 1978), p. 23. Statement and testimony of William H. Webster, *H.R. 6588 Hearings*, pp. 50-58; address by Frank H. Perez, Office for Combating Terrorism, Department of State, before the Conference on Terrorism sponsored by the Institute de Questions Internationales, Madrid, Spain, June 10, 1982: "Terrorist Target: The Diplomat," in U.S. Department of State, Bureau of Public Affairs, *Current Policy*, no. 402 (June 10, 1982).

46. *Foreign and Military Intelligence*, p. 166; Zuehlke, "What Is Counterintelligence?" p. 26.

47. One counterintelligence specialist has described four other types of security operations: (1) "defensive source programs," in which sources within an institution presumed under threat observe the actions of others who might be vulnerable to foreign intelligence approaches; (2) countermeasures employed to identify technical devices planted by adversary services to collect information; (3) security education programs; (4) special vulnerability assessments for sensitive installations and activities. Zuehlke, "What Is Counterintelligence?" pp. 26-27.

48. See the various materials describing CI techniques in *Surveillance*, pp. 113-81.

49. See Central Intelligence Agency, Office of Public Affairs, *Intelligence: The Acme of Skill* (Washington, D.C.), p. 28. Covert action is there described as a "special activity

conducted abroad in support of US foreign policy objectives and executed so that the role of the United States Government is not apparent or not acknowledged publicly. Covert action is distinct from the intelligence gathering function . . . [It] often gives the United States a foreign policy option between diplomatic and military action."

50. Angelo Codevilla, "Covert Action and Foreign Policy," in Godson, *Covert Action*, p. 82.

51. Arthur M. Schlesinger, Jr., *The Imperial Presidency* (New York: Popular Library, 1973), p. 167. See also H. Bradford Westerfield, *The Instruments of America's Foreign Policy* (New York: Crowell, 1963), pp. 401-54; Hilsman, *To Move A Nation*, pp. 75-88; Henry Kissinger, *White House Years* (Boston and Toronto: Little, Brown, 1979), pp. 661-83; Thomas Powers, *The Man Who Kept the Secrets: Richard Helms and the CIA* (New York: Knopf, 1979), p. 236-38.

52. Presentation given at Bowdoin College, Brunswick, Maine, to the Seminar on Intelligence for Teaching Faculty, National Strategy Information Center, July 19, 1982. An earlier (1968) summary by Mr. Bissell was published in Victor Marchetti and John D. Marks, *The CIA and the Cult of Intelligence* (New York: Knopf, 1974), pp. 381, 387.

53. Examples are: Agee, *Inside the Company*; Marchetti and Marks, *CIA and the Cult of Intelligence;* Stockwell, *In Search of Enemies;* and Frank Snepp, *Decent Interval* (New York: Random House, 1977).

54. U.S. Congress, Senate, Select Committee to Study Governmental Operations with Respect to Intelligence Activities, *An Interim Report; Alleged Assassination Plots Involving Foreign Leaders,* S. Rept. 94-465, 94 Cong. 1 sess. (1975) (hereafter cited as *Interim Report*).

55. *Foreign and Military Intelligence.*

56. This program was broadcast on Feb. 27, 1977.

57. John Marks, *The CIA and Mind Control: The Search for the Manchurian Candidate* (New York: McGraw-Hill, 1980); Tad Szulc, "Putting the Bite Back in CIA," *New York Times Magazine,* Apr. 6, 1980, p. 28. On Nicaragua, see, e.g., Joanne Omang, "Reagan Defends U.S. Right to Use Covert Activity," *Washington Post,* Oct. 20, 1983, p. A1.

58. See, for example, Theodore G. Shackley, "The Uses of Paramilitary Covert Action in the 1980's," in Godson, *Covert Action*, p. 133.

59. Allen W. Dulles, *The Craft of Intelligence* (New York: Harper and Row, 1963), pp. 223, 232.

60. Ibid., pp. 235, 236.

61. George W. Ball, *Diplomacy for a Crowded World: An American Foreign Policy* (Boston and Toronto: Little, Brown, 1976), pp. 219-20; Kissinger, *White House Years*, pp. 658-59.

62. Cline, *Secrets, Spies, and Scholars*, pp. 97-98.

63. *Foreign and Military Intelligence*, pp. 563-64.

64. Codevilla, "Covert Action and Foreign Policy," p. 179.

65. Recent works include: on domestic intelligence, Donner, *Age of Surveillance*; on intelligence collection, Rhodri Jeffreys-Jones, *American Espionage: From Secret Service to CIA* (New York: Free Press, 1977); on intelligence generally, Thomas F. Troy, *Donovan and the CIA: A History of the Establishment of the Central Intelligence Agency* (Frederick, Md: Univ. Press of America, 1981).

66. Henry M. Wriston, *Executive Agents in American Foreign Relations* (Baltimore: Johns Hopkins Univ. Press, 1929); idem, "The Special Envoy," *Foreign Affairs* 38 (Jan. 1960): 219-20.

67. In their modern forms these arguments are summarized in *Foreign and Military Intelligence,* pp. 34-35; statement of Kevin T. Maroney, deputy assistant attorney general, Criminal Division, Department of Justice, in U.S., Congress, House, Committee on Internal Security, *Domestic Intelligence Operations for Internal Security Purposes: Hearings before the*

Committee, 93 Cong. 2 sess. (1974), Part 1: 3332-35 (hereafter cited as *Internal Security Hearings*).

68. Act of February 9, 1793, 1 Stst. 300.

69. Tyrus G. Fain, et al., eds. *The Intelligence Community: History, Organization, and Issues* (New York: Bowker, 1977), p. 3.

70. For a history of domestic intelligence organizations, see U.S. Congress, Senate, Select Committee to Study Governmental Operations with Respect to Intelligence Activities, *Final Report,* Book 2: *Intelligence Activities and the Rights of Americans,* pp. 21-28; (hereafter cited as *Intelligence Activities and the Rights of Americans);* and Book 3: *Supplementary Detailed Staff Reports on Intelligence Activities and the Rights of Americans,* 94 Cong. 2 sess. (1976), pp. 375-559 (hereafter cited as *Supplementary Staff Reports).*

71. The provision is now found in a Sept. 6, 1966, codification of laws relating to the FBI, 28 USC 531-37; it is sec. 533.

72. Statement of J. Edgar Hoover, *Internal Security Hearings,* pp. 3688, 3689.

73. Collected at pp. 3697-98 of *Internal Security Hearings.*

74. These and associated directives pertinent to the OSS are collected in Troy, *Donovan and the CIA,* pp. 423-65.

75. R. Harris Smith, *OSS: The Secret History of America's First Central Intelligence Agency* (New York: Dell, 1972), p. 361.

76. 50 USC 403.

77. The Church Committee finally concluded that the original intent of Congress did include espionage activities. *Foreign and Military Intelligence,* p. 127.

78. "Congressional Authorization for the Central Intelligence Agency to Conduct Covert Action," *Foreign and Military Intelligence, Appendix I,* pp. 475, 477. See also statement of Clark Clifford, former chairman of the President's Foreign Intelligence Advisory Board and former secretary of defense, in *S. 2525 Hearings,* pp. 7-8.

79. In 1949, Congress passed the Central Intelligence Agency Act of 1949 (50 USC 403a-403j). It was an enabling act containing administrative provisions necessary for the conduct of the agency's mission, including waiver of normal restrictions placed on governmental acquisition of material, on hiring of personnel, and on accounting for funds. The Senate's investigation in 1976 found that, although Congress as a body in 1949 knew generally that some kinds of secret CIA operations were being facilitated by this legislation, the act cannot be read as approval of the "full repertoire" of activity that had gained sanction within the executive. *Foreign and Military Intelligence,* pp. 492-96.

80. U.S. Congress, House, Permanent Select Committee on Intelligence, *U.S. Intelligence Agencies and Activities: Intelligence Costs and Fiscal Procedures: Hearings before the Permanent Select Committee on Intelligence,* 94 Cong. 1 sess. (1975), part 1:383-85.

81. President Ford's executive order excluded Intelligence Community Staff elements from the formal definition of the intelligence community. U.S. President, Executive Order 11905, *U.S. Foreign Intelligence Activities, Federal Register* 41, no. 34 (Feb. 19, 1976):7701, sec. 2(b) (hereafter cited as EO 11905). President Reagan's includes them: EO 12333, sect. 3.4(f).

82. EO 12333, sec. 3.4(f).

83. EO 12333, sec. 1.4.

84. These descriptions of functions are summarized from EO 12333 and from the CIA publication *Intelligence: The Acme of Skill.*

85. See, for example, J. Edgar Hoover, *A Study of Communism* (New York: Holt, Rinehart and Winston, 1962).

86. Anthony Cave Brown, *The Last Hero: Wild Bill Donovan* (New York: Times Books, 1982), p. 786. See also Troy, *Donovan and the CIA;* and Smith, *OSS.*

Chapter 3

1. An early example of this was the 1949 agreement delimiting the investigative duties of the FBI and the counterintelligence elements of the several armed services. The agreement, with subsequent amendments, appears in *Internal Security Hearings*, pp. 3369-83.

2. See for instance, the discussion of NSC directives concerning the conduct and coordination of covert action operations in *Foreign and Military Intelligence*, pp. 48-53.

3. One compilation of newspaper stories gathered from all over the nation concerning alleged operational excesses includes 350 pages of newspaper extracts. Judith F. Buncher, et al., eds. *The CIA and the Security Debate, 1971-1975* (New York: Facts on File, 1976).

4. Sherman Kent's book *Strategic Intelligence for American World Policy* (Princeton: Princeton Univ. Press, 1949) has been recognized as a landmark study in this genre. See also Roger Hilsman, "Intelligence and Policymaking in Foreign Affairs," *World Politics* 5 (Oct. 1952): 1.

5. One major study, for instance, scrutinized "doctrines" about what intelligence agencies ought to produce and how they ought to produce it. It argued that the then-prevailing focus on compilation of descriptive data was far too narrow and clearly insufficient to support policymakers' needs. Roger Hilsman, Jr., *Strategic Intelligence and National Decisions* (Glencoe, Ill.: Free Press, 1956).

6. Ransom, *Central Intelligence and National Security*, p. 77.

7. See, e.g., Ransom, *The Intelligence Establishment* (Cambridge: Harvard Univ. Press, 1970), p. 236, noting the continuing lack of well-defined organizational purposes.

8. Ransom, *Central Intelligence and National Security*, pp. 79-82.

9. Ibid., p. 82.

10. Ransom, *Intelligence Establishment*, p. 235.

11. Ransom, *Central Intelligence and National Security*, pp. 201-4.

12. Ibid., p. 84.

13. Ibid., 145-46.

14. Ibid., p. 184. See also pp. 206-8.

15. Paul W. Blackstock, *The Strategy of Subversion: Manipulating the Politics of Other Nations* (Chicago: Quadrangle Books, 1964), pp. 41-42.

16. Ibid., p. 184.

17. Ibid., p. 292.

18. Ibid., p. 321.

19. Ibid., p. 184. See also p. 187.

20. Ibid., p. 188.

21. Ibid., p. 190.

22. Ibid., pp. 95-120.

23. Ibid., pp. 135-36.

24. Ibid., pp. 275, 235-36, 278-80.

25. Hilsman, *To Move a Nation*.

26. Ibid., pp. 64-67.

27. Ibid., pp. 74-81.

28. Ibid., pp. 73-74, 85.

29. Lyman B. Kirkpatrick, Jr., *The Real CIA* (New York: Macmillan, 1968), pp. 1-4.

30. Ibid., pp. 289-91.

31. David Wise and Thomas B. Ross, *The Espionage Establishment* (New York: Random House, 1967), pp. 154-56.

32. Quoted in *Foreign and Military Intelligence*, p. 452.

33. The first revelations were published in Christopher H. Pyle, "CONUS Intelligence: The Army Watches Civilian Politics," *Washington Monthly* (Jan. 1970), p. 4. Restrictions were announced in U.S. Department of the Army, AGDA-A(M) Letter, 1 June 1971, Subject: Acquisition of Information Concerning Persons and Organizations Not Affiliated with the Department of Defense. Army Regulation 380-13, *Acquisition and Storage of Information Concerning Non-Affiliated Persons and Organizations, 30 September 1974.* On the congressional investigation, see U.S. Congress, Senate, Committee on the Judiciary, *Military Surveillance of Civilian Politics: A Report of the Subcommittee on Constitutional Rights of the Committee on the Judiciary,* 93 Cong. 1 sess. (1973).

34. David Wise, *The American Police State: The Government against the People* (New York: Random House, 1976) p. 185.

35. Prominent examples are Marchetti and Marks, *CIA and the Cult of Intelligence;* Agee, *Inside the Company.*

36. L. Fletcher Prouty, *The Secret Team: The CIA and Its Allies in Control of the United States and the World* (Englewood Cliffs, N.J.: Prentice-Hall, 1973).

37. An excellent example is Nelson Blackstock's COINTELPRO. See also the collection of articles "exposing" CIA activities in Howard Frazier, ed., *Uncloaking the CIA* (New York: Free Press, 1978).

38. Ray S. Cline, for instance, provided insightful and knowledgeable analysis in *Secrets, Spies, and Scholars.*

39. See *Intelligence Activities and the Rights of Americans;* and *Supplementary Staff Reports.*

40. See the reports on these activities in "Rattling Skeletons in the CIA Closet," *Time,* Jan. 8, 1975, p. 44; Marchetti and Marks, *CIA and the Cult of Intelligence* pp. 226, 232-35; "Reforming the Secret Agencies," *Nation,* Jan. 24, 1975, p. 67.

41. See, e.g., the discussion of "NSA Surveillance Programs" in Morton H. Halperin, et al., *The Lawless State: The Crimes of the U.S. Intelligence Agencies* (New York: Penguin Books, 1976), pp. 172-82.

42. Marchetti and Marks, *CIA and the Cult of Intelligence,* pp. 229-37.

43. "Brutal Intelligence," *New Republic,* Dec. 6, 1975, p. 5; "Our Keystone Kops in Havana," *Nation,* Jan. 24, 1976, p. 68.

44. Agee, *Inside the Company,* pp. 561-92, 114, 127-28; Marchetti and Marks, *CIA and the Cult of Intelligence,* p. 19.

45. Morton H. Halperin, "CIA, Denying What's Not in Writing,: *New Republic,* Oct. 4, 1975, pp. 11-12.

46. John H. F. Shattuck, *Rights of Privacy* (Skokie, Ill.: National Textbook Co., 1977), pp. 69-70.

47. U.S. Congress, House, Committee on the Judiciary, *Hearings before the Subcommittee on Courts, Civil Liberties, and the Administration of Justice,* 94 Cong. 1 sess. (1975), p. 181.

48. Ibid.

49. 277 U.S. 438 (1928).

50. *Silverman* v. *United States,* 365 U.S. 505 (1961).

51. 389 U.S. 347 (1967), and 388 U.S. 41 (1967), respectively.

52. 389 U.S. at 358, footnote 23. See also Justice Stewart's remarks in *Giordano* v. *United States,* 394 U.S. at 314 (1967). White's view is in 389 U.S. at 362.

53. 18 USC 2516 (1968), sec. (3).

54. 407 U.S. 297 (1972).

55. 494 Fed. 593 (2nd Cir.) *(en banc)* (1974), cert. den. 419 U.S. 881 (1974).

56. See *United States* v. *Clay,* 430 Fed. 165 (5th Cir. 1970), reversed on other grounds, 403 U.S. 698 (1971); *Zweibon* v. *Mitchell,* 363 F. Supp. 936 (D.C. District 1973).

57. *Supplementary Staff Reports,* pp. 819-21.

58. 410 F. Supp. 144 (1976).

59. *Bivens* v. *Six Unknown Named Agents*, 403 U.S. 388 (1971).

60. It was, in fact, the "general rule" concerning official immunity. *Barr* v. *Matteo*, 360 U.S. 564, 575 (1959).

61. Martin Shapiro, *The Pentagon Papers and the Courts: A Study in Foreign Policymaking and Freedom of the Press* (San Francisco: Chandler, 1972), p. 26.

62. Scholars were beginning to make recommendations in this regard, too. See, e.g., Lee H. Hamilton and Michael H. Van Dusen, "Making the Separation of Powers Work," *Foreign Affairs* 57 (Fall 1978): 17; Douglas J. Bennet, Jr., "Congress in Foreign Policy: Who Needs it?" *Foreign Affairs* 57 (Fall 1978): 40.

63. 32 USC 2422 (PL 93-559, sec. 662).

64. The amendment did expand the number of committees responsible for intelligence oversight, adding the two foreign relations committees to the Armed Services and Appropriations committees of both houses. There was some sentiment in Congress, however, after the notification requirement had been in place for more than a year, that the degree of compliance by the executive was questionable. See the remarks of Congressman Michael Harrington in *The CIA: Past Transgressions and Future Controls*, Monograph on National Security Affairs (Providence: Brown Univ., 1975), pp. 22-24.

65. See Sanford J. Ungar, "The Intelligence Tangle," *Atlantic* (April 1976), p. 34.

66. U.S. Congress, House, Select Committee on Intelligence, *Recommendations of the Final Report of the House Select Committee on Intelligence*, H. Rept. 94-833, 94 Cong. 2 sess. (1976).

67. "Reflections on the Quarter," *Orbis* (Winter 1976) p., 1247. See also the critical remarks of Congressman Michael Harrington in *The CIA*, pp. 28-29. Critics were also quick to point out that even in the midst of the intelligence debate, 122 members of the House had voted against conducting the inquiry at the outset.

68. Ungar, "Intelligence Tangle," p. 34.

69. "Entering the 1984 Decade," *Time*, Mar. 24, 1975, p. 26.

70. The committee's concept of its mandate is described early in its *Interim Report*, pp. 1-2.

71. Ibid., pp. 264-67.

72. Ibid., p. 11.

73. Ibid., p. 261.

74. *Foreign and Military Intelligence*, pp. 56-57.

75. Ibid., p. 57.

76. *Interim Report*, pp. 258-59.

77. *Intelligence Activities and the Rights of Americans*, pp. 1-3.

78. Ibid., p. 6.

79. *Foreign and Military Intelligence*, pp. 441-56.

80. Senator Inouye, chairman of the new committee, so indicated in a speech reported in *Washington Post*, Sept. 23, 1976, p. 1. After a year, the committee issued a brief report reconfirming the existence of the oversight procedures and explaining its mechanics. The report also asserted that the intelligence agencies were at last well-controlled and that national security interests justified retention and exercise of their properly supervised capabilities. U.S. Congress, Senate, Select Committee on Intelligence, Report No. 95-217, 95 Cong. 1 sess. (1977), pp. 13, 26 (hereafter cited as *Senate Report 95-217*).

81. See the letter to the editor of *New York Times* (Nov. 16, 1977, p. A 28) by Senator Walter Huddleston, who headed the subcommittee that was drafting the proposed statute, attributing legislative delays to the drawn-out process of coordination with the executive.

82. Emerging views were illustrated in sections 161 and 162 of H.R. 4173, 95 Cong., 1 sess. (introduced by Rep. Dellums of California), and paragraph 2(b) of H.R. 6051, 95 Cong. 1 sess. (introduced by Rep. Badillo of New York).

83. U.S. Congress, House, Committee on International Relations, *Congress and Foreign Policy – 1976*, Committee Print (Washington, D.C.: GPO, 1977), pp. 220-21.

84. This discussion is summarized from *Senate Report 95-217*.

85. Ibid., p. 1.

86. Ibid., p. 23.

87. The text of the proposal is printed in full in *Congressional Record*, Feb. 10, 1978, p. E 533, sects. 114, 131-39.

88. *Senate Report 95-217*, pp. 30-31.

89. Ibid., pp. 6-7. The Ford Administration had argued for a formula similar to the one appearing in the 1968 Omnibus Crime Control and Safe Streets Act (discussed earlier).

90. *Washington Post*, Apr. 30, 1977, p. A 6. (It would not, for instance, reach the facts in the *Berlin Democratic Club* case.)

91. See, e.g., remarks of Senator Birch Bayh, included in White House press release, *Remarks of the President upon Signing of the Intelligence Executive Order 12036*, Jan. 24, 1978 (Washington, D.C.: White House), p. 3.

92. See the Jan. 1976 argument by Secretary of State Kissinger for the lifting of congressional restrictions on U.S. aid (including covert action) to political factions within Angola, "Implications of Angola for Future U.S. Foreign Policy," statement by Secretary of State Kissinger before the Subcommittee on African Affairs of the Senate Committee on Foreign Relations, in Richard B. Stebbins and Elaine P. Adam, *American Foreign Relations, 1975: A Documentary Record* (New York: New York Univ. Press, 1977), pp. 605-7, 617-18.

93. Secretary of State Kissinger appealed for just that sort of solidarity on policy toward Angola. Ibid., p. 618.

94. See the critique of CIA activity in Africa, especially Angola, by Tony Monteiro, "The CIA in Africa," in Frazier, *Uncloaking the CIA*, p. 126.

95. See, e.g., Richard J. Barnet, *Roots of War* (New York: Penguin Books, 1972).

96. Stockwell, *In Search of Enemies*, pp. 252-53.

97. This perspective is expressed in *Intelligence Activities and the Rights of Americans*, pp. 1-5. See also Morton H. Halperin, "National Security and Civil Liberties," *Foreign Policy* 21 (Winter 1975-1976): 125; and Shattuck, *Rights of Privacy*, pp. 69-70.

98. Halperin, "National Security and Civil Liberties," pp. 129-30.

99. *Intelligence Activities and the Rights of Americans*, p. 291.

100. Ibid., p. 4.

101. *Intelligence Activities and the Rights of Americans*, p. 1.

102. An overview of these arguments can be obtained from Harry Rositzke, "America's Secret Operations: A Perspective," *Foreign Affairs* 53 (Jan. 1975): 334; Scoville, "Is Espionage Necessary," p. 482; and Godfrey, "Ethics and Intelligence," p. 624. See also Stockwell, *In Search of Enemies*, p. 254; and the views of former Senator Frank Church in *Foreign and Military Intelligence*, p. 564.

103. Ernest Lefever, "Can Covert Action Be Just?" *Policy Review* 12 (Spring 1980): 115.

104. See, e.g., Adler, "Executive Command and Control in Foreign Policy," p. 671.

105. Louis Henkin, *Foreign Affairs and the Constitution* (New York: Norton, 1975), p. 32.

106. The wartime ethos and legacy is described in Smith, OSS.

107. Ball, *Diplomacy for a Crowded World*, p. 228.

108. Arthur Schlesinger and other critics of the "imperial presidency" have treated the intelligence advantage as a crucial one tipping the intragovernmental balance of power toward the executive; Schlesinger, *Imperial Presidency*, p. 166.

109. *Intelligence Activities and the Rights of Americans*, p. 292.

Chapter 4

1. *Public Papers of the Presidents of the United States: Gerald R. Ford, August 9 to December 31, 1974* (Washington, D.C.: G.P.O., 1975), pp. 150-51.

2. Ibid., p. 156.

3. In addition to the vice-president, the members appointed to the panel were: John T. Conner, former U.S. secretary of commerce and at the time chairman and chief executive officer of Allied Chemical Corporation; C. Douglas Dillon, then a director of Dillon, Read, and formerly U.S. secretary of the treasury, U.S. ambassador to France, and U.S. under secretary of state; Erwin N. Griswold, then a Washington lawyer and formerly U.S. solicitor general and dean of the Harvard Law School; Joseph Lane Kirkland, secretary-treasurer of the AFL-CIO; Lyman L. Lemnitzer (general, U.S. Army, retired), former chairman of the Joint Chiefs of Staff and former supreme allied commander in Europe; Ronald Reagan, former governor of California and former president of the Screen Actors Guild; and Edgar F. Shannon, Commonwealth Professor of English at the University of Virginia and former president of that university. See U.S. President, Executive Order 11828, *Commission on CIA Activities within the United States,* Jan. 4, 1975, *Weekly Compilation of Presidential Documents* 11, no. 2 (Jan. 13, 1975):24-25.

4. U.S. President, Commission on CIA Activities within the United States, *Report to the President by the Commission on CIA Activities within the United States* (Washington D.C.: G.P.O. 1975), p. 80 (hereafter cited as *Rockefeller Commission Report*).

5. *Rockefeller Commission Report,* p. XI.

6. News conference of Mar. 17, 1975, *Public Papers of the Presidents of the United States: Gerald R. Ford, 1975,* p. 368.

7. Ibid., pp. 789-90.

8. *Weekly Compilation of Presidential Documents* 11, no. 2 (Jan. 13, 1975): 23, 24.

9. *Public Papers of the Presidents of the United States: Gerald R. Ford, 1975,* pp. 1513-14.

10. Ibid., pp. 550-51.

11. William Colby, director of Central Intelligence at the time, has indicated that President Ford himself hoped to limit damage to the intelligence community by appointing this highly-visible investigatory panel and drawing its charter narrowly. William Colby and Peter Forbath, *Honorable Men: My Life in the CIA* (New York: Simon and Schuster, 1978), pp. 398-400. Colby's account is consistent with that provided by President Ford in Gerald R. Ford, *A Time To Heal* (New York: Harper and Row, 1979), pp. 229-30.

12. *Weekly Compilation of Presidential Documents* 11, no.2 (Jan. 13, 1975): 24.

13. William Colby's account indicates that the president by this time knew of the so-called "family jewels" list, a CIA-prepared list of past activities the agency thought might be challengeable by critics. Colby and Forbath, *Honorable Men,* pp. 398-400.

14. *Rockefeller Commission Report,* pp. 3-5.

15. Ibid., p. 5.

16. Ibid., p. 48.

17. Ibid., p. 55.

18. Ibid., p. 58.

19. Ibid.

20. Ibid., p. 62.

21. NSC direction was accomplished almost entirely through announcement of basic policies in National Security Council Intelligence Directives (NSCIDS), and in decisions about allocation of resources to and within the intelligence community. The general policy pronouncements were very broad decisions about, and delegations of, authority. They often assigned additional responsibilities to the CIA and to other intelligence agencies pursuant to

the 1947 National Security Act. In some cases, NSC guidance had declared specifically where and how the CIA should undertake particular operations, but more typically it did not. Ibid., p. 71.

22. The Forty Committee was chaired by the assistant to the president for national security affairs and included (among others) the director of Central Intelligence, the chairman of the Joint Chiefs of Staff, and representatives of the secretaries of state and defense.

23. For a more extensive discussion of OMB roles, see also the report of the Senate's investigating committee, *Foreign and Military Intelligence,* pp. 66-70.

24. *Rockefeller Commission Report,* p. 77.

25. The commission recognized arguments that for several reasons inherent in the nature of the judiciary, the courts were at best a clumsy instrument of control. Judges were generally reluctant to interefere with activities closely related to foreign affairs, and most of the CIA's activities were unarguably foreign intelligence operations. Secrecy, moreover, effectively shielded CIA operations from potential challengers who might otherwise take their complaints to court. Ibid., p. 78.

26. Ibid., p. 83.

27. Ibid.

28. Ibid., pp. 87-88.

29. Ibid., p. 95

30. The agency knew, as well, of the public and congressional sensitivities that would be aroused if the operation was discovered. Because of those sensitivities the agency's inspector general, when he learned of the operation in 1960, recommended preparation of a cover story to be used in the event of public disclosure. The issue of legality – criminal misuse of the mail – was not then raised. During a 1971 briefing on the operation, then-Postmaster General Blount thought momentarily about reviewing the legality of the project, but then discarded the idea because such an inquiry would intrude upon the interests of compartmentation of knowledge about operational activity. Ibid., pp. 101-10.

31. Ibid., p. 149.

32. Other activities scrutinized included electronic eavesdropping (e.g., telephone taps on reporters suspected of obtaining "leaked" sensitive intelligence information), physical surveillances, surreptitious entry into homes, and examination of income tax records.

33. *Rockefeller Commission Report,* pp. 7-8.

34. Ibid.

35. Ibid., p. 10.

36. Ibid., p. 12.

37. For example, collecting foreign intelligence from witting sources within the United States, and coordinating protection of intelligence sources and methods. Ibid., pp. 12-13.

38. Ibid., p. 13.

39. Ibid., pp. 12-13.

40. Ibid., p. 19.

41. Ibid., p. 33.

42. One member of the commission, Erwin Griswold, was not satisfied with the report's recommendations. His "minority view," appearing in a footnote to the report (p. 81) anticipated major themes of criticism soon to appear in other forums where investigative charters were not so narrowly drawn and where dissonance about the imperative of national security would be quite pronounced.

43. News conference of June 9, 1975, *Public Papers of the Presidents of the United States: Gerald R. Ford, 1975,* p. 789.

44. Testimony of Leon Friedman, professor of law, Hofstra University, in *Surveillance*, p. 187.

45. Testimony of John H.F. Shattuck, ibid., p. 107.

46. For an overview of the "pressure group" politics that emerged on intelligence issues, see Roy Godson, "The Role of Pressure Groups," in Ernest W. Lefever and Roy Godson, eds., *The CIA and the American Ethic: An Unfinished Debate* (Washington, D.C.: Ethics and Public Policy Center, 1979), p. 67.

47. Testimony of Kevin T. Maroney, *Surveillance*, p. 458.

48. Testimony of Dean Rusk, ibid., p. 427.

49. The procedure was outlined in testimony of FBI Dirctor Clarence Kelley, ibid., p. 471.

50. Testimony of Dean Rusk, ibid., p. 430.

51. Ibid., p. 435.

52. In an exchange with Congressman Robert Drinan, who was pressing for closer judicial scrutiny of executive proposals for operations, Mr. Rusk said: "In this pretty mean and dirty game that is going on in the world in which many governments participate, I cannot help but − I cannot quite get out of my mind Leo Durocher's remark that 'nice guys finish last.' " Ibid., pp. 438-39.

53. U.S., Congress, Senate, Select Committee to Study Governmental Operations with Respect to Intelligence Activities, *Interim Report*, pp. 281-85.

54. Ibid., p. 1.

55. EO 11905.

56. *Weekly Compilation of Presidential Documents* 12, no. 8 (Feb. 23, 1976): 227-33 (hereinafter cited as *WCPD* 12/8).

57. Ibid., p. 228.

58. Ibid., p. 230.

59. EO 11905, sec. 1.

60. EO 11905, sec. 5.

61. *WCPD* 12/8, p. 228.

62. Ibid., See also EO 11905, sec. 3(a), concerning NSC functions.

63. See, e.g., the analysis in Cline, *Secrets, Spies, and Scholars* pp. 238-39.

64. EO 11905, sec. 3(c).

65. Ibid., sec. 6.

66. *WCPD* 12/8, p. 228.

67. This term was defined as "the gathering, analysis, dissemination, or storage of nonpublicly-available information without the informed express consent of the subject of the information."

68. The restrictions are contained in section 5 of the order.

69. EO 11905, sec. 3(d) (1) (XII).

70. *WCPD* 12/8, p. 243.

71. Ibid., p. 244.

72. Ibid., p. 243.

73. See, e.g., *Public Papers of the Presidents of the United States: Gerald R. Ford, 1975*, pp. 1506-07.

74. Ibid., p. 550. See also the president's Mar. 23, 1976, letter to Congress on proposed legislation on the use of electronic surveillance to obtain foreign intelligence information: *Public Papers of the Presidents of the United States, Gerald R. Ford, 1976-1977*, 1:793-94.

75. The FBI measures are examined in James T. Elliff, *The Reform of FBI Intelligence Operations* (Princeton: Princeton Univ. Press, 1979).

76. These rules did not cover FBI efforts to counter foreign espionage or other activities of foreign intelligence services. Nor did these "domestic" regulations apply to cases of "ordinary crime," for which law enforcement rules would still apply.

77. The investigations were to be limited to activities of individuals or groups intended to accomplish any of five purposes: overthrowing the federal government or the government of a state; interfering with the activities within the United States of foreign governments or their representatves; influencing governmental policies by interfering by force or violence with governmental functions or interstate commerce; depriving individuals of their civil rights; and creating domestic violence or rioting when such violence or rioting would necessitate as a countermeasure the use of federal armed forces. Testimony of Edward H. Levi in U.S. Congress, Senate, Select Committee to Study Governmental Operations with Respect to Intelligence Activities, *Hearings before the Senate Select Committee to Study Governmental Operations with Respect to Intelligence Activities*, vol. 6: *Intelligence Activities, Federal Bureau of Investigation,* 94 Cong. 1 sess. (1975), pp. 313, 317 (hereafter cited as *Church Committee Hearings*).

78. See, e.g., Herbert Romerstein, "Soviet Intelligence in the United States," and Arnold Beichman and Roy Godson, "Legal Constraints and Incentives," in Godson, pp. 161, 193-94, 281, 286-87.

79. *Church Committee Hearings,* 6: 320-24.

80. Under these rules, scattered parts of which were later forced onto the public record by lawsuits, the attorney general had authority to approve written requests for domestic electronic surveillance, the investigative technique most feared by civil liberties activists. Before granting approval he had to find probable cause to believe that the person "targeted" (but not, it should be noted, others involved) was an agent of a foreign power and that the use of the technique was necessary for one of the following reasons: (1) to protect the nation against actual or potential attack or other hostile acts of a foreign power; (2) to obtain foreign intelligence information deemed essential to the security of the nation; (3) to protect national security information against foreign intelligence activities; or (4) to obtain information relating to foreign affairs essential to the security of the nation. See *S. 2525 Hearings,* pp. 767-90.

81. *Church Committee Hearings,* 6: 328-29.

Chapter 5

1. See, e.g., "Senate Panel Inquires into CIA 'Bug' Reports," *Washington Post,* Dec. 14, 1976, p. 20.

2. See, e.g., "That 38-Year Investigation," *Washington Post,* Sept. 27, 1976, p. A 26. Typical of the effort to publicize the revelations generated by lawsuits was Nelson Blackstock's *COINTELPRO,* a compilation and analysis of FBI documents released in litigation.

3. Columnist Tom Wicker argued that intelligence officials would attempt to roll back the Ford Administration's new rules: "Spooks vs. Zilsh," *New York Times,* Dec. 10, 1976, p. 27. See also David Binder, "U.S. Intelligence Officials Apprehensive of New Shakeups under Carter," *New York Times,* Dec. 13, 1976, p. 43.

4. Prominent among these critics was Robert L. Borosage, "The Tyranny of Intelligence," *Nation,* Mar. 13, 1976, p. 296.

5. See, e.g., *Intelligence Activities and the Rights of Americans,* pp. 296-97; and *Foreign and Military Intelligence,* pp. 426-27. Other observers, though not members of Congress, were of the same mind. See, for instance, the views of former Director of Central Intelligence William E. Colby in "Reorganizing the CIA: Who and How," *Foreign Policy* 23 (Summer 1976): 53.

6. See the views of Senator John Tower in *Foreign and Military Intelligence,* pp. 573-76.

7. Compare the views of Senator John Tower, ibid., later restated in "Congress versus the President: The Formulation and Implementation of American Foreign Policy," *Foreign Affairs* 60 (Winter 1981-1982): 229-46; with those of Sanford J. Ungar, "The Intelligence Tangle," *Atlantic*, Apr. 1976, pp. 31, 41; and William Colby, "Reorganizing the CIA."

8. See the exchange on this point between Senators Bayh and Garn in U.S. Congress, Senate, Select Committee on Intelligence, *Nomination of E. Henry Knoche: Hearing before the Select Committee on Intelligence on Nomination of E. Henry Knoche to be Deputy Director of Central Intelligence*, 94 Cong. 2 sess. (1976), pp. 9-10 (hereafter cited as *Knoche Hearing*).

9. Peter Szanton and Graham Allison, "Reorganizing the CIA: Who and How," *Foreign Policy* 23 (Summer 1976): 63. See also Ungar, "Intelligence Tangle," p. 40.

10. William E. Colby, "The View from Langley," in Robert L. Borosage and John Marks, eds., *The CIA File* (New York: Grossman Publishers, 1976), p. 181. This was a speech before a most hostile audience, the Fund for Peace Conference on the CIA and Covert Action.

11. Walter F. Mondale, "Reorganizing the CIA: Who and How," *Foreign Policy* 23 (Summer 1976): 57-59.

12. The administration argued, for instance, against any tightening of the standard, prescribed in the 1974 Hughes-Ryan Amendment, for initiating covert action operations: that a proposed operation be "important to the national security." Critics were pressing at the time for an "essentiality" standard, which they thought might eliminate some questionable operations or proposals. Critics also pressed for more congressional involvement in the review of operational proposals prior to their implementation. The administration resisted this, too, as unfeasible and possibly harmful. *Knoche Hearing* ("E.H. Knoche Responses to Additional Interrogatories Submitted by Senator Gary Hart"), pp. 27-29.

13. *Public Papers of the Presidents: Jimmy Carter, 1977*, 242-43. These remarks were made in a February 24, 1977, meeting with employees of the Department of State. See also James T. Wooten, "Carter Says Foreign Sources are Questioning Their Safety in Providing Secrets after CIA Reports," *New York Times*, Feb. 25, 1977, p. 9.

14. David Binder, "U.S. Intelligence Officials Apprehensive of New Shakeups under Carter," *New York Times*, Dec. 13, 1976, p. 43.

15. Theodore C. Sorensen, *Watchmen in the Night: Presidential Accountability after Watergate* (Cambridge: MIT Press, 1975). See especially pp. 109-13 on the intelligence agencies.

16. The affidavits, filed in the Ellsberg case and the associated *New York Times* case, appear in U.S. Congress, Senate, Select Committee on Intelligence, *Nomination of Theodore C. Sorensen: Hearing before the Select Committee on Intelligence on Nomination of Theodore C. Sorensen to Be Director of Central Intelligence*, 95 Cong. 1 sess. (1977), pp. 18-30 (hereafter cited as *Sorensen Hearings*).

17. Remarks of Senators Jake Garn, William Hathaway, and Howard Baker, *Sorensen Hearings*, pp. 2-3, 4-5, and 10-11, respectively.

18. Ibid., p. 34 (Sorensen testimony).

19. Ibid., p. 33.

20. U.S. Congress, Senate, Select Committee on Intelligence, *Nomination of Admiral Stansfield Turner: Hearings before the Select Committee on Intelligence on Nomination of Admiral Stansfield Turner to Be Director of Central Intelligence*, 95 Cong. 1 sess. (1977), p. 4 (hereafter cited as *Turner Hearings*).

21. Ibid., p. 5.

22. Carter's inaugural address had announced America's "absolute" moral commitment to advancement of human rights. *Public Papers of the Presidents: Jimmy Carter, 1977*, p. 1. See also his remarks at the United Nations on Mar. 17, 1977, ibid., pp. 444, 446; and at a Clinton, Mass., town meeting, ibid., pp. 382, 385.

23. *Turner Hearings*, pp. 6, 26-27.

24. Turner balked, however, at a proposal that would give Congress up to ten days' advance notice; ibid., pp. 17, 29.

25. Ibid., pp. 12-13.

26. Immediately after his inauguration the president announced to the other nations of the world that, under his leadership, U.S. power and influence would be guided at home and abroad by a desire to shape a "more humane world responsive to human aspirations." *Public Papers of the Presidents: Jimmy Carter, 1977*, pp. 4-5.

27. Ibid., pp. 921-22.

28. Ibid.

29. Ibid., pp. 925, 928.

30. Announcement of the proposal was made at a White House meeting attended by members of the Senate Select Committee on Intelligence and the House and Senate Judiciary Committees. Remarks of several attendees are in ibid., pp. 923-27.

31. Ibid., p. 921.

32. Ibid., p. 928.

33. Testimony of Stansfield Turner, U.S. Congress, Senate, Select Committee on Intelligence, *Foreign Intelligence Surveillance Act of 1978: Hearings before a Subcommittee of the Select Committee on Intelligence on S. 1566*, 95 Cong. 2 sess., 1977, p. 47 (hereafter cited as *S. 1566 Hearings*).

34. Officials later designated to perform this duty were: the secretaries of state and defense, the DCI, the deputies of those officials, and the director of the FBI. U.S. Congress, Senate, Select Committee on Intelligence, *Implementation of the Foreign Intelligence Surveillance Act of 1978*, S. Rept. 96-379, 96 Cong. 1 sess. (1979), p. 8.

35. *S. 1566 Hearings*, pp. 2-4.

36. Ibid., p. 6 (remarks of Senator Bayh).

37. Ibid., p. 7 (remarks of Senator Biden).

38. Ibid., pp. 14-15.

39. Testimony of Griffin Bell in U.S. Congress, House, Permanent Select Committee on Intelligence, *Foreign Intelligence Electronic Surveillance: Hearings before a Subcommittee of the Permanent Select Committee on Intelligence*, 95 Cong. 2 sess. (1978), p. 35 (hereafter cited as *Electronic Surveillance Hearings*).

40. American Civil Liberties Union attorneys, and representatives of several lawyers' associations, were prominent among the critics. See *S. 1566 Hearings*, pp. 87-88, 99, 110, 178; testimony of Professor Arthur S. Miller, National Law Center, George Washington University, *Electronic Surveillance Hearings*, p. 138. See also Robert H. Bork, "Reforming Foreign Intelligence," *Wall Street Journal*, Mar. 9, 1978, p. 24.

41. 92 Stat. 1783. Perhaps the most important modification to the original Carter proposal was the addition of a provision, at the insistence of members of the House of Representatives, authorizing warrantless (i.e., conducted without judicial approval) surveillance of communications of "official" foreign powers, where the contents of the communications were transmitted by means used exclusively between or among such powers. In these cases the attorney general, who was in effect the final approving official, was required to certify that there was no substantial likelihood that the surveillance would acquire the contents of a communication to which a United States person was a party. He was additionally required to send a copy of that certification to the FISA court. See U.S. Congress, House, *Foreign Intelligence Surveillance Act of 1978: Conference Report*, H. Rept. 95-1720, 95 Cong. 2 sess. (1978), pp. 24-25.

42. The ACLU, in particular, argued that Americans abroad must be protected, too. *S. 2525 Hearings*, p. 559.

43. Section 108 of the act also provided for congressional oversight of the implementa-

tion of the act through semiannual reports by the attorney general to the intelligence committees concerning electronic surveillances undertaken pursuant to the new procedure. Congress was especially concerned that the intelligence committees be fully informed in this area. U.S. Congress, Senate, Select Committee on Intelligence, *Foreign Intelligence Surveillance Act of 1978: Report Together with Additional Views on S. 1566*, S. Rept. 95-701, 95 Cong. 2 sess. (1978), pp. 67-68.

44. His remarks (on Oct. 25, 1978) appear in *Public Papers of the Presidents: Jimmy Carter, 1978*, pp. 1853-54.

45. Leslie Maitland, "A Closed Court's One-Issue Caseload," *New York Times*, Oct. 14, 1982, p. B 16, quoting an administration official.

46. John Osborne, "White House Watch – Remaking Foreign Policy," *New Republic*, Oct. 1, 1977, p. 12; Rowland Evans and Robert Novak, "A Charter for the New CIA," *Washington Post*, Sept. 12, 1977, p. A 23.

47. Executive Order 11985, *United States Foreign Intelligence Activities*, May 13, 1977, *Public Papers of the Presidents: Jimmy Carter, 1977*, p. 880; and Executive Order 11994, *United States Foreign Intelligence Activities*, June 1, 1977, ibid., pp. 1051-52.

48. See, for example, analyses in Pat M. Holt, "Carter's Spy Reshuffle – Plus and Minus," *Christian Science Monitor*, Aug. 17, 1977, p. 31; "Turner Disavows Any Intention to Become Intelligence Czar," *Aviation Week and Space Technology*, Aug. 15, 1977, p. 17; and Nicholas M. Horrock, "Under Turner, Spy Business Is Not What It Was," *New York Times*, Oct. 30, 1977, p. 4 E.

49. "Announcement of Decisions on the Organization and Functions of the Community," *Public Papers of the Presidents: Jimmy Carter, 1977*, pp. 1421-23.

50. See, e.g., "T.V. Guide Editor Admits to 'Dull' Ties with CIA," *Washington Post*, Sept. 28, 1977, p. 12; John M. Crewdson, "400 Newsmen Aided CIA, Magazine Says," *New York Times*, Sept. 12, 1977, p. 1; and John M. Crewdson, "CIA: Secret Shaper of Public Opinion," ibid., Dec. 25, 1977, p. 1.

51. *Public Papers of the Presidents: Jimmy Carter, 1978*, pp. 189-91.

52. U.S. President, Executive Order 12036, *United States Intelligence Activities*, *Federal Register* 43, no. 18 (Jan. 26, 1978): 3675 (hereafter cited as EO 12036).

53. Turner and Thibault, "Intelligence: The Right Rules," pp. 122, 126.

54. Ibid., pp. 126-27.

55. See the laudatory remarks of Senator Walter D. Huddleston, who was heading the parallel effort in Congress to draft a comprehensive charter, in *Washington Post*, Nov. 11, 1977, p. 2.

56. EO 12036, sect. 1-302.

57. EO 12036, sects. 1-706, 3-302.

58. EO 12036, sect. 3-305.

59. EO 12036, sect. 1-601(j).

60. Turner and Thibault, "Intelligence: The Right Rules," p. 136.

61. EO 12036, sect. 3-305: "Such procedures shall ensure compliance with law, protect constitutional rights and privacy, and ensure that any intelligence activity within the United States or directed against any United States person is conducted by the least intrusive means possible. The procedures shall also ensure that any use, dissemination, and storage of information about United States persons acquired through intelligence activities is limited to that necessary to achieve lawful governmental purposes."

62. EO 12036, sect. 1-304.

63. EO 12036, sect. 1-304 (d).

64. EO 12036, sect. 1-6.

65. EO 12036, sects. 3-402 and 3-403.

66. EO 12036, sect. 3-401.

67. With regard to the controversy about opening of citizens' mail, for just one example, the directive announced that "No agency within the Intelligence Community shall open mail or examine envelopes in United States postal channels, *except in accordance with applicable statutes and regulations.*" EO 12036, sect. 2-205 (emphasis added).

68. EO 12036, sec. 2-201 (b). The order provided that if the specified operations would require a warrant when undertaken for law enforcement purposes, then they "shall not be undertaken against a United States person without a judicial warrant, unless the President has authorized the type of activity involved and the Attorney General has both approved the particular activity and determined that there is probable cause to believe that the United States person is an agent of a foreign power."

69. EO 11905, sect. 5b (6).

70. EO 12036, sect. 2-207.

71. Compare EO 11905, sect. 5b(7), with EO 12036, sect. 2-208.

72. Compare EO 11905, sect. 5g, with EO 12036, sect. 2-305.

73. See, for example, reservations expressed in "Shaping Tomorrow's CIA," *Time,* Feb. 6, 1978, pp. 15-18.

74. Even though the prohibition of assassination, for example, was clear and categorical, Admiral Turner indicated that at least in his mind there existed some cases where the president, *in extremis,* might grant an exception (e.g., in a hijacking situation). He was therefore uncomfortable with the prospect of flat statutory prohibitions. Ibid.

75. See, for example, the testimony of Rep. Larry McDonald, lamenting the civil liberties bias of President Carter's order, in U.S. Congress, Senate, Select Committee on Intelligence, *Nomination of Ambassador Frank Carlucci; Hearings before the Select Committee on Intelligence on Nomination of Ambassador Frank C. Carlucci to Be Deputy Director of Central Intelligence Agency,* 95 Cong. 2 sess. (1978), pp. 29-30, 35 (hereafter cited as *Carlucci Hearings*).

76. Interview with William Casey, *U.S. News and World Report,* Mar. 8, 1982, pp. 23-26.

77. In addition to the proposed intelligence community charter discussed here, there was also an effort to write a domestic charter for the FBI. This also entailed a process of bargaining between the Senate Intelligence Committee and the executive. See, e.g., Charles R. Babcock, "Court Ruling Stirs Debate on Intelligence Charters," *Washington Post,* July 4, 1979, p. 22; David Burnham, "Rights Group Lawyers See F.B.I. Charter Bill as 'Seriously Flawed,' " *New York Times,* Oct. 11, 1979, p. A 14. Since the principles involved in both efforts were the same, and since the intelligence community charter proposal encompassed more national capabilities than the domestic proposal, the focus here will be on the former.

78. *Carlucci Hearings,* p. 2.

79. Senator Walter D. Huddleston, letter to the editor, *New York Times,* Nov. 16, 1977, p. A 28, published under the heading "Intelligence Agency Legislation: Why the Delay."

80. It was introduced in the Senate on Feb. 9, 1978, and in the House (as H.R. 11245) on Mar. 2, 1978. See the text in *Congressional Record,* Feb. 10, 1978, pp. 533-64.

81. *S. 2525 Hearings.*

82. S. 2525, sect. 114.

83. S. 2525, sects. 131(a), (e), and (g).

84. S. 2525, sect. 141(b).

85. S. 2525, sect. 151(f) (2), (g) (1), and (f) (5), and sect. 153.

86. S. 2525, sects. 311, 321, 341, and 351.

87. S. 2525, sect. 131 (covert action and collection) and sect. 141 (counterintelligence and counterterrorism).

88. S. 2525 sect. 141(a).

89. S. 2525, sects. 131(a), 141(a), and 203(4). In sect. 205(a) (see also sects. 212 and 215) the attorney general's duties were specified as (1) to approve regulations or procedures issued by the intelligence agencies to implement the charter; (2) to evaluate all statutes and executive directives on intelligence activities for impact on individual rights; (3) to supervise the FBI; (4) to review or approve intelligence activities as required by the charter; and (5) to report annually in writing to both congressional intelligence committees on the intelligence activities he or his designee had approved.

90. S. 2525, sects. 151 and 152.

91. The basic authority statement is in S. 2525, sect. 111(a); also see sects. 134 and 135(a).

92. S. 2525, sect. 132.

93. "Carlucci Says CIA Has Not Used Reporters, Clerics, or Academics," *New York Times,* Feb. 1, 1980, p. 1.

94. Charles Mohr, "Carter Said to Seek Leeway in C.I.A. Bill," *New York Times,* Feb. 1, 1980, p. 1.

95. S. 2525, sect. 136(a) (1) through (3). The emergency exception for the prohibition on assassination dealt only with periods of declared war or War Powers Act situations (sect. 134).

96. S. 2525, sect. 131(c) through (e).

97. S. 2525, sects. 131(c)(4) and 211 through 232.

98. See testimony in *S. 2525 Hearings,* pp. 525, 533, 551, and 579-81.

99. Ibid., p. 322-26.

100. Ibid., p. 194.

101. Ibid., pp. 216-20. Stilwell became deputy under secretary of defense in the Reagan Administration, with responsibilities that included intelligence policy.

Chapter 6

1. A major functionary on the House Intelligence Committee's staff and a prominent participant with subcommittee members at these hearings was Herbert Romerstein, whose criticisms of recently imposed constraints were soon afterwards published in Godson, *Counterintelligence,* p. 161.

2. Remarks of Morgan F. Murphy, chairman of the Subcommittee on Legislation, Permanent Select Committee on Intelligence, in U.S. Congress, House, *Espionage Law and Leaks: Hearings before a Subcommittee of the Permanent Select Committee on Intelligence,* 96 Cong. 1 sess. (1979), pp. 1-2.

3. Ibid., pp. 2-3.

4. Ibid., p. 3.

5. Prepared statement of Anthony A. Lapham, general counsel, Central Intelligence Agency, ibid., pp. 12-13, 23.

6. Statement of Daniel P. Silver, general counsel, National Security Agency, ibid., p. 25.

7. Ibid., p. 59.

8. Ibid., p. 90.

9. Statement of Thomas I. Emerson, Yale Law School, ibid., p. 168. See also statement of Harold Edgar and Benno Schmidt, Jr., Columbia Law School, ibid., p. 114.

10. The Freedom of Information Act, 5 USC 552, was effective on Feb. 19, 1975; the Privacy Act, 5 USC 552a, was effective on Sept. 25, 1975.

11. See the letter of William H. Webster, director of the Federal Bureau of Investigation, to the Subcommittee on Legislation of the House Permanent Select Committee on Intelligence, June 19, 1979, *FOIA Hearings,* p. 65. The exceptions to disclosure

requirements included: matters specifically authorized to be kept secret, according to criteria established in an executive order, in the interest of national defense or foreign policy; investigatory records compiled for law enforcement purposes; and internal personnel rules and practices of the agency concerned, as well as intra- and interagency memoranda and letters not made available to the public except as required in litigation.

12. *FOIA Hearings,* pp. 2-12.

13. Ibid., pp. 9-10 (remarks of Congressman Robert McClory).

14. Ibid., pp. 24-25, 62.

15. Prepared statement of Philip B. Heymann, assistant attorney general, Criminal Division, Department of Justice, in U.S. Congress, House, Permanent Select Committee on Intelligence, *Graymail Legislation: Hearings before a Subcommittee of the Permanent Select Committee on Intelligence,* 96 Cong. 1 sess. (1979), p. 4. The argument that classified information was required to protect litigants' interests also arose in civil suits where government employees were sued for damages by plaintiffs who claimed their constitutional rights had been violated.

16. Ibid., p. 41.

17. Jimmy Carter, *Keeping Faith: Memoirs of a President* (New York: Bantam Books, 1982), p. 465.

18. Tad Szulc, "Shaking Up the CIA," *New York Times Magazine,* July 29, 1979, p. 13. For congressional scrutiny of this "warning failure," see U.S. Congress, House, Permanent Select Committee on Intelligence, *Iran: Evaluation of U.S. Intelligence Performance prior to November 1978* (Washington, D.C.: GPO, 1979).

19. Remarks to reporters on Dec. 28, 1979, *Public Papers of the Presidents: Jimmy Carter, 1979,* p. 2287.

20. Carter, *Keeping Faith,* p. 483.

21. Ibid., p. 509.

22. "No Longer a Secret," *New York Times,* Oct. 26, 1982, p. B 6. See also Charles Mohr, "Schlesinger Assails a Charter for the CIA," ibid., Apr. 3, 1980, p. A 11, on administration attitudes concerning waivers of restrictions in the executive order.

23. Carter, *Keeping Faith,* p. 475.

24. State of the Union Address to Congress, Jan. 23, 1980, *Public Papers of the Presidents: Jimmy Carter, 1980-1981,* p. 196.

25. Tad Szulc, "Putting the Bite Back in CIA," *New York Times Magazine,* Apr. 6, 1980, p. 28.

26. State of the Union Message, *Public Papers of the Presidents: Jimmy Carter, 1980-1981,* p. 164.

27. Ibid., p. 155. See also the president's remarks in a Jan. 30, 1980, news conference: *Public Papers of the Presidents: Jimmy Carter, 1980-1981,* p. 241; State of the Union Message, in ibid., p. 167.

28. State of the Union Address, Jan. 23, 1980, in ibid., pp. 194, 195.

29. Ibid., p. 198.

30. *Public Papers of the Presidents, Jimmy Carter, 1980-1981,* p. 241.

31. Remarks of Congressman McClory in U.S. Congress, House, Permanent Select Committee on Intelligence, *Proposals to Criminalize the Unauthorized Disclosure of the Identities of Undercover United States Intelligence Officers and Agents: Hearings before a Subcommittee of the Permanent Select Committee on Intelligence,* 96 Cong. 2 sess. (1980), pp. 7-8 (hereafter cited as *Identities Protection Hearings*).

32. Ibid., pp. 4, 6. Administration officials had been conducting an active lobbying campaign with leaders of Congress, hoping to solidify support for such measures as this. Richard Burt, "President Seeking to Ease C.I.A. Curbs," *New York Times,* Jan. 11, 1980, p. A 1.

33. *Identities Protection Hearings,* p. 9. See also the statement of Senator Lloyd Bentsen in ibid., pp. 149-51.

34. Ibid., pp. 11-12.

35. Ibid., pp. 28-29.

36. These fears had surfaced in the Senate Intelligence Committee as much as a year earlier. George Lardner, Jr., "Intelligence Charter: Time May Run Out as Spies Argue," *Washington Post,* Feb. 14, 1979, p. A 10.

37. *Identities Protection Hearings,* p. 74.

38. See, for example, the exchange between Congressman C. W. Bill Young and two civil liberties spokesmen, the ACLU's Berman and Morton Halperin of the Center for National Security Studies, ibid., p. 77.

39. *Soviet Covert Action Hearings.* This statement of purpose is taken from initial remarks of the subcommittee chairman, Rep. Les Aspin (p. 1).

40. Ibid., p. 2 (statement of Rep. Ashbrook).

41. Ibid., p. 52 (testimony by Ladislav Bittman, a former Czechoslovakian intelligence official).

42. See the prepared statement of Sen. Daniel Patrick Moynihan, U.S. Congress, Senate, Select Committee on Intelligence, *National Intelligence Act of 1980: Hearings before the Senate Select Committee on Intelligence on S. 2284,* 96 Cong. 2 sess. (1980), p. 9 (hereafter cited as *S. 2284 Hearings*).

43. Lardner, "Intelligence Charter."

44. Ibid.

45. Charles Mohr, "White House and Panel Near Accord on CIA Rules," *New York Times,* Jan. 15, 1980, p. A 16.

46. See, e.g., "Fast Relief for Intelligence Headaches," *New York Times,* Jan. 16, 1980, p. A 24 (editorial); see also "In Defense of Intelligence," ibid., Apr. 4, 1980, p. A 24 (editorial).

47. *S. 2284 Hearings,* pp. 5-6.

48. Prepared statement of Admiral Stansfield Turner, ibid., pp. 15-22.

49. Prepared statement of Daniel J. Murphy, deputy under secretary of defense (policy review), ibid., pp. 69-72.

50. Ibid., pp. 477-78, 129-30.

51. See, e.g., testimony of Athan G. Theoharis, professor of American history, Marquette University, ibid., pp. 249-50. The bill would generally have required agencies to release only personal data on individual requestors. See also statement of Jerry Berman, American Civil Liberties Union, ibid., p. 147.

52. Statement of Peter Weiss, vice-president, Center for Constitutional Rights, ibid., pp. 465-70.

53. See Tom Wicker, "The C.I.A. Triumphant," *New York Times,* May 6, 1980, p. A 27.

54. Charles Mohr, "Experts to Redraft C.I.A. 'Charter Bill,' " *New York Times,* Apr. 2, 1980, p. A 12. See also Charles Mohr, "Intelligence Agency Charter," ibid., Apr. 25, 1980, p. A 20.

55. The committee's decision was explained later in U.S. Congress, Senate, Select Committee on Intelligence, *Intelligence Identities Protection Legislation: Hearings before the Select Committee on Intelligence on S. 2216, Et Al.,* 96 Cong. 2 sess. (1980), p. 1 (remarks of the chairman, Senator Bayh) (hereafter cited as *S. 2216 Hearings*). See also U.S. Congress, Senate, Select Committee on Intelligence, *Identities Protection Act,* S. Rept., 96-896, 96 Cong. 2 sess. (1980), p. 5 (cited hereafter as *S. Rept. 96-896*).

56. U.S. Congress, House, Permanent Select Committee on Intelligence, *Intelligence Oversight Act of 1980,* H. Rept. 96-1153, 96 Cong., 2 sess. (1980).

57. *S. 2216 Hearings*. For reaction to the Carter Administration's support for the bill, see Tom Wicker, "Killing Freedom to Save It," *New York Times*, Sept. 5, 1980, p. A 23.

58. *S. Rept. 96-896*, pp. 10-11.

59. U.S. Congress, Senate, Select Committee on Intelligence, *Intelligence Reform Act of 1981: Hearing before the Senate Select Committee on the Intelligence Reform Act of 1981*, 97 Cong., 1 sess., 1981.

60. Charles Mohr, "Congress Settles for a Draw in New Intelligence Charter," *New York Times*, Sept. 28, 1980, p. E 5. See also "Retreat from Intelligence," ibid., May 6, 1980, p. A 26 (editorial).

61. Judith Miller, "Reagan Urged to Reorganize U.S. Intelligence," *New York Times*, Dec. 8, 1980, p. A 1; Jay Peterzell, "The Intelligence Transition," *First Principles* (Center for National Security Studies), Jan. 1981, p. 1.

62. See, e.g., Graham Allison, "An Intelligence Agenda," *New York Times*, Dec. 21, 1980, p. E 17; see also Ray S. Cline's emphatic earlier views: "Rebuilding American Intelligence," *New York Times*, Dec. 20, 1979, p. A 27.

63. See, e.g., Morton H. Halperin, "How Reagan Can Improve the Intelligence Product," *Washington Post*, Feb. 5, 1981, p. A 19; Khalid B. Sayeed, "A Set of Values for U.S. Intelligence," *New York Times*, Jan. 7, 1981, p. A 19 (letter to the editor).

64. U.S. Congress, Senate, Select Committee on Intelligence, *Nomination of William J. Casey: Hearing before the Select Committee on Intelligence on Nomination of William J. Casey to Be Director of Central Intelligence*, 97 Cong. 1 sess. (1981), pp. 16-26.

65. Ibid., p. 32.

66. Ibid., pp. 40-41 (remarks of Senators Moynihan and Huddleston).

67. See the reiteration of themes supportive of intelligence agencies in U.S. Congress, Senate, Select Committee on Intelligence, *Nomination of Admiral Bobby R. Inman: Hearing before the Select Committee on Intelligence on Nomination of Admiral Bobby R. Inman to be Deputy Director of Central Intelligence*, 97 Cong. 1 sess. (1981).

68. U.S. Congress, House, Permanent Select Committee on Intelligence, *H.R. 4, the Intelligence Identities Protection Act: Hearings before a Subcommittee of the Permanent Select Committee on Intelligence*, 97 Cong. 1 sess. (1981).

69. *Intelligence Reform Act of 1981*.

70. The Intelligence Identities Protection Act of 1982, Public Law 97-200, June 23, 1982, 96 Stat. 122. For a restatement of arguments opposing it, see "The Spy Bill Wrapped in the Flag," *New York Times*, Mar. 4, 1982, p. A 22 (editorial).

71. See, e.g., Mr. Casey's letter to the editor of *New York Times*, published Oct. 1, 1982 (p. A 31), arguing that FOIA provisions continue to threaten important security interests. See also the countervailing position in the response by Morton Halperin, *New York Times*, Oct. 10, 1982, p. E 16.

72. Major national newspapers published detailed descriptions and analyses of the proposed directive. See, e.g., Robert Pear, "Intelligence Groups Seek Power to Gain Data on U.S. Citizens," *New York Times*, Mar. 10, 1981, p. A 1; and "The Hidden War," *Wall Street Journal*, Mar. 26, 1981, p. 26.

73. Kenneth Bass, "Deja Vu, C.I.A.-Wise," *New York Times*, Mar. 12, 1981, p. A 23; "Son of Operation CHAOS," ibid., Mar. 12, 1981, p. A 22.

74. Under the Carter order, searches and surreptitious entries, for instance, could be conducted without a judicial warrant if the president had approved the general type of activity involved and if the attorney general had authorized its use in a specific operation. The draft Reagan directive gave the attorney general the responsibility formerly assigned to the president, and allowed delegation of approval authority to agency heads.

75. Pear, "Intelligence Groups Seek Power."

76. At about this time the administration was beginning to incorporate concern about

terrorism into its description of broad foreign policy challenges. See, e.g., U.S. Department of State, Bureau of Public Affairs, "A New Direction in U.S. Foreign Policy," *Current Policy* 275 (Apr. 24, 1981) (speech by Secretary Haig); and "International Terrorism," *Current Policy* 285 (June 10, 1981): (statement by Under-secretary of State Richard T. Kennedy).

77. Charles Mohr, "C.I.A. Aide Clarifies Stand on Restraint," *New York Times*, Mar. 12, 1981, p. A 17.

78. Hedrick Smith, "President Opposes Domestic C.I.A. Role," *New York Times*, Mar. 18, 1981, p. A 1.

79. John Shattuck of the American Civil Liberties Union, quoted in Charles Mohr, "A.C.L.U. Says Efforts to Combat Terrorism Hold Threat to Rights," *New York Times*, May 19, 1981, p. B 11.

80. See Judith Miller, "Administration Studying New Plan on Bolstering Intelligence Agencies," *New York Times*, May 21, 1981, p. A 1.

81. See, e.g., U.S. Department of State, Bureau of Public Affairs, "Soviet Active Measures: Forgery, Disinformation, Political Operations," no. 88, Oct. 1981.

82. See Judith Miller, "Reagan Draft Order Said to Allow Wider Intelligence Activity in U.S.," *New York Times*, Oct. 6, 1981, p. A 1.

83. "Panel Challenges Breadth of C.I.A. Guidelines," *New York Times*, Oct. 14, 1981, p. A 23; "Senate Committee Challenges Breadth of Intelligence Order," ibid., Oct. 15, 1981, p. A 20.

84. Senator David Durenberger, quoted in Judith Miller, "Panel Opposes Plan to Permit Domestic Spying," *New York Times*, Oct. 28, 1981, p. A 1. See the views of Senators Moynihan, Durenberger, and Wallop, quoted in Judith Miller, "Three Senators Warn President on C.I.A.," *New York Times*, Nov. 5, 1981, p. A 19.

85. See the remarks of Senator Patrick Leahy and Jerry Berman of the American Civil Liberties Union, quoted in Judith Miller, "Putting It All Together, Critics Spell 'Big Brother,' " *New York Times*, Nov. 15, 1981, p. E 2.

86. Mark Lynch, American Civil Liberties Union attorney, quoted in Miller, "Putting It All Together."

87. *Weekly Compilation of Presidential Documents* 17, no. 49 (Dec. 7, 1981): 1335-36.

88. Address before the American Bar Association in New Orleans, U.S., Department of State, Bureau of Public Affairs, "A Strategic Approach to Foreign Policy," *Current Policy* 305 (Aug. 11, 1981): 3.

89. EO 12333 sect. 2.2.

90. EO 12036, sect. 2.1 (emphasis added).

91. EO 12333, sect. 1.1.

92. U.S., President, Executive Order 12334, *President's Intelligence Oversight Board,* issued Dec. 4, 1981, *Weekly Compilation of Presidential Documents* 17, no. 49 (Dec. 7, 1981): 1348-49.

93. EO 12333, sect. 1.1(c).

94. See "A Strategic Approach to Foreign Policy," *Current Policy* 305 (Aug. 11, 1981): 4.

95. U.S. Department of Defense, *Annual Report to the Congress, Fiscal Year 1983: Report of Secretary of Defense Caspar W. Weinberger to the Congress on the FY 1983 Budget, FY 1984 Authorization Request, and FY 1983-1987 Defense Programs,* Feb. 8, 1982, pp. I-22, I-23. A study by the National Academy of Sciences reinforced that conclusion. See Philip M. Boffey, "Security of U.S. Said to Be Hurt by Data Leaks," *New York Times*, Oct. 1, 1982, p. A 1. See also David Burnham, "Government Restricting Flow of Information to the Public," *New York Times*, Nov. 15, 1982, p. A 1 for a discussion of reaction to administration initiatives meant to preclude leakage of know-how to the Soviets.

96. Compare EO 12036, sect. 1-303, with EO 12333, sect. 1.2.

97. The relevant provision of EO 12036, sect. 1-304(e), has no counterpart in EO 12333.

98. EO 12333, sect. 1.2(b).

99. Robert E. Hunter, *Presidential Control of Foreign Policy: Management or Mishap,* The Washington Papers, no. 91, (New York: Praeger, 1982), pp. 109, 112-14.

100. Turner and Thibault, "Intelligence: The Right Rules," pp. 122, 127.

101. EO 12036, sect. 1-302.

102. The specific rule was that if a judicial warrant would be required to use intrusive techniques for law enforcement purposes, then such techniques could not be used against a United States person for foreign intelligence purposes unless the president had authorized the type of activity and the attorney general had approved the specific proposal and had determined that there was probable cause to believe that the person was an agent of a foreign power. EO 12036, sect. 2-201(b).

103. EO 12333, sect. 2.5.

104. Compare EO 12036, sect. 1-303, with EO 12333, sect. 1.2.

105. EO 12333, sect. 2.4, 3.2.

106. See the analysis by Daniel B. Silver in *Intelligence Report* 4, no. 5 (May 1982): 2, published by the American Bar Association's Standing Committee on Law and National Security, Chicago, Ill.

107. The Carter order's definition (EO 12036, sect. 4-214) included U.S. citizens, permanent resident aliens, unincorporated associations organized in the United States or "substantially composed of" U.S. citizens or permanent resident aliens, or corporations incorporated within the United States. The Reagan order (EO 12333, sect. 3.4[i]) stated: "United States person means a United States citizen, an alien known by the intelligence agency concerned to be a permanent resident alien, an unincorporated association substantially composed of United States citizens or permanent resident aliens, or a corporation incorporated in the United States, except for a corporation directed and controlled by a foreign government or governments."

108. EO 12333, sect. 3.4(h).

109. See, e.g., Silver, *Intelligence Report,* p. 6.

110. EO 12036, sect. 2-201.

111. EO 12333, sect. 2.4: "Agencies within the Intelligence Community shall use the least intrusive techniques feasible within the United States or directed against United States persons abroad."

112. For just one more example, the new rules on undisclosed participation in organizations within the United States discarded the Carter requirement that the types of participation be approved by the attorney general and described in a public document. Compare EO 12036, sect. 2-207(c) with EO 12333, sect. 2.9.

113. "C.I.A. Changes Spy Operations to Add Security," *New York Times,* Feb. 2, 1982, p. A 1.

114. Interview with William J. Casey, director of Central Intelligence, *U.S. News and World Report,* Mar. 8, 1982, pp. 23-26. See also Richard Halloran, "U.S. Seeks Reforms for Military Data," *New York Times,* June 13, 1982, p. 19, describing the outlines of Secretary of Defense Weinberger's program for improving Defense intelligence.

115. Inman's remarks, in a speech to the American Newspaper Publishers' Association, were summarized in Wallace Turner, "Inman Calls U.S. Intelligence 'Marginally Capable,' " *New York Times,* Apr. 28, 1982, p. A 16.

116. Casey interview, *U.S. News and World Report,* Mar. 8, 1982, pp. 23-26.

117. See, e.g., Philip Geyelin, "Covert Action – and Reaction," *Washington Post,* Mar. 2, 1982, p. 17.

118. *Congressional Quarterly Weekly Report* 40, no. 41 (Oct. 9, 1982): 2670.

119. Leslie Gelb, "Reagan Backing Covert Actions, Officials Assert," *New York Times,* Mar. 14, 1982, p. A 1; "Senior Intelligence officials" quoted in Philip Taubman, "U.S. Backing Raids against Nicaragua," *New York Times,* Nov. 3, 1982, p. A 6; see also Alan Riding, "Nicaragua Rebels Build Up Strength," ibid., Nov. 7, 1982, p. A 17. Throughout 1983 this "covert" action was thoroughly and openly debated in Congress, in the media, and in academic journals.

120. Russell Watson with David C. Martin, "Is Covert Action Necessary," *Newsweek,* Nov. 8, 1982, pp. 53, 54. See also Philip Taubman, "Casey and His C.I.A. on the Rebound," *New York Times Magazine,* Jan. 16, 1983, pp. 20, 47, 62.

121. See the analysis of a federal court of appeals decision about NSA interception of American citizens' communications, ruling in NSA's favor and overruling a district court decision, in David Burnham, "Courts Says U.S. Spy Agency Can Tap Overseas Messages," *New York Times,* Nov. 7, 1982, p. 28.

122. See, e.g., Philip Taubman, "Inman Resignation Tied to Debate on Widening Intelligence Activity," *New York Times,* Apr. 23, 1982, p. A 1.

123. See, e.g., John Shattuck, "Civil Rights Are Safer in Congress' Hands," *New York Times,* Nov. 3, 1982, p. A 27; Victor S. Navasky, "Why Sue the C.I.A.?" ibid., Oct. 26, 1982, p. A 29; and "Letter Sweaters and Spies," *Progressive,* Jan. 1983, pp. 11-12.

Chapter 7

1. For discussion of the renewed emphasis on keeping secrets, see Sissela Bok, "Secrecy vs. Security," *New York Times,* Feb. 23, 1983, p. A 23. Administration attitudes on new FBI rules are surveyed in Robert Pear, "More Freedom for the FBI Causes Some Critics to Worry," ibid., Mar. 13, 1983, p. E 3; Leslie Maitland, "Eased FBI Curbs Touch Off Dispute," ibid., May 14, 1983, p. 8; and Nat Hentoff, "A Spectre Hoovering over F.B.I.," ibid., Mar. 24, 1983, p. A 31. On covert action, see the remarks of President Reagan defending the capability in Joanne Omang, "Reagan Defends U.S. Right to Use Covert Activity," *Washington Post,* Oct. 20, 1983, p. A 1.

2. James MacGregor Burns, *Leadership* (New York: Harper and Row, 1978), p. 432.

3. Samuel P. Huntington, *American Politics: The Promise of Disharmony* (Cambridge: Harvard Univ. Press, 1981).

4. Stanley Hoffman, *Primacy or World Order: American Foreign Policy since the Cold War* (New York: McGraw-Hill, 1978), p. 227.

5. See, e.g., the appraisal in James Chace, "Is a Foreign Policy Consensus Possible?" *Foreign Affairs* 57 (Fall 1978): 1, 16: "We may simply have to learn to conduct foreign policy for a very long time without a single unifying theme on which to base broad national consensus."

6. See Godfrey, "Ethics and Intelligence," p. 624.

7. See the public opinion data summarized in Daniel Yankelovich, "Farewell to 'President Knows Best,' " in *America and the World, 1978 (Foreign Affairs* 57, no. 3) (New York: Council on Foreign Relations, 1979), p. 670; and Daniel Yankelovich and Larry Kaagan, "Assertive America," in William P. Bundy, ed., *America and the World, 1980 (Foreign Affairs* 59, no. 3) (New York: Pergamon Press, 1981), p. 696.

8. Kenneth W. Thompson, *Morality and Foreign Policy* (Baton Rouge: Louisiana State Univ. Press, 1980), pp. 20-21, 28.

9. John Courtney Murray, S.J., *We Hold These Truths: Catholic Reflections on the American Proposition* (Garden City, N.Y.: Image Books, 1964), pp. 265, 266.

10. Ibid., p. 272.

11. Kenneth W. Thompson, *Ethics and National Purpose* (New York: Council on Religion and International Affairs, 1957), p. 17.

12. Harry R. Davis and Robert C. Good, eds., *Reinhold Neibuhr on Politics* (New York: Charles Scribner's Sons, 1960), p. 333.

13. Ernest Lefever, "Can Covert Action Be Just?" *Policy Review* 12 (Spring 1980): 115. See also his letter to the editor of the *New York Times Magazine,* Feb. 20, 1983, p. 78.

14. See the arguments summarized in Scott D. Breckinridge, "Clandestine Intelligence: International Law," *International Studies Notes* 9 (Summer 1982): 8. See also Richard Falk, "CIA Covert Operations and International Law," in Borosage and Marks, *CIA File,* p. 142.

15. See, e.g., Paul W. Blackstock, *The Strategy of Subversion: Manipulating the Politics of Other Nations* (Chicago: Quadrangle Books, 1964), pp. 287-92; and Hilsman, *To Move a Nation,* p. 85.

16. A good example of the kind of assessment required is Weissman, "CIA Covert Action in Zaire and Angola," p. 263.

17. Adda B. Bozeman, "Covert Action and Foreign Policy," in Godson, *Covert Action,* p. 70.

18. Turner and Thibault, "Intelligence: The Right Rules," p. 122.

19. Ibid., p. 124.

20. In April 1984 there was an outcry of protest from some members of the Senate Intelligence Committee, who felt that they had not been briefed in sufficient detail about CIA involvement in the mining of Nicaraguan ports. CIA Director William Casey and the committee quickly agreed on steps to avoid such difficulty in the future. See Helen Dewar, "Casey Apologizes to Hill for Lapse on Port Mining," *Washington Post,* April 27, 1984, p. A 1.

21. Admiral Turner argues this position in "Intelligence: The Right Rules," p. 138.

22. See, e.g., David Truman, *The Governmental Process: Political Interests and Public Opinion,* 2nd ed. (New York: Knopf, 1971), pp. 416-21, summarizing the scholarship on development of a *modus vivendi* between regulators and regulated in a number of contexts. See also Herbert Kaufman, *The Administrative Behavior of Federal Bureau Chiefs* (Washington, D.C.: Brookings Institution, 1981), pp. 68-71.

23. See, e.g., Morris S. Ogul, *Congress Oversees the Bureaucracy: Studies in Legislative Supervision* (Pittsburgh: Univ. of Pittsburgh Press, 1976), pp. 185-86; and Lawrence C. Dodd and Richard L. Schott, *Congress and the Administrative State* (New York: John Wiley and Sons, 1979), pp. 170-84, 211.

24. Randall B. Ripley, *Congress: Process and Policy,* 2nd ed. (New York: W. W. Norton, 1978), p. 372.

Selected Bibliography

UNITED STATES GOVERNMENT DOCUMENTS

Congress

House. *Foreign Intelligence Surveillance Act of 1978: Conference Report*. H. Rept. 95-1720. 95 Cong. 2 ses., 1978.

House. Permanent Select Committee on Intelligence. *Disclosure of Funds for Intelligence Activities: Hearings before a Subcommittee of the Permanent Select Committee on Intelligence*. 95 Cong. 2 sess., 1978.

House. Permanent Select Committee on Intelligence. *Espionage Laws and Leaks: Hearings before a Subommittee of the Permanent Select Committee on Intelligence*. 96 Cong. 1 sess., 1979.

House. Permanent Select Committee on Intelligence. *Foreign Intelligence Electronic Surveillance: Hearings before a Subcommittee of the Permanent Select Committee on Intelligence on H.R. 5794, H.R. 9745, H.R. 7308, and H.R. 5632, the Foreign Intelligence Surveillance Act of 1977*. 95 Cong. 2 sess., 1978.

House. Permanent Select Committee on Intelligence. *H.R. 4, The Intelligence Identities Protection Act: Hearings before a Subcommittee of the House Permanent Select Committee on Intelligence*, 97 Cong. 1 sess., 1981.

House. Permanent Select Committee on Intelligence. *H.R. 6588, the National Intelligence Act of 1980: Hearings before a Subcommittee of the House Permanent Select Committee on Intelligence*. 96 Cong. 2 sess., 1980.

House. Permanent Select Committee on Intelligence. *Impact of the Freedom of Information Act and the Privacy Act on Intelligence Activities: Hearing before a Subcommittee of the House Permanent Select Committee on Intelligence*. 96 Cong. 1 sess., 1979.

House. Permanent Select Committee on Intelligence. *Intelligence Oversight Act of 1980*. H. Rept. 96-1153. 96 Cong. 2 sess., 1980.

House. Permanent Select Committee on Intelligence. *Iran: Evaluation of U.S. Intelligence Performance prior to November 1978*. Staff report. 96 Cong. 1 sess., 1979.

House. Permanent Select Committee on Intelligence. *Proposals to Criminalize the Unauthorized Disclosure of the Identities of Undercover United States Intelligence Officers and Agents: Hearings before a Subcommittee of the Permanent Select Committee on Intelligence*. 96 Cong. 2 sess., 1980.

House. Permanent Select Committee on Intelligence. *Soviet Active Measures: Hearings before the Permanent Select Committee on Intelligence.* 97 Cong. 2 sess., 1982.

House. Permanent Select Committee on Intelligence. *Soviet Covert Action (The Forgery Offensive): Hearings before the Subcommittee on Oversight of the Permanent Select Committee on Intelligence.* 96 Cong. 2 sess., 1980.

House. Permanent Select Committee on Intelligence. *Report to the House.* H. Rept. 95-1795. 95 Cong. 2 sess., 1978.

House. Permanent Select Committee on Intelligence. *Report to the House.* H. Rept. 96-1475. 96 Cong. 2 sess., 1980.

House. Permanent Select Committee on Intelligence. *The CIA and the Media: Hearings before a Subcommittee of the Permanent Select Committee on Intelligence.* 95 Cong. 1 and 2 sess., 1977-1978.

House. Select Committee on Intelligence. *U.S. Intelligence Agencies and Activities: Committee Proceedings: Hearings before the House Select Committee on Intelligence.* 94 Cong. 1 sess., 1975

House. Select Committee on Intelligence. *U.S. Intelligence Agencies and Activities: Committee Proceedings II: Hearings before the House Select Committee on Intelligence.* 94 Cong. 1 sess., 1975.

House. Select Committee on Intelligence. *U.S. Intelligence Agencies and Activities: Domestic Intelligence Programs: Hearings before the House Select Committee on Intelligence.* 94 Cong. 1 sess., 1975.

House. Select Committee on Intelligence. *U.S. Intelligence Agencies and Activities: Intelligence Costs and Fiscal Procedures: Hearings before the House Select Committee on Intelligence.* 94 Cong. 1 sess., 1975.

House. Select Committee on Intelligence. *U.S. Intelligence Agencies and Activities: Risks and Control of Foreign Intelligence: Hearings before the House Select Committee on Intelligence.* 94 Cong. 1 sess., 1975.

House. Select Committee on Intelligence. *U.S. Intelligence Agencies and Activities: The Performance of the Intelligence Community: Hearings before the House Select Committee on Intelligence.* 94 Cong. 1 sess., 1975.

Senate. Select Committee on Intelligence. *Activities of "Friendly" Foreign Intelligence Services in the United States: A Case Study. Report of the Senate Committee on Intelligence.* 95 Cong. 2 sess., 1978.

Senate. Select Committee on Intelligence. *Annual Report.* S. Rept. 95-217. 95 Cong. 1 sess., 1977.

Senate. Select Committee on Intelligence. *Annual Report.* S. Rept. 96-141. 96 Cong. 1 sess., 1979.

Senate. Select Committee on Intelligence. *Annual Report.* S. Rept. 97-193. 97 Cong. 1 sess., 1981.

Senate. Select Committee on Intelligence. *Foreign Intelligence Surveillance Act of 1978: Hearings before a Subcommittee of the Senate Select Committee on Intelligence on S. 1566.* 95 Cong. 2 sess., 1978.

Senate. Select Committee on Intelligence. *Foreign Intelligence Surveillance Act of 1978: Report Together with Additional Views to Accompany S. 1566.* S. Rept. 95-701. 95 Cong. 2 sess., 1978.

Senate. Select Committee on Intelligence. *Implementation of the Foreign Intelligence Surveillance Act of 1978.* S. Rept. 96-379. 96 Cong. 1 sess., 1979.

Senate. Select Committee on Intelligence. *Intelligence Identities Protection Act*. S. Rept. 96-896. 96 Cong. 2 sess., 1980.

Senate. Select Committee on Intelligence. *Intelligence Identities Protection Legislation: Hearings before the Select Committee on Intelligence on S. 2216, Et Al*. 96 Cong. 2 sess., 1980.

Senate. Select Committee on Intelligence. *Intelligence Oversight Act of 1980*. S. Rept. 96-730. 96 Cong. 1 sess., 1980.

Senate. Select Committee on Intelligence. *Intelligence Reform Act of 1981: Hearings before the Select Committee on Intelligence on the Intelligence Reform Act of 1981*. 97 Cong. 1 sess., 1981.

Senate. Select Committee on Intelligence. *National Intelligence Act of 1980: Hearings before the Senate Select Committee on Intelligence on S. 2284*. 96 Cong. 2 sess., 1980.

Senate. Select Committee on Intelligence. *National Intelligence Reorganization and Reform Act of 1978: Hearings before the Senate Select Committee on Intelligence on S. 2525*. 95 Cong. 2 sess., 1978.

Senate. Select Committee on Intelligence. *Nomination of Admiral Bobby R. Inman: Hearing before the Select Committee on Intelligence on Nomination of Admiral Bobby R. Inman to Be Deputy Director of Central Intelligence*. 97 Cong. 1 sess., 1981.

Senate. Select Committee on Intelligence. *Nomination of Admiral Stansfield Turner: Hearings before the Select Committee on Intelligence on Nomination of Admiral Stansfield Turner to Be Director of Central Intelligence*. 95 Cong. 1 sess., 1977.

Senate. Select Committee on Intelligence. *Nomination of Ambassador Frank C. Carlucci: Hearings before the Select Committee on Intelligence on Nomination of Ambassador Frank C. Carlucci to Be Deputy Director of Central Intelligence Agency*. 95 Cong. 2 sess., 1978.

Senate. Select Committee on Intelligence. *Nomination of E. Henry Knoche: Hearing before the Select Committee on Intelligence on Nomination of E. Henry Knoche to Be Deputy Director of Central Intelligence*. 94 Cong. 2 sess., 1976.

Senate. Select Committee on Intelligence. *Nomination of John N. McMahon: Hearing before the Senate Select Committee on Nomination of John N. McMahon to Be Deputy Director of Central Intelligence*. 97 Cong. 2 sess., 1982.

Senate. Select Committee on Intelligence. *Nomination of Theodore C. Sorensen: Hearing before the Select Committee on Intelligence on Nomination of Theodore C. Sorensen to Be Director of Central Intelligence*. 95 Cong. 1 sess., 1977.

Senate. Select Committee on Intelligence. *Nomination of William J. Casey: Hearing befoe the Select Committee on Intelligence on Nomination of William J. Casey to Be Director of Central Intelligence*. 97 Cong. 1 sess., 1981.

Senate. Select Committee on Intelligence. *Principal Findings on the Capabilities of the United States to Monitor the SALT II Treaty*. 96 Cong. 1 sess., 1979.

Senate. Select Committee on Intelligence. *Report Together with Additional Views to Accompany S. 2216, the Intelligence Identities Protection Act*. S. Rept. 96-896. 96 Cong 2 sess., 1980.

Senate. Select Committee to Study Governmental Operations with Respect to Intelligence Activities. *An Interim Report: Alleged Assassination Plots Involving Foreign Leaders*. S. Rept. 94-465. 94 Cong. 1 sess., 1975.

Senate. Select Committee to Study Governmental Operations with Respect to

Intelligence Activities. *Covert Action in Chile, 1967-1973.* 94 Cong. 1 sess., 1975.
Senate. Select Committee to Study Governmental Operations with Respect to Intelligence Activities. *Final Report,* S. Rept. 94-755, 94 Cong. 2 sess., 1976. Book I: *Foreign and Military Intelligence.* Book II: *Intelligence Activities and the Rights of Americans.* Book III: *Supplementary Detailed Staff Reports on Intelligence Activities and the Rights of Americans.* Book IV: *Supplementary Detailed Staff Reports on Intelligence and Military Intelligence.* Book V: *The Investigation of the Assassination of President John F. Kennedy: Performance of the Intelligence Agencies.* Book VI: *Supplementary Report on Intelligence Activities.*
Senate. Select Committee to Study Governmental Operations with Respect to Intelligence Activities. *Hearings before the Senate Select Committee to Study Governmental Operations With Respect to Intelligence Activities,* 94 Cong. 1 sess., 1975. Vol. I: *Unauthorized Storage of Toxic Agents.* Vol. II: *Huston Plan.* Vol. III: *Internal Revenue Service.* Vol. IV: *Mail Opening.* Vol. V: *The National Security Agency and Fourth Amendment Rights.* Vol. VI: *Federal Bureau of Investigation.* Vol. VII: *Covert Action.*

Executive

Commission on CIA Activities within the United States. *Report to the President by the Commission on CIA Activities within the United States.* Washington, D.C.: GPO, 1975.
Commission on the Organization of Government for the Conduct of Foreign Policy [The "Murphy Commission"]. *Report of the Commission.* Vol. 7: *Appendix U: Intelligence Functions Analyses.* Washington, D.C.: GPO, 1975.
President. Executive Order 11905. *United States Foreign Intelligence Activities. Federal Register* 41, no. 34 (19 Feb. 1976): 7701-38.
President. Executive Order 12036. *United States Intelligence Activities. Federal Register* 43, no. 18 (26 Jan. 1978): 3675-92.
President. Executive Order 12333. *United States Intelligence Activities. Federal Register* 46, no. 235 (8 Dec. 1981): 55941-54.
President. *Public Papers of the Presidents of the United States: Gerald R. Ford, 1974, 1975* [Books I and II], *1976-1977* [Books I-III]. Washington, D.C.: Office of the *Federal Register,* National Archives and Records Service.
President. *Public Papers of the Presidents of the United States: Jimmy Carter, 1977* [Books I and II], *1978, 1979* [Books I and II], *1980-1981.* Washington, D.C.: Office of the *Federal Register,* National Archives and Records Service.
President. *Public Papers of the Presidents of the United States: Ronald Reagan, 1981.* Washington, D.C.: Office of the *Federal Register,* National Archives and Records Service.

BOOKS

Agee, Philip. *Inside the Company: CIA Diary.* New York: Stonehill, 1975.
_____, and Wolf, Louis, eds. *Dirty Work: The CIA in Western Europe.* Introduction by Philip Agee. Seacaucus, N.J.: Lyle Stuart, 1978.

Ambrose, Stephen E. *Ike's Spies: Eisenhower and the Espionage Establishment.* Garden City, N.Y.: Doubleday, 1981.

Appleton, Sheldon. *United States Foreign Policy: An Introduction with Cases.* Boston: Little, Brown, 1968.

Ball, George W. *Diplomacy for a Crowded World: An American Foreign Policy.* Boston and Toronto: Little, Brown, 1976.

Beard, Charles A. *The Idea of National Interest: An Analytical Study in American Foreign Policy.* New York: Macmillan, 1934.

Berman, Jerry J., and Halperin, Morton H., eds. *The Abuses of the Intelligence Agencies.* Washington, D.C.: Center for National Security Studies, 1975.

Blackstock, Nelson. *COINTELPRO: The FBI's Secret War on Political Freedom.* New York: Vintage Books, 1976.

Blackstock, Paul W. *The Strategy of Subversion: Manipulating the Politics of Other Nations.* Chicago: Quadrangle Books, 1964.

————. *Agents of Deceit: Frauds, Forgeries and Political Intrigue among Nations.* Chicago: Quadrangle Books, 1964.

————, and Schaf, Frank L., Jr. *Intelligence, Espionage, Counter-Espionage, and Covert Operations: A Guide to Information Sources.* Detroit: Gale Research, 1978.

Blum, Richard H., ed. *Intelligence and Espionage in a Free Society: A Report by the Planning Group on Intelligence and Security to the Policy Council of the Democratic National Committee.* New York: Praeger, 1972.

Borosage, Robert L., and Marks, John, eds. *The CIA File.* New York: Grossman, 1976.

Buncher, Judith F., et al., eds. *The CIA and the Security Debate, 1971-1975.* New York: Facts on File, 1976.

Carter, Jimmy. *Keeping Faith: Memoirs of a President.* New York: Bantam Books, 1982.

Cline, Ray S. *Secrets, Spies, and Scholars: Blueprint of the Essential CIA.* Washington, D.C.: Acropolis Books, 1976.

————. *The CIA: Reality vs. Myth.* Washington, D.C.: Acropolis Books, 1983.

Colby, William, and Forbath, Peter. *Honorable Men: My Life in the CIA.* New York: Simon and Schuster, 1978.

Corson, William, R. *The Armies of Ignorance: The Rise of the American Intelligence Empire.* New York: Dial Press, 1977.

Crabb, Cecil V., Jr. *Policymakers and Critics: Conflicting Theories of American Foreign Policy.* New York: Praeger, 1976.

————. *American Foreign Policy in the Nuclear Age.* 4th ed. New York: Harper and Row, 1983.

Davis, Harry R., and Good, Robert C., eds. *Reinhold Neibuhr on Politics: His Political Philosophy and Its Application to Our Age as Expressed in His Writings.* New York: Charles Scribner's Sons, 1960.

de Silva, Peer. *Sub Rosa: The CIA and the Uses of Intelligence.* New York: New York Times Book Co., 1978.

Destler, I.M. *Presidents, Bureaucrats, and Foreign Policy: The Politics of Organizational Reform.* Princeton, N.J.: Princeton Univ. Press, 1972.

Donner, Frank J. *The Age of Surveillance: The Aims and Methods of America's Political Intelligence System.* New York: Vintage Books, 1981.

Dulles, Allen W. *The Craft of Intelligence*. New York: Harper and Row, 1963.

Elliff, James T. *The Reform of FBI Intelligence Operations*. Princeton: Princeton Univ. Press, 1979.

Fain, Tyrus G., et al., eds. *The Intelligence Community: History, Organization, and Issues*. New York and London: Bowker, 1977.

Ford, Gerald R. *A Time To Heal*. New York: Harper and Row, 1979.

Frazier, Howard, ed. *Uncloaking the CIA*. New York: Free Press, 1978.

Gaddis, John Lewis. *Strategies of Containment: A Critical Appraisal of Postwar American National Security Policy*. New York and Oxford: Oxford Univ. Press, 1982.

Godson, Roy, ed. *Intelligence Requirements for the 1980's: Elements of Intelligence*. Washington, D.C.: National Strategy Information Center, 1980.

————. *Intelligence Requirements for the 1980's: Analysis and Estimates*. Washington, D.C.: National Strategy Information Center, 1980.

————. *Intelligence Requirements for the 1980's: Counterintelligence*. Washington, D.C.: National Strategy Information Center, 1980.

————. *Intelligence Requirements for the 1980's: Covert Action*. Washington, D.C.: National Strategy Information Center, 1981.

————. *Intelligence Requirements for the 1980's: Clandestine Collection*. Washington, D.C.: National Strategy Information Center, 1982.

Halperin, Morton H., et al. *The Lawless State: The Crimes of the U.S. Intelligence Agencies*. New York: Penguin Books, 1976.

Hartz, Louis. *The Liberal Tradition in America: An Interpretation of American Political Thought since the Revolution*. New York: Harcourt, Brace, 1955.

Henkin, Louis. *How Nations Behave: Law and Foreign Policy*. New York: Praeger, 1968.

————. *Foreign Affairs and the Constitution*. New York: Norton, 1975.

Hilsman, Roger. *To Move a Nation: The Politics of Foreign Policy in the Administration of John F. Kennedy*. Garden City, N.Y.: Doubleday, 1967.

————. *The Politics of Policymaking in Defense and Foreign Affairs*. New York: Harper and Row, 1971.

Hoffman, Stanley. *Primacy or World Order: American Foreign Policy since the Cold War*. New York: McGraw-Hill, 1978.

Huntington, Samuel P. *The Common Defense: Strategic Programs in National Politics*. New York and London: Columbia Univ. Press, 1961.

————. *American Politics: The Promise of Disharmony*. Cambridge: Belknap Press of Harvard Univ. Press, 1981.

Jeffreys-Jones, Rhodri. *American Espionage: From Secret Service to CIA*. New York: Free Press, 1977.

Jordan, Amos A., and Taylor, William J., Jr. *American National Security: Policy and Process*. Baltimore: Johns Hopkins Univ. Press, 1981.

Kegley, Charles W., Jr., and Wittkopf, Eugene R. *American Foreign Policy: Pattern and Process*. New York: St. Martin's Press, 1979.

Kent, Sherman. *Strategic Intelligence for American World Policy*. Princeton: Princeton Univ. Press, 1949.

Kim, Young Hum, ed. *The Central Intelligence Agency: Problems of Secrecy in a Democracy*. Lexington, Mass.: Heath, 1968.

Kirkpatrick, Lyman B., Jr. *The Real CIA*. New York: Macmillan, 1968.

————. *The U.S. Intelligence Community: Foreign Policy and Domestic Activities*. New York: Hill and Wang, 1973.

Kissinger, Henry A. *White House Years*. Boston and Toronto: Little, Brown, 1979.

————. *Years of Upheaval*. Boston and Toronto: Little, Brown, 1982.

Langguth, A.J. *Hidden Terrors*. New York: Random House, 1978.

Lefever, Ernest W., and Godson, Roy, eds. *The CIA and the American Ethic: An Unfinished Debate*. Washington, D.C.: Ethics and Public Policy Center, 1979.

McGarvey, Patrick J. *CIA: The Myth and the Madness*. New York: Saturday Review Press, 1972.

Mansfield, Harvey G., ed. *Congress against the President*. Montpelier, Vt.: Capital City Press, 1975.

Marchetti, Victor, and Marks, John D. *The CIA and the Cult of Intelligence*. New York: Knopf, 1974.

Marks, John. *The CIA and Mind Control: The Search for the Manchurian Candidate*. New York: McGraw-Hill, 1980.

Melanson, Richard A. *Neither Cold War Nor Detente: Soviet-American Relations in the 1980's*. Charlottesville: Univ. Press of Virginia, 1982.

Merritt, Richard L., ed. *Foreign Policy Analysis*. Toronto and London: Lexington Books, 1975.

Meyer, Cord. *Facing Reality: From World Federalism to the CIA*. New York: Harper and Row, 1980.

Morgan, Richard E. *Domestic Intelligence: Monitoring Dissent in America*. Austin and London: Univ. of Texas Press, 1980.

Murray, John Courtney. *We Hold These Truths: Catholic Reflections on the American Proposition*. New York: Image Books, 1964.

Phillips, David Atlee. *The Night Watch*. New York: Atheneum, 1977.

Poelchau, Warner, ed. *White Paper Whitewash: Interviews with Philip Agee on the CIA and El Salvador*. New York: Deep Cover Books, 1981.

Powers, Thomas. *The Man Who Kept the Secrets: Richard Helms and the CIA*. New York: Knopf, 1979.

Prouty, Fletcher L. *The Secret Team: The CIA and Its Allies in Control of the United States and the World*. Englewood Cliffs, N.J.: Prentice-Hall, 1973.

Ransom, Harry Howe. *Central Intelligence and National Security*. Cambridge: Harvard Univ. Press, 1958.

————. *The Intelligence Establishment*. Cambridge: Harvard Univ. Press, 1970.

Ray, Ellen, et al., eds. *Dirty Work II: The CIA in Africa*. Seacaucus, N.J.: Lyle Stuart, 1979.

Roosevelt, Kermit. *Countercoup: The Struggle for the Control of Iran*. New York: McGraw-Hill, 1979.

Rositzke, Harry. *The CIA's Secret Operations: Espionage, Counterespionage, and Covert Action*. New York: Reader's Digest Press, 1977.

Rossiter, Clinton. *Alexander Hamilton and the Constitution*. New York: Harcourt, Brace and World, 1964.

Rowan, Ford. *Techno Spies*. New York: G.P. Putnam's Sons, 1978.

Sapin, Burton M. *The Making of United States Foreign Policy*. New York and Washington: Praeger, 1966.

Schlesinger, Arthur M., Jr. *The Imperial Presidency.* New York: Popular Library, 1973.

Seabury, Paul. *Power, Freedom, and Diplomacy: The Foreign Policy of the United States of America.* New York: Vintage Books, 1967.

Shackley, Theodore. *The Third Option: An American View of Counterinsurgency Operations.* New York: McGraw-Hill, 1981.

Shapiro, Martin. *The Pentagon Papers and the Courts: A Study in Foreign Policymaking and Freedom of the Press.* San Francisco: Chandler, 1972.

Shattuck, John H.F. *Rights of Privacy.* Skokie, Ill.: National Textbook Co., 1977.

Smith, R. Harris. *OSS: The Secret History of America's First Central Intelligence Agency.* New York: Dell, 1972.

Sorensen, Theodore C. *Watchmen in the Night: Presidential Accountability after Watergate.* Cambridge, Mass., and London: MIT Press, 1975.

Stockwell, John. *In Search of Enemies: A CIA Story.* New York: Norton, 1978.

Theoharis, Athan. *Spying on Americans: Political Surveillance from Hoover to the Huston Plan.* Philadelphia: Temple Univ. Press, 1978.

Thompson, Kenneth W. *Ethics and National Purpose.* New York: Council on Religion and International Affairs, 1957.

————. *Morality and Foreign Policy.* Baton Rouge and London: Louisiana State Univ. Press, 1980.

Troy, Thomas F. *Donovan and the CIA: A History of the Establishment of the Central Intelligence Agency.* Frederick, Md: Univ. Press of America, 1981.

Ungar, Sanford J. *FBI.* Boston: Little, Brown, 1976.

Varg, Paul A. *Foreign Policies of the Founding Fathers.* East Lansing: Michigan State Univ. Press, 1963.

Vocke, William C. *American Foreign Policy: An Analytical Approach.* New York: Free Press, 1976.

Waltz, Kenneth N. *Theory of International Politics.* Reading, Mass.: Addison-Wesley, 1979.

Wise, David. *The American Policy State: The Government against the People.* New York: Random House, 1976.

————, and Ross, Thomas B. *The Espionage Establishment.* New York: Random House, 1967.

Wriston, Henry M. *Executive Agents in American Foreign Relations.* Baltimore: Johns Hopkins Univ. Press, 1929.

ARTICLES

In Journals

Adelman, Kenneth L. "A Clandestine Clan." *International Security* 5 (Summer 1980): 152-71.

Adler, Emanuel. "Executive Command and Control in Foreign Policy: The CIA's Covert Activities." *Orbis* 23 (Fall 1979): 671-96.

Andrew, Christopher. "Whitehall, Washington, and the Intelligence Services." *International Affairs* 53 (July 1977): 390-404.

Baldwin, Hanson. "The Future of Intelligence." *Strategic Review* 4 (Summer 1976): 6-24.

Barnds, William J. "Intelligence and Foreign Policy: Dilemmas of a Democracy." *Foreign Affairs* 47 (Jan. 1969): 281-95.

Bax, Frans R. "The Legislative-Executive Relationship in Foreign Policy: New Partnership or New Competition?" *Orbis* 20 (Winter 1977): 881-904.

Beichman, Arnold. "Can Counterintelligence Come In from the Cold?" *Policy Review* 15 (Winter 1981): 93-101.

Bennett, Douglas, J., Jr. "Congress in Foreign Policy: Who Needs It?" *Foreign Affairs* 57 (Fall 1978): 40-50.

Blackstock, Paul W. "The Intelligence Community under the Nixon Administration." *Armed Forces and Society* 1 (Winter 1975): 231-50.

Caraley, Demetrios, et al. "American Political Institutions after Watergate – A Discussion." *Political Science Quarterly* 89 (Winter 1974-1975): 713-49.

Claude, Inis L., Jr. "Prospects for an American Renewal." *Orbis* 20 (Spring 1976): 137-46.

Cline, Ray S. "Policy without Intelligence." *Foreign Policy* 17 (Winter 1974-1975): 121-35.

Colby, William E. "Reorganizing the CIA: Who and How." *Foreign Policy* 23 (Summer 1976): 53-63.

―――. "Intelligence Secrecy and Security in a Free Society." *International Security* 1 (Fall 1976): 3-14.

Cooper, Chester L. "The CIA and Decisionmaking." *Foreign Affairs* 50 (Jan. 1972): 223-36.

Cronin, Thomas E. "A Resurgent Congress and the Imperial Presidency." *Political Science Quarterly* 95 (Summer 1980): 209-37.

Destler, I.M. "Congress as Boss?" *Foreign Policy* 42 (Spring 1981): 167-80.

Ellsworth, Robert F., and Adelman, Kenneth L. "Foolish Intelligence." *Foreign Policy* 36 (Fall 1979): 147-59.

Emerson, Thomas. "Control of Government Intelligence Agencies – The American Experience." *Political Quarterly* 53 (July-Sept. 1982): 273-91.

Godfrey, E. Drexel, Jr. "Ethics and Intelligence." *Foreign Affairs* 56 (Apr. 1978): 624-42.

Halperin, Morton H. "National Security and Civil Liberties." *Foreign Policy* 21 (Winter 1975-1976): 125-60.

Hamilton, Charles V. "America in Search of Itself: A Review Essay." *Political Science Quarterly* 97 (Fall 1982): 487-93.

Hamilton, Lee H., and Van Dusen, Michael H. "Making the Separation of Powers Work." *Foreign Affairs* 57 (Fall 1978): 17-39.

Hilsman, Roger. "On Intelligence." *Armed Forces and Society* 8 (Fall 1981): 129-43.

Huntington, Samuel P. "American Ideals versus American Institutions." *Political Science Quarterly* 97 (Spring 1982): 1-37.

Johnson, Loch K. "Controlling the Quiet Option." *Foreign Policy* 39 (Summer 1980): 143-53.

Katzenbach, Nicholas DeB. "Foreign Policy, Public Opinion, and Secrecy." *Foreign Affairs* 52 (Oct. 1973): 1-19.

Lefever, Ernest W. "Moralism and U.S. Foreign Policy." *Orbis* 16 (Summer 1972): 396-410.

―――. "Can Covert Action Be Just?" *Policy Review* 12 (Spring 1980): 115-22.

Marks, John. "On Being Censored." *Foreign Policy* 15 (Summer 1974): 93-108.

Moore, John Norton. "Law and National Security." *Foreign Affairs* 51 (Jan. 1973): 408-21.

Morgenthau, Hans J. "The Founding Fathers and Foreign Policy: Implications for the Late Twentieth Century." *Orbis* 20 (Spring 1976): 15-25.

Neuchterlein, Donald E. "The Concept of 'National Interest': A Time for New Approaches." *Orbis* 23 (Spring 1979): 73-92.

Ransom, Harry Howe. "Strategic Intelligence and Foreign Policy." *World Politics* 27 (Oct. 1974): 131-46.

――――. "Being Intelligent about Secret Intelligence Agencies." *American Political Science Review* 74 (Mar. 1980): 141-48.

Rositzke, Harry. "America's Secret Operations: A Perspective." *Foreign Affairs* 53 (Oct. 1975): 334-51.

Schlesinger, Arthur, Jr. "Congress and the Making of Foreign Policy." *Foreign Affairs* 51 (Oct. 1972): 78-113.

Scoville, Herbert. "Is Espionage Necessary for Our Security?" *Foreign Affairs* 54 (Apr. 1976): 482-95.

Seabury, Paul. "The Moral Purposes and Philosophical Bases of American Foreign Policy." *Orbis* 20 (Spring 1976): 3-14.

Sigal, Leon V. "Official Secrecy and Informal Communication in Congressional-Bureaucratic Relations." *Political Science Quarterly* 90 (Spring 1975): 71-92.

Sondermann, Fred A. "The Concept of National Interest." *Orbis* 21 (Spring 1977): 121-38.

Spector, Ronald. "The Twilight of the Secret Agent." *Armed Forces and Society* 7 (Summer 1981): 657-60.

Theoharis, Athan G. "The FBI's Stretching of Presidential Directives, 1936-1953." *Political Science Quarterly* 91 (Winter 1976-1977): 649-72.

Thompson, Kenneth W. "American Foreign Policy: Values Renewed or Discovered." *Orbis* 20 (Spring 1976): 123-35.

Tower, John G. "Congress versus the President: The Formulation and Implementation of American Foreign Policy." *Foreign Affairs* 60 (Winter 1981-1982): 229-46.

Turner, Stansfield, and Thibault, George. "Intelligence: The Right Rules." *Foreign Policy* 48 (Fall 1982): 122-38.

Weissman, Stephen R. "CIA Covert Action in Zaire and Angola: Patterns and Consequences." *Political Science Quarterly* 94 (Summer 1979): 263-86.

Wolfers, Arnold. "The Pole of Power and the Pole of Indifference." *World Politics* 4 (Oct. 1951): 39-63.

Yost, Charles W. "The Instruments of American Foreign Policy." *Foreign Affairs* 50 (Oct. 1971): 59-68.

Zeidenstein, Harvey G. "The Reassertion of Congressional Power: New Curbs on the President." *Political Science Quarterly* 93 (Fall 1978): 393-409.

In Compilations

Barnds, William J. "Intelligence Functions." In U.S. Commission on the Organization of Government for the Conduct of Foreign Policy, *Report of the Commission, Vol. 7: Appendix U: Intelligence Functions Analyses*, pp. 7-20. Washington, D.C.: GPO, 1975.

_____. "Intelligence and Policymaking in an Institutional Context." In U.S. Commission on the Organization of Government for the Conduct of Foreign Policy, *Report of the Commission, Vol. 7: Appendix U: Intelligence Functions Analyses*, pp. 21-40. Washington, D.C.: GPO, 1975.

Belcher, Taylor G. "Clandestine Operations." In U.S. Commission on the Organization of Government for the Conduct of Foreign Policy, *Report of the Commission, Vol. 7: Appendix U: Intelligence Functions Analyses*, pp. 67-76. Washington, D.C.: GPO, 1975.

Blackstock, Paul W. "Intelligence, Covert Operations, and Foreign Policy." In U.S. Commission on the Organization of Government for the Conduct of Foreign Policy, *Report of the Commission, Vol. 7: Appendix U: Intelligence Functions Analyses*, pp. 95-102. Washington, D.C.: GPO, 1975.

Cline, Ray S. "The Future of U.S. Foreign Intelligence Operations." In *The United States in the 1980's*, ed. Peter Duignan and Alvin Rabushka, pp. 469-96. Stanford: Hoover Institution on War, Revolution, and Peace, 1980.

George, Alexander L., and Keohane, Robert. "The Concept of National Interests: Uses and Limitations." In U.S. Commission on the Organization of Government for the Conduct of Foreign Policy, *Report of the Commission, Vol. 2: Appendix D: Use of Information*, pp. 64-74. Washington, D.C.: GPO, 1975.

Good, Robert C. "National Interest and Moral Theory: The "Debate" among Contemporary Political Realists." In *Foreign Policy in the Sixties: The Issues and Instruments*, pp. 271-92. Baltimore: Johns Hopkins Press, 1965.

Greene, Fred. "The Intelligence Arm: The Cuban Missile Crisis." In *Foreign Policy in the Sixties: The Issues and Instruments*, ed. Roger Hilsman and Robert C. Good, pp. 127-40. Baltimore: Johns Hopkins Press, 1965.

Halperin, Morton H., and Stone, Jeremy J. "Secrecy and Covert Intelligence Collection and Operations." In *National Security Policy-Making: Analyses, Cases, and Proposals*, ed. Morton H. Halperin, pp. 165-82. Lexington, Mass.: Heath, 1975.

Hilsman, Roger. "Intelligence through the Eyes of the Policymaker." In *Surveillance and Espionage in a Free Society*, ed. Richard H. Blum, pp. 163-77. New York: Praeger, 1972.

Karas, Thomas H. "Secrecy as a Reducer of Learning Capacity in the U.S. Foreign Policy Bureaucracy." In *Foreign Policy Analysis*, ed. Richard L. Merritt, pp. 95-99. Toronto and London: Lexington Books, 1975.

Kent, Sherman. "Meaning and Method of Intelligence." In *Elements of American Foreign Policy*, ed. L. Larry Leonard, pp. 127-31. New York: McGraw-Hill, 1953.

Marshall, Charles B. "The National Interest." In *Readings in American Foreign Policy*, ed. Robert A. Goldwin, with Ralph Lerner and Gerald Stourzh, pp. 664-73. New York: Oxford Univ. Press, 1959.

Nogee, Joseph L. "Congress and the Presidency: The Dilemmas of Policy-Making in a Democracy." In *Congress, the Presidency and American Foreign Policy*, ed. John Spanier and Joseph Nogee, pp. 189-300. New York: Pergamon Press, 1981.

Ransom, Harry Howe. "Can the Intelligence Establishment Be Controlled in a Democracy?" In *Surveillance and Espionage in a Free Society*, ed. Richard H. Blum. New York: Praeger, 1972.

————. "Congress and the Intelligence Agencies." In *Congress against the President*, ed. Harvey C. Mansfield, Sr., pp. 153-66. Montpelier, Vt.: Capital City Press, 1975.

————. "Congress and American Secret Intelligence Agencies." In U.S. Commission on the Organization of Government for the Conduct of Foreign Policy, *Report of the Commission*, vol. 7: *Appendix U: Intelligence Functions Analyses*, pp. 87-94. Washington, D.C.: GPO, 1975.

Robinson, Thomas W. "National Interests." In *International Politics and Foreign Policy: A Reader in Research and Theory*, ed. James N. Rosenau, pp. 182-90. New York: Free Press, 1969.

Smith, Russell Jack. "Intelligence Support for Foreign Policy in the Future." In U.S. Commission on the Organization of Government for the Conduct of Foreign Policy, *Report of the Commission*, Vol. 7: *Appendix U: Intelligence Functions Analyses*, pp. 77-86. Washington, D.C.: GPO, 1975.

Spanier, John. "Congress and the Presidency: The Weakest Link in the Policy Process." In *Congress, the Presidency and American Foreign Policy*, ed. John Spanier and Joseph Nogee, pp. ix-xxxii. New York: Pergamon Press, 1981.

Swift, Richard N. "Morality and Foreign Policy." In *Foreign Policy Analysis*, Richard L. Merritt, pp. 15-19. Toronto and London: Lexington Books, 1975.

Thompson, Kenneth W. "Human Rights and Soviet-American Relations." In *Neither Cold War nor Detente: Soviet-American Relations in the 1980's*, ed. Richard A. Melanson, pp. 134-50. Charlottesville, Univ. Press of Virginia, 1982.

In Other Periodicals

Epstein, Edward Jay. "The War within the CIA." *Commentary* 66 (Aug. 1978): 35-39.

————. "The Spy War." *New York Times Magazine*, Sept. 28, 1980, p. 34.

Glazer, Nathan. "American Values and American Foreign Policy." *Commentary* 62 (July 1976): 32-37.

Kalven, Jamie, "Security and Secrecy." *Bulletin of the Atomic Scientists* (Oct. 1982): 16-17.

Oseth, John M. "Intelligence Controls and the National Interest." *Parameters: Journal of the U.S. Army War College* 11 (Dec. 1981): 34-42.

Szulc, Tad. "Shaking Up the C.I.A." *New York Times Magazine*, July 29, 1979, p. 13.

Taubman, Philip. "Casey and His C.I.A. on the Rebound." *New York Times Magazine*, Jan. 16, 1983, p. 20.

Wilson, James Q. "Buggings, Break-ins and the FBI." *Commentary* 65 (June 1978): 52-58.

Index

absolute immunity: of government officials from lawsuit, 57

Adams, John Quincy, 189 n. 9

Afghanistan: CIA aid to freedom fighters in, 29, 161; U.S. reaction to Soviet invasion of, 138-39, 143

Ailes, Stephen, 94

Alien and Sedition Acts, 23

Allende, Salvatore, xiii, 2, 27, 71. *See also* Chile

American Civil Liberties Union: on need for controls, 88; on 1978 charter controls, 129-30; in 1979 House hearings, 135; in House hearings on identities protection, 141; on 1980 charter bill, 145

American Creed, 9, 10

American ideals: as central debate theme, 67-68, 171-72

Angola: CIA operation in, 200 n. 92

Annapolis (U.S. Naval Academy), 106

army intelligence activity: restrictions on, 198 n. 33

assassination: Senate investigation of, 28-29; public concern about, 52; 1975 Senate inquiry into, 59-60; prohibition of, in Executive Order 12036, 121; in 1978 charter proposal, 126; and controls generally, 179-80

Association of Former Intelligence Officers, 130

attorney general: and 1976 FBI guidelines, 91, 100-102; in Ford Administration, 93, 96-97; in Carter Administration, 112, 115-17; in 1978 charter proposal, 125, 128-29; in Reagan Administration, 158

Bayh, Birch, 107

Bay of Pigs invasion, xiii, 46

Ball, George, 30, 69

Bell, Griffin: and electronic surveillance controls, 108, 110; on constraints, 143; on 1980 charter, 144

Berger v. *New York,* 54

Berlin Democratic Club, et al., v. *Brown,* 56-57

Berman, Jerry, 141

Biden, Joseph: on electronic surveillance controls, 110; in 1979 House hearings, 135

Bissell, Richard M., Jr., 27-28

Blackstock, Paul: contributions to intelligence critique, 45-47

Boland, Edward, 141

Bozeman, Adda, 181

Brown, Seyom, 190 n. 18

Brzezinski, Zbigniew, 112

budget process, 63, 80

Bureau of Intelligence and Research, 14, 39

Bush, George, 91

Carlucci, Frank C.: on human intelligence, 17; on impact of Freedom of Information and Privacy Acts 136

Carter, Jimmy: on general need for intelligence, 105; views on value-based controls, 106-7; reaction to Iran and Afghanistan crises, 138-39; 1979-1980 program to strengthen the agencies, 139, 140; on need for congressional charter, 139; overview of administration, 169-70; commitment to human rights, 205 n. 22, 206 n. 26

Casey, William J.: nomination as DCI, 148; on restoring operational capability, 161; on Freedom of Information Act, 212 n. 71

Castro, Fidel, 28

CBS television, 29

Center for National Security Studies, 130

Central America: CIA operations in, 29, 161

Central Intelligence Agency, 14, 77-78, 83, 134; accomplishments of, ix-xi; Truman criticism of, xi; covert action operations by, 27, 29; in National